Nontaxation and Representation

Does oil make countries autocratic? Can foreign aid make countries democratic? Does taxation lead to representation? In this book, Kevin M. Morrison develops a novel argument about how government revenues of all kinds affect political regimes and their leaders. Contrary to conventional wisdom, Morrison illustrates that taxation leads to instability, not representation. With this insight, he extends his award-winning work on nontax revenues to encompass foreign aid, oil revenue, intergovernmental grants, and borrowing, and he shows that they lead to decreased taxation, increased government spending, and increased political stability. Looking at the stability of democracies and dictatorships as well as leadership transitions within those regimes, Morrison incorporates cross-national statistical methods, formal modeling, a quasi-experiment, and case studies of Brazil, Kenya, and Mexico to build his case. This book upends many common hypotheses and policy recommendations, providing the most comprehensive treatment of revenue and political stability to date.

Kevin M. Morrison is an assistant professor of public policy and political science at the University of Pittsburgh. He is the coauthor of *The Future of Development Assistance: Common Pools and International Public Goods* (1999). Morrison's academic work has been published in the *American Economic Journal: Applied Economics*, *Business & Politics*, *Comparative Political Studies*, *Comparative Politics*, *Development Policy Review*, *Electoral Studies*, *International Organization*, *Perspectives on Politics*, *Public Choice*, *Review of International Organizations*, and the *World Bank Research Observer*. His article in *International Organization* won the 2009 Robert O. Keohane Award for best paper in that journal by an untenured professor. His opinions and commentary have appeared in the *Durham Herald-Sun*, the *Financial Times*, the *International Herald Tribune*, the *Raleigh News & Observer*, and Slate.com.

To those who have taught me,
especially Mom, Dad, Marcela, and Lorenzo

Cambridge Studies in Comparative Politics

Other Books in the Series

Ben W. Ansell, *From the Ballot to the Blackboard: The Redistributive Political Economy of Education*
Leonardo R. Arriola, *Multi-Ethnic Coalitions in Africa: Business Financing of Opposition Election Campaigns*
David Austen-Smith, Jeffry A. Frieden, Miriam A. Golden, Karl Ove Moene, and Adam Przeworski, eds., *Selected Works of Michael Wallerstein: The Political Economy of Inequality, Unions, and Social Democracy*
Andy Baker, *The Market and the Masses in Latin America: Policy Reform and Consumption in Liberalizing Economies*
Lisa Baldez, *Why Women Protest: Women's Movements in Chile*
Stefano Bartolini, *The Political Mobilization of the European Left, 1860–1980: The Class Cleavage*
Robert Bates, *When Things Fell Apart: State Failure in Late-Century Africa*
Mark Beissinger, *Nationalist Mobilization and the Collapse of the Soviet State*
Nancy Bermeo, ed., *Unemployment in the New Europe*

continued after the index

Nontaxation and Representation

The Fiscal Foundations of Political Stability

KEVIN M. MORRISON
University of Pittsburgh

CAMBRIDGE
UNIVERSITY PRESS

CAMBRIDGE
UNIVERSITY PRESS

32 Avenue of the Americas, New York NY 10013-2473, USA

Cambridge University Press is part of the University of Cambridge.

It furthers the University's mission by disseminating knowledge in the pursuit of education, learning and research at the highest international levels of excellence.

www.cambridge.org
Information on this title: www.cambridge.org/9781107076778

First published 2015

A catalogue record for this publication is available from the British Library

Library of Congress Cataloguing in Publication data
Morrison, Kevin M.
Nontaxation and representation : the fiscal foundations of political stability / Kevin M. Morrison, University of Pittsburgh.
pages cm. – (Cambridge studies in comparative politics)
Includes bibliographical references and index.
ISBN 978-1-107-07677-8 (hardback)
1. Political stability – Economic aspects. 2. Representative government and representation – Economic aspects. 3. Democracy – Economic aspects. 4. Economic assistance – Political aspects. 5. Fiscal policy. 6. Taxation. 7. Revenue. I. Title.
JC330.2.M68 2014
320.01–dc23 2014020961

ISBN 978-1-107-07677-8 Hardback
ISBN 978-1-107-43399-1 Paperback

Contents

Tables

Figures

Acknowledgments

This book marks the culmination of a project that began about ten years ago, and the preparation of these acknowledgments has been a reminder of how extremely fortunate I have been along the way.

Let me begin with the people who have been most directly involved in the production of this book. Certainly foremost is Stephan Litschig, who was my coauthor on the article (Litschig and Morrison 2013) that formed the basis of Chapter 5. It was such a pleasure to work with him, and I am grateful for his agreeing to make the article a chapter in this book. I am also greatly indebted to the two reviewers solicited by Cambridge University Press, who provided insightful and constructive comments that immeasurably improved the manuscript. One of them, Erik Wibbels, self-revealed after the review process was complete. I hope the other reviewer will do the same at some point, so that I can thank her or him in person. Finally, I am very grateful to Lewis Bateman and Shaun Vigil at Cambridge, and to Bindu Vinod at Newgen Knowledge Works, for overseeing the review of the manuscript and production of the book. Shaun connected me with David Cox, who accurately and efficiently produced the four maps in the book.

This book presents a new argument, but not surprisingly it builds on my prior work related to the topic. In particular, substantial portions of four previously published articles appear here, particularly in Chapters 4, 5, and 6. In chronological order, they are my 2009 article entitled "Oil, Nontax Revenue, and the Redistributional Foundations of Regime Stability," in *International Organization* 63(Winter): 107–38; my 2011 article entitled "Nontax Revenue, Social Cleavages, and Authoritarian Stability in Mexico and Kenya: 'Internationalization, Institutions, and Political Change' Revisited," in *Comparative Political Studies* 44(6): 719–46; my 2012 article entitled "What Can We Learn About the 'Resource Curse' from Foreign Aid?" in the *World*

Bank Research Observer 7(1): 52–73; and my 2013 article with Stephan Litschig entitled "The Effect of Intergovernmental Grants on Education Outcomes and Poverty Reduction," in the *American Economic Journal: Applied Economics* 5(4): 206–40. I am grateful to the American Economic Association, Cambridge University Press, Oxford University Press, and SAGE for permission to reprint this material.

The work for these articles and the rest of the project was funded by a variety of sources. These include the National Science Foundation, the U.S. Department of Education, Duke University, Cornell University, and the University of Pittsburgh. I have also received institutional support from Duke University's Department of Political Science, Princeton University's Niehaus Center for Globalization and Governance, Cornell University's Department of Government, and the University of Pittsburgh's Graduate School of Public and International Affairs. Any opinions, findings, conclusions, or recommendations expressed in this book are mine and do not necessarily reflect the views of the National Science Foundation or any other of these entities.

Among other things, this financial support funded superb research assistance by Jian Cui, Jonas Gamso, and Jikuo Lu, and especially Dylan Fagan and Youcef Msaid, the last two of whom helped, respectively, with data collection and formal modeling. It also funded fieldwork in Kenya and Mexico, where I had temporary affiliations with the Centro de Investigación y Docencia Económicas in Mexico City and the African Economic Research Consortium in Nairobi.

My fieldwork was also made infinitely easier and more pleasurable by the generosity and company of certain individuals. I am not sure what I would have done in Nairobi without the friendship of Jeni Klugman and her family, and especially the generosity of Alfred Dube, who shared his house with us. In Mexico I was at home because of my wonderful family: Fernando, Chacha, Gabriela, and Alberto (and now Valentina!). Everyone should be so lucky as to have the in-laws that I have.

Finally, I am greatly indebted to many people who have provided helpful comments or support on this project along the way. They include Daron Acemoglu, Despina Alexiadou, Chris Anderson, Daniel Benjamin, Carles Boix, David Brady, Tim Büthe, Francesco Caselli, Antonio Ciccone, Steve Coate, Jeff Colgan, David Davis, Rajeev Dehejia, John Doces, Allan Drazen, Oeindrila Dube, Peter Enns, Marcel Fafchamps, Jim Fearon, Claudio Ferraz, Albert Fishlow, Brian Fried, Patricia Funk, James Galbraith, José Garcia Montalvo, Joyee Ghosh, Clark Gibson, Marcela González Rivas, Robin Grier, Justin Grimmer, Torben Iversen, William Jack, Pierre Jaquet, Nate Jensen, Emmanuel Jimenez, Seth Jolly, Philip Keefer, Robert Keohane, Mushtaq Khan, Herbert Kitschelt, Stephen Knack, Wojciech Kopczuk, Anton Korinek, Dan Kselman, David Lee, Fernanda Leite Lopez de Leon, Leigh Linden, Stephan Litschig, John Londregan, Bentley MacLeod, Beatriz Magaloni, Helen Milner, Mary

Morrison, Tom Morrison, Gaia Narciso, Akbar Noman, Brendan Nyhan, Kevin O'Rourke, Tom Pepinsky, Steve Pischke, Dina Pomeranz, Giacomo Ponzetto, Kiki Pop-Eleches, Karen Remmer, Michael Ross, Nita Rudra, Bernard Salanié, Alberto Simpser, Matt Singer, Dan Slater, Alastair Smith, Albert Solé-Ollé, Chukwuma Soludo, Pilar Sorribas-Navarro, David Soskice, David Stasavage, Joseph Stiglitz, Alessandro Tarozzi, Cameron Thies, Miguel Urquiola, Nicolas van de Walle, Pedro Vicente, James Vreeland, Till von Wachter, Camber Warren, Mark Watson, Chris Way, Steven Wilkinson, Francis Wilson, and Nimrod Zalk, as well as numerous anonymous reviewers. David Samuels graciously shared with us his Brazilian electoral data for the work in Chapter 5. In addition to all of these people, numerous others have asked helpful questions or given insightful comments at presentations of this project in dozens of universities and conferences over the years. In particular, drafts of chapters here were presented at the meetings of the American Political Science Association and the Midwest Political Science Association. I am grateful to all of these individuals.

This book is dedicated to those who have taught me throughout my life. As I watch my son grow up, I realize how much of what we know is learned early, and how much is cumulative, and I feel truly thankful to have had such an incredible number of great teachers from elementary school through graduate school. Those who were teaching me as the ideas in this book began to take shape include John Aldrich, Chris Gelpi, Scott de Marchi, Mike Munger, and Emerson Niou, and especially my dissertation committee of Karen Remmer, Bob Keohane, Herbert Kitschelt, and David Soskice. I owe a particularly great debt to Bob Keohane for his critiques and backing over the years, and most of all to Karen Remmer, my advisor and mentor. I can only hope that someday I will be able to demonstrate to my students some small share of the professionalism, incisiveness, caring, and true grit that Karen has demonstrated to me.

Ideally, of course, one never stops having great teachers around, and this was brought home to me while I was at Cornell and had the privilege of getting to know Steve Coate. Without question, the greatest influences on the advances in this book compared to my prior work were my taco lunches with Steve (not to mention his willingness to comment on repeated drafts). I am immensely grateful for his support, ideas, and friendship.

Finally, there are those who have simply taught me everything: Mom, Dad, Marcela, and Lorenzo. I have rewritten this paragraph more than any other in the book, trying to express the vastness of what I feel for each of them, including my gratitude for their endless support throughout this project and so much else. After all the revisions, I keep coming back to a phrase that my grandfather Scotty taught me, and on which I cannot improve: *sine qua non.*

1

Introduction

1.1 Revenue Paradoxes

Almost by definition, developing country governments do not have enough money. Their countries have staggering needs – from widespread poverty to political instability – many of which seemingly could be helped by an influx of funds. Not surprisingly, therefore, it is commonplace among those concerned about the development of poor countries to hear laments about how international donors do not give enough foreign aid. Certainly they give nothing close to the 0.7 percent of their annual gross national product (GNP) that they first promised in a United Nations General Assembly Resolution in 1970, and which has been reaffirmed in various international agreements since. If they did, foreign aid would jump from about $100 billion per year to about $250 billion per year, and the massive windfall to developing countries would likely be greeted with great fanfare by many (e.g., Sachs 2005).[1]

What would happen instead if the extra $150 billion did not come from aid, but from some other source? What would be the difference? In fact, a similar scenario has happened in recent years, with record-high prices for oil and other natural commodities generating massive revenues for many developing countries. Although commodity prices have fallen with the recent global economic crisis, they still are likely to remain at historically high levels for the foreseeable future (International Monetary Fund 2011). And many countries that stand to reap the benefits of these higher prices are exactly the ones facing financing gaps in meeting their Millennium Development Goals (Overseas Development Institute 2006).[2]

[1] This calculation is based on figures in Organization for Economic Co-operation and Development (OECD) (2008).

[2] The eight Millennium Development Goals were developed at the United Nations Millennium Summit in 2000, and include halving extreme poverty. Available at: http://www.un.org/millenniumgoals/.

However, instead of great fanfare, these billions of dollars from natural resources have been greeted by many observers with a great deal of trepidation. Although there has been some hope that this windfall will have a beneficial development impact, there has been far more emphasis in the international community on how countries need to avoid the "curse" that apparently comes with natural resources (e.g., Overseas Development Institute 2006). Venezuela's oil minister in the early 1960s, Juan Pablo Pérez Alfonzo, famously went so far as to call his country's oil the "devil's excrement," a term that served as the title of a *Foreign Policy* article on the dangers of the resource curse (Naím 2009). Is there really that much difference between $150 billion generated by foreign aid and $150 billion generated by natural resources?

This juxtaposition of the possibilities of receiving revenue from oil or aid reveals just one of several apparent paradoxes in the literature on revenue and political development. Consider another example: the conventional wisdom that oil is bad for democracy (Ross 2001; Friedman 2006). If this is the case, then pro-democracy observers should be happy that, for example, Mexico's oil deposits are rapidly decreasing.[3] However, Mexico's political regime, widely seen as having transitioned to democracy in 2000, faces long-standing problems of economic inequality as well as newer challenges, most notably widespread violence as a result of organized crime groups. Is it really true that Mexico's democratic regime would be better off without millions of dollars in oil revenue?

The paradoxes are not limited to the effects of oil and aid. Take another example from the literature on revenue and political development, the famous adage that "taxation leads to representation" (e.g., Bates and Lien 1985; Huntington 1991; Bräutigam, Fjeldstad, and Moore 2008). An important body of work has focused on how rising tax burdens in Europe several centuries ago helped lead to more representative institutions on that continent, and this thinking has been quite influential in explaining democratization in other parts of the world. As a result, one might think that higher levels of taxation are good for democracy, and this is indeed what some studies suggest (Ross 2004). But how can we reconcile this with the history of Latin America and elsewhere, where democracy has been repeatedly overthrown by wealthy elites unhappy with the level of redistributive taxation (e.g., O'Donnell 1973; Stepan 1985; Drake 1996; Collier 1999b)? Indeed, this history has led to a different – and also quite influential – body of theoretical work arguing that this fear of taxation is a systematic reason for the overthrow of democracies (Boix 2003; Acemoglu and Robinson 2006). Are these two different and quite prominent theoretical approaches to taxation and representative government reconcilable?

This book attempts to answer these questions by providing a synthetic and complete account of how different types of revenue relate to one another and to political instability, here defined as the likelihood of a change in a country's

[3] *The Wall Street Journal,* April 5, 2007, A1.

leadership or political regime (for example, from dictatorship to democracy). Although the question of why some political regimes are more stable than others is one of the oldest – and still most active – areas of political science, such an account is still missing. Most works in this area have tended to ignore government finances, assigning explanatory importance instead to factors such as accidents of history (O'Donnell, Schmitter, and Whitehead 1986; Olson 1993), level of development (Lipset 1959; Przeworski et al. 2000), economic performance (Diamond and Linz 1989), authoritarian institutions (Geddes 1999), and splits within the ruling regime (O'Donnell and Schmitter 1986; Przeworski 1991). The works that have addressed government finance have often done so indirectly, such as the theories of regime stability that revolve around patronage or government spending (van de Walle 2001; Bueno de Mesquita et al. 2003), pacts by elites regarding the benefits of government office (Karl 1990; Burton, Gunther, and Higley 1992), protests over the cutting of government benefits (Bratton and van de Walle 1997), "neoliberal" economic reform more generally (Przeworski 1991; Haggard and Kaufman 1995), or redistributional struggles between elites and citizens (Moore 1966; Rueschemeyer, Stephens, and Stephens 1992; Boix 2003; Acemoglu and Robinson 2006). The size and source of government revenue in all of these theories are likely to have major implications, although these implications are usually left unexplored.[4]

To help fill this gap in the literature, this book first revises one of the most well-known theories relating tax revenue to political stability – the argument that taxation leads to representation – and then uses this new framework to explain the political effects of nontax revenue sources such as oil and foreign aid. I argue that the canonical examples of increasing levels of taxation leading to democratization – such as England's Glorious Revolution and the rebellion of the colonists in the United States – are examples of the broader tendency for rising taxation to destabilize political regimes and their leaders. In other words, while higher levels of taxation may indeed lead to representation by destabilizing authoritarian regimes, as it did in these cases, it can also lead away from representation by destabilizing democracies. Having established this result, the book goes on to argue that nontax revenues enable governments to reduce their taxation levels while increasing government spending, thereby increasing the stability of democracies, dictatorships, and their leaders.

In sum, taxation hurts regimes and leaders, spending helps them, and nontax revenue increases political stability by facilitating the lowering of taxes and increasing spending. In making this argument, this book brings together and rationalizes the disparate literature on tax and nontax revenues, providing a systematic account of how the size and type of all government revenues combine to affect political stability.

[4] There are important exceptions, such as Smith (2008) and Bueno de Mesquita and Smith (2010).

1.2 Nontax Revenue around the World

Although tax revenue is a familiar concept, most readers may be unfamiliar with nontax revenue. Therefore, before delving into more details about this book's argument, it is helpful to discuss what nontax revenue entails, and how important it is around the world. I consider nontax revenue to consist of money a government can spend without having to tax its citizens. Most revenues from oil can be considered nontax revenues since the majority of government revenue generated from oil comes not through taxes (such as on foreign companies), but rather through state-owned companies, which control an estimated 75 percent of the world's oil production and 90 percent of its reserves (Ivanhoe 2000; Tordo, Tracy, and Arfaa 2011). Nontax revenue also includes foreign aid, borrowing, intergovernmental grants at the subnational level, and all other revenue besides taxation (for example, other state-owned enterprise revenue, fines, and so forth). This is obviously quite a diverse category of revenue, and it should be noted at the outset that – despite various scholars' claims that some of these revenues might have something in common (Bräutigam 2000; Svensson 2000; Moore 2001; Therkildsen 2002; Collier 2006; Morrison 2007; Smith 2008) – asserting that they can be aggregated into one category constitutes a hypothesis in its own right. Therefore, I take steps in my empirical analysis throughout this book to ensure that this hypothesis is valid.

However, if aggregating seemingly different types of revenue into one category seems unintuitive at first, consider that research on taxation and political regimes has primarily focused on aggregate taxation (Cheibub 1998; Ross 2004), despite the evident differences that exist between various forms of taxes.[5] Much insight, similarly, has been gained by focusing on aggregate government spending, discounting differences between various kinds of expenditure (Rodrik 1998; Rodden 2003). Research on nontax revenue to date (although generally not positioned as such) has instead focused primarily on disaggregated types of revenue, such as oil revenues or foreign aid.[6] Similar to works that focus on aggregate taxation and spending, this book offers evidence that leverage can be gained by aggregating different kinds of nontax revenue.

Given this encompassing theoretical definition of nontax revenue, the simplest way of calculating the aggregate value of such revenue is to subtract total tax revenue from total expenditures (Morrison 2007, 2009).[7] This gives

[5] Important exceptions, of course, exist (Timmons 2005; Scheve and Stasavage 2010; Timmons 2010).

[6] There are certainly important exceptions, dating back to Mahdavy's (1970: 428) work on the *rentier* state, which he defined broadly as one that received substantial rents from "foreign individuals, concerns or governments." More recent contributions in this tradition include Smith (2008), Bueno de Mesquita and Smith (2010), Ahmed (2012), and my own work (Morrison 2007, 2009).

[7] The best available data on revenue and spending is from the IMF's *Government Finance Statistics* (GFS). Unfortunately for researchers interested in revenue over a long time period,

a direct measure of the revenue other than tax revenue that a government can use to finance expenditures in a given period.

Nontax revenue defined in this way is critical to many countries and leaders in the world. It accounts for an average of 27 percent of national government expenditures, and in some countries it accounts for the large majority of expenditures, as Figure 1.1 details.[8] As further evidence of their importance, these nontax revenues are also large relative to the size of economies. Figure 1.2 lists some major components of revenue as a share of gross domestic product (GDP) by region, as well as the specific definitions of these variables used in the statistical analysis throughout the book. Included are tax revenue and two of the major components of nontax revenue: foreign aid receipts and an approximation of income from state-owned enterprises (this latter variable includes income from state-owned oil companies). The table also lists the regional averages of oil exports as a share of GDP, a commonly used indicator of oil dependence (Ross 2001; Smith 2004).

Whereas theories of taxation and spending are easily perceived to have widespread relevance around the world, theories involving foreign aid, for example, are usually perceived to have more limited geographic scope. The same could be said for theories about the effects of oil. However, comparing the various indicators in Figures 1.1 and 1.2 serves notice that the geographical coverage (extension) of a theory of nontax revenue is likely to be much broader than a theory focused on aid or oil exclusively. For instance, while many oil revenues will be included in my nontax revenue variable, the correlation between my nontax revenue variable and oil exports as a share of GDP is only 0.18. Whereas the Middle East is the region with the most of both nontax revenue and oil, its oil/GDP ratio is almost three times that of the next highest region, and twenty times that of the lowest ranked region. In contrast, the Middle East's nontax revenue/GDP ratio is only about 1.5 times that of the next highest region, and only about four times that of the lowest ranked region. In other words, while the Middle East looks exceptional from the perspective of oil, it looks more like other regions when it comes to nontax revenue. Similar

in the beginning of the 2000s, the IMF changed the way it categorizes government finance (International Monetary Fund 2001). Obviously, this means that the newer categorization is only available for a limited time period. However, the data for the previous coding by the IMF is available over the period of 1973–2001. Therefore, to analyze a longer time-series, I use the previous coding of revenue and spending in this book. The previous coding is detailed in International Monetary Fund (1986).

8 The data from the International Monetary Fund that are used to calculate these variables are unfortunately missing for many countries and years. In order to examine whether these absences were systematic, I ran regressions with a dichotomous variable as the dependent variable, measuring 1 if data for nontax revenue were missing and zero if they were present. The independent variables I included were: regime transition, economic growth, GDP per capita, urban population, ethno-linguistic fractionalization, population density, past political instability, the age of the regime, whether or not the country was democratic, and oil exports as a share of GDP. None of these were significant predictors of missing data.

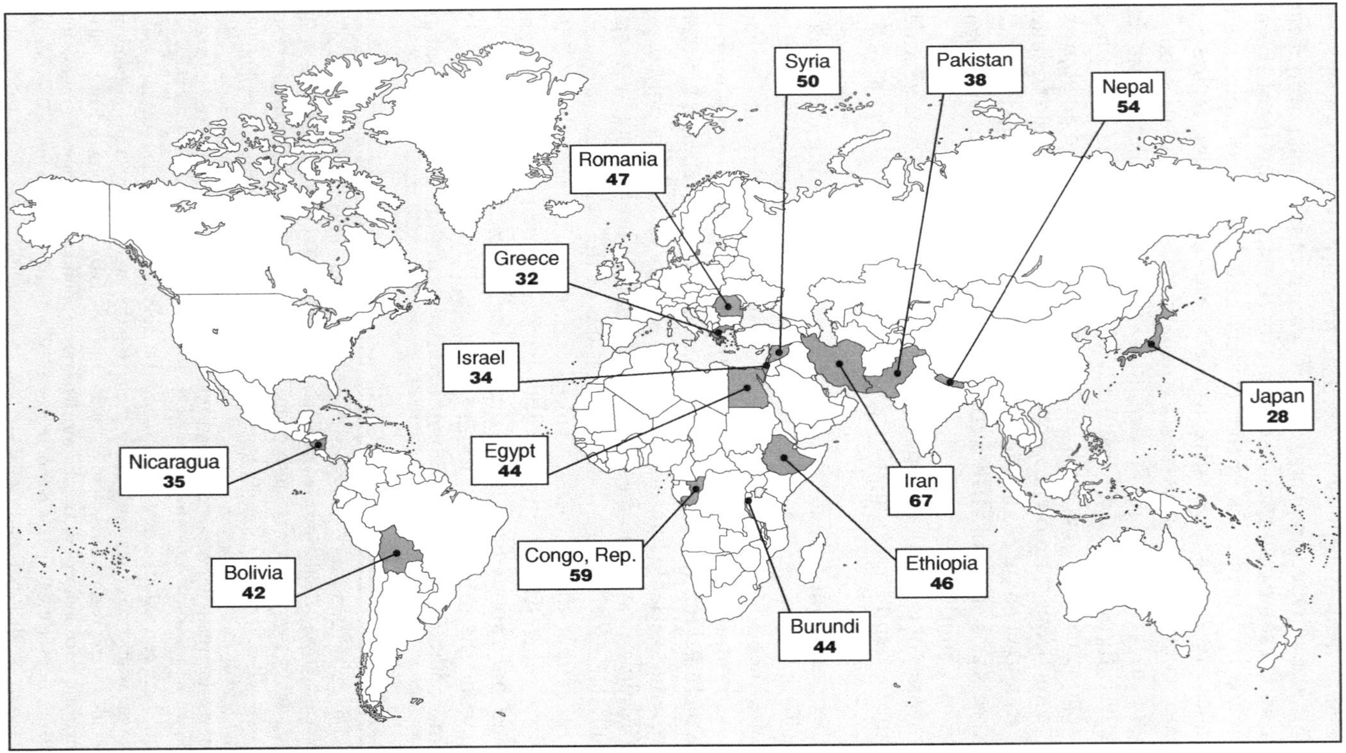

FIGURE 1.1. The importance of nontax revenue in some countries' revenue streams.

Notes: Numbers are the average percent of total expenditure covered by nontax revenue for observations in my sample covering 1973–2001. 100 = 100 percent. Calculated using data from the International Monetary Fund's (IMF's) *Government Finance Statistics* (GFS).

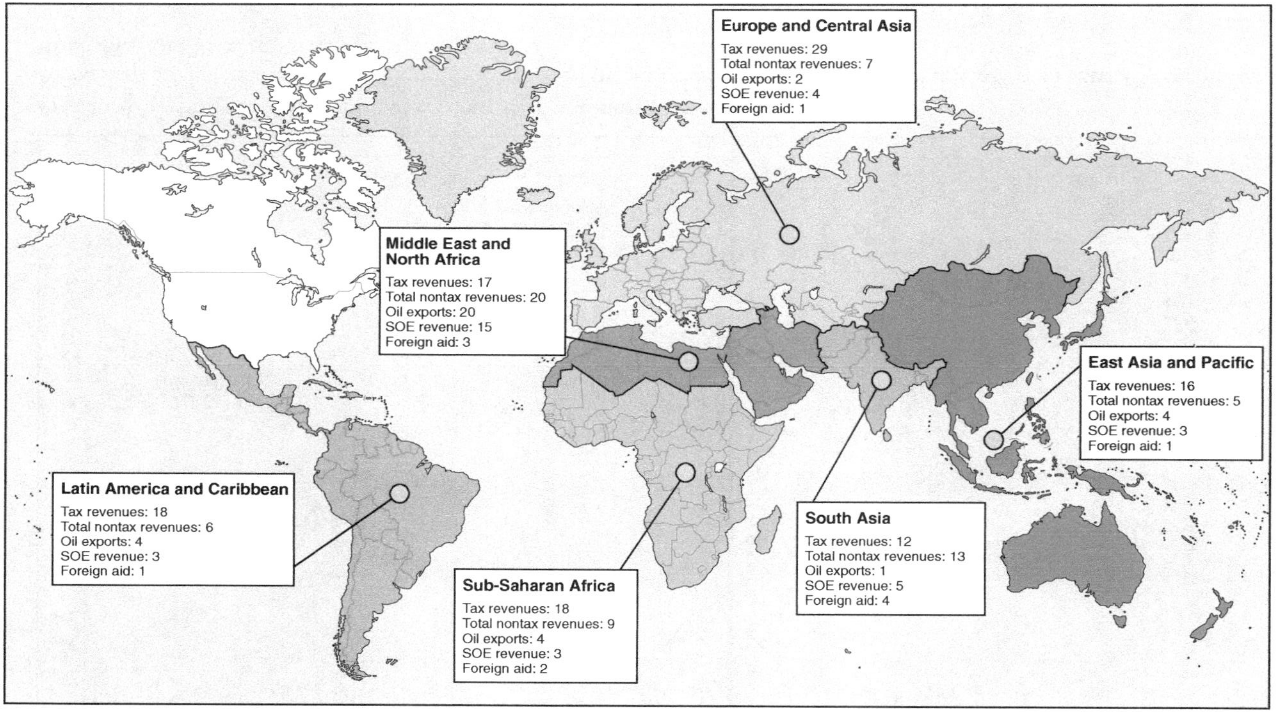

FIGURE 1.2. The importance of nontax revenue in economic terms.

Notes: Variables as a percentage of GDP. Regional breakdowns are as defined by the World Bank. Oil exports as a share of GDP are from the World Bank. "Tax revenues" as defined by the IMF's (1986) *Government Finance Statistics* (GFS) are "compulsory, unrequited payments to government" (p. 118). "State-owned enterprise revenue" is approximated here by the variable "nontax revenue" in the GFS. Although this category also includes administrative fees and charges, the majority of this revenue is the government's "entrepreneurial and property income." "Foreign aid" is the "grants" variable in the GFS, and includes "all nonrepayable unrequited payments received from other governments or programs, for general budget support, or any other purpose" (p. 130). "Total nontax revenues" are as defined in the text. 100 = 100 percent.

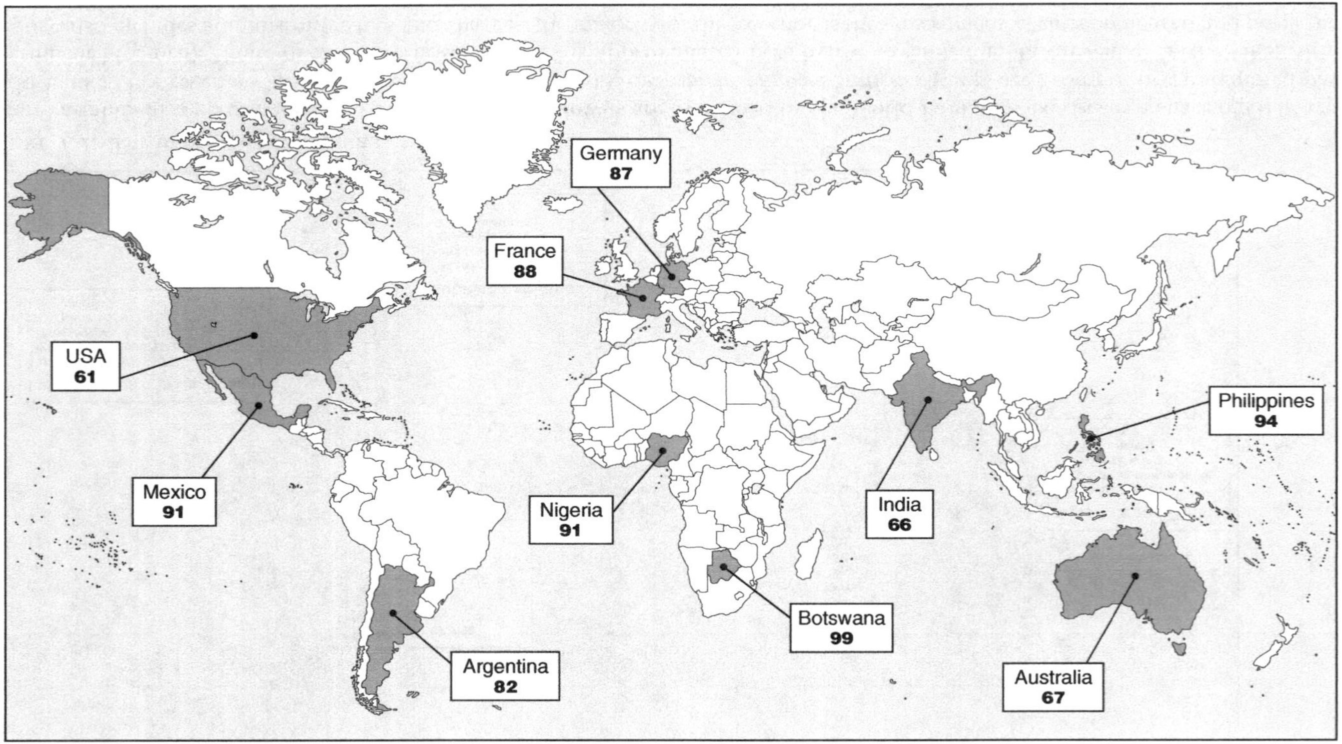

FIGURE 1.3. Percent of subnational revenue that is nontax revenue.

Notes: Source is Rodden (2004). Figures are attained by subtracting from 100 his variable of "own source" revenue as a share of total state and local revenue. 100 = 100 percent.

comparisons can be made between the geographical coverage of theories of nontax revenue and foreign aid.

Indeed, the importance of nontax revenue for political stability appears even greater when one considers that subnational governments also often receive large amounts of nontax revenue. These subnational governments are subject to the same kinds of leadership turnover as national governments, and many countries also exhibit important differences in terms of democracy and authoritarianism at the subnational level (O'Donnell 1993; Benton 2012). Federal systems throughout the world rely on intergovernmental grants to finance local governments, and the majority of these local governments receive much more in grants than they pay out in taxes that fund the grants (Broadway 2008). Using data from Rodden (2004), Figure 1.3 presents some examples of the extent to which subnational governments around the world rely on revenues that are not "own-source." That is, the ratios approximate the role of nontax revenue in financing these local governments. Given their high levels, it is not surprising that studies of the effects of these revenues are increasingly drawing on the literature of the resource curse (Gervasoni 2010; Brollo et al. 2013).

In sum, these figures underline the importance of both tax and nontax revenue to governments around the world. Nontax revenue is at least as important as tax revenue to many governments, highlighting the need for an encompassing theoretical approach for understanding the political impact of these kinds of revenue.

1.3 Toward a Theory of Revenue and Regime Stability: An Outline of the Book

In Chapter 2, I begin my exploration of revenue and stability by focusing exclusively on tax revenue and spending. Attempting to reconcile existing arguments about taxation and political stability, the chapter brings several literatures together into a broader argument. Instead of positing that taxation leads to or undermines certain kinds of political systems, as is the norm in the literature, I hypothesize that taxation is destabilizing to all political regimes and leaders – whether democratic or authoritarian – just as government spending is stabilizing to them. Using cross-national time-series analysis, I find support for this argument, demonstrating that increased taxation destabilizes both democracies and dictatorships, and that government spending stabilizes them. I also show that the same relationship holds for leaders in authoritarian countries. In addition to providing a new perspective on the existing work on taxation and representation, the chapter provides an essential result for the rest of the book.

With this understanding of how taxation and spending relate to political stability, Chapter 3 turns to nontax revenue, developing an argument for how it relates to taxation and spending. Building a simple model that draws from literature on government finance, I demonstrate that nontax revenue should tend to decrease taxation and increase spending across a wide variety of different contexts, including different political regimes and different tax systems. Crucially, I also develop an argument about why different kinds of nontax revenue, including foreign aid, are likely to work similarly. Then, using cross-national time-series analysis of all countries and years for which data are available, I demonstrate that nontax revenue is indeed associated with lower taxation and increased spending.

The implication of these two chapters is that nontax revenue should stabilize national political regimes and their leaders. In Chapter 4, I return to the discussion in Chapter 2 about the effects of taxation and spending, and explain why under most circumstances this implication should indeed hold. I also present two case studies of Mexico and Kenya to illustrate the argument. Then, using cross-national time-series analysis of all countries and years for which data are available, I demonstrate that higher levels of nontax revenue lead to reduced levels of regime transition in both democracies and dictatorships. Finally, I show that nontax revenue's stabilizing effect extends to political leaders, as higher levels of nontax revenue result in longer leadership tenure in authoritarian regimes.

Chapter 4 therefore completes the theoretical framework of the book. Rationalizing the disparate literatures on tax and nontax revenues, Chapters 2 through 4 present the argument that taxation hurts political regimes and their leaders, spending helps them, and nontax revenue stabilizes them by enabling them to reduce taxes and increase spending.

Chapter 5 continues the empirical analysis of the book's theory in three important ways. First, it examines the links between revenue and democratic leadership stability, which (for reasons discussed in Chapters 2 and 4) the data used elsewhere in this book cannot do. Second, it analyzes the hypotheses regarding revenue and political stability using a design-based research strategy as opposed to a model-based one (Dunning 2010). And third, it examines the link between revenue and stability at the subnational level, indicating that the theory advanced in the rest of this book applies at this level as well.

Specifically, Chapter 5 examines the links between revenue, spending, and the stability of democratic incumbents in Brazil, analyzing the effects that particular intergovernmental transfers had on taxes, spending, and municipal reelection in the 1980s. Certain federal transfers were allocated to municipalities on the basis of population thresholds, an allocation strategy that created "jumps" in per capita transfers to municipalities just over the thresholds. With the use of a particular method of analysis (regression discontinuity), these jumps enable the identification of a causal effect of these transfers on taxation, spending, and the probability of reelection in municipalities. Consistent with the theory in the book, nontax revenue – in the form of intergovernmental transfers – increased stability in the sense that municipalities that received more of these transfers had higher rates of mayoral party reelection, owing to the effects of that revenue on their need and ability to tax and spend. For various reasons discussed in Chapter 5, Brazil during the time period under study represents a "least likely" case in which to find a stabilizing effect of nontax revenue, suggesting that the findings might be even stronger elsewhere.

The empirical tests in this book therefore provide an array of supporting evidence for the overall argument: taxation hurts political regimes and their leaders, spending helps them, and nontax revenue stabilizes them by enabling them to reduce taxes and increase spending. *Nontaxation and Representation* concludes with Chapter 6, outlining the implications of that evidence. Most importantly, of course, this book provides a framework by which to understand the effects of all kinds of revenue on political stability. However, in addition to the implications for theories about taxes, oil, aid, and other revenues, the argument and evidence here have implications for theoretical development more broadly. For example, the results suggesting the interchangeability of nontax revenues have particular implications for how such revenues are studied and theorized, and also suggest new frontiers for research. The framework in this book also suggests that benefits can be gained from studying regime transitions in general, rather than just focusing (separately) on transitions to democracy or transitions to authoritarian regimes. Finally, this book's theory and findings have some normative implications concerning how we interpret greater stability in democratic regimes.

Having gone through the theoretical implications, Chapter 6 concludes with some policy implications of this book's argument for the "curse" of natural resources mentioned at the beginning of this Introduction. Although the book contends that nontax revenues have similar effects on political stability, current international policies regarding two chief sources of nontax revenue – natural resources and foreign aid – diverge sharply. Whereas foreign aid policy used to resemble today's international policies toward natural resources, dissatisfaction with the results of that approach have led aid donors to change their tactics. Chapter 6 explores the reasons and results of these different policies and suggests a new direction for international policies aimed at avoiding the resource curse.

2

Taxation Leads to Instability, Not Representation

2.1 Introduction

Human beings seem to prefer getting something for nothing. Surveys fairly consistently show that taxation is unpopular, but people do not want government spending cut, despite the apparent problem of reconciling these preferences within a given budget (Free and Cantril 1967; Sears and Citrin 1985; Bowler and Donovan 1995; Hansen 1998). Correspondingly, empirical work has shown that raising taxes is politically dangerous for democratically elected officials (Paler 2013), tending to result in a higher probability of them not being reelected (Niemi, Stanley, and Vogel 1995; Sobel 1998). Spending, by contrast, does just the opposite: it helps incumbents return to office (Levitt and Snyder 1997; Akhmedov and Zhuravskaya 2004; Litschig and Morrison 2013).

This chapter builds on this insight to make a straightforward argument: taxation hurts political regimes and their leaders whereas spending helps them. Given the apparent unpopularity of taxation and popularity of spending, one might think that this hypothesis would be fairly uncontroversial. However, while existing scholarship tends to agree that greater government spending helps both regimes and their leaders stay in power, the literature on taxation is more complicated.

Most famously, as mentioned in the Introduction, "it is widely thought that taxation promotes representation" (Herb 2003). The basic thrust of work on this topic – even the phrase "taxation leads to representation" – gives more positive overtones to the role of taxation in democracies than the unpopularity of taxation would lead one to expect. As this chapter discusses, the studies in this literature pay almost no attention to the possibility that taxation's role in making authoritarian regimes unstable may be just one example of a broader phenomenon in which higher levels of taxes make *all* political regimes more unstable. This possibility is strengthened by the fact that there is a literature focusing on the dangers of taxation for democratic regimes. However, the works in this other literature, which are focused on the redistributional cleavages that underlie conflict about political regimes, never engage the "taxation and representation" literature.

As a first step toward building a theory of how revenue affects political stability, this chapter attempts to bring these and other literatures together into an overarching argument about the role of taxation and spending in that stability. The next part of the chapter reviews various perspectives on the effects of taxation and spending, building the theoretical background for the hypothesis that taxation destabilizes political regimes and their leaders while spending stabilizes them. The third section turns to empirical analysis, conducting a cross-sectional time-series analysis of the hypothesized relationships. The results provide the first systematic examination of the role of taxation and spending on the stability of *both* democracies and dictatorships, showing that taxation destabilizes – and spending stabilizes – both.

The fourth section supplements these findings with a more in-depth look at the effects of taxation and spending on leadership transitions in authoritarian regimes. As mentioned earlier, several studies have shown that taxation hurts – and spending helps – the political fortunes of incumbents in democratic regimes, but we know little about how these affect leaders in authoritarian regimes. And in fact, because my theoretical approach makes different predictions about taxation's effect on leaders than the taxation-leads-to-representation approach does, analyzing this effect helps adjudicate between the approaches. I find that taxation leads to a greater probability of authoritarian leader transition, whereas spending diminishes the probability.

In sum, the findings suggest that taxation leads to greater political instability for democracies, dictatorships, and their leaders, whereas spending stabilizes them. A final section concludes, setting the stage for the role of nontax revenue discussed in the following chapters.

2.2 Theoretical Perspectives on Spending, Taxation, and Stability

Almost a century ago, Schumpeter (1918 [1991]: 101) famously wrote, "The public finances are one of the best starting points for an investigation of society, especially though not exclusively of its political life." Many scholars have followed his lead, seeking greater insight into political regimes by analyzing the dynamics of their public finances (e.g., Brennan and Buchanan 1980; Levi 1988). This section reviews and attempts to synthesize several of the main approaches to spending and taxation in the literature.

2.2.1 *Spending*

Scholars tend to agree that spending is good for political regimes and leaders, whether democratic or authoritarian. Essentially, spending helps solidify support from the base of a regime or leader, as well as buy off potential threats.

Although the particular mechanisms differ, the central idea throughout the literature on the effect of spending is that both supporters and threatening groups are less likely to try to overturn a regime or throw out a leader if money is being spent on them. Almost always this is because the switch to an alternative regime or leader is potentially costly.

Consider the theory of Acemoglu and Robinson (2006) with regard to threats to authoritarian regimes. In their approach and others (e.g., Boix 2003), the threat to authoritarian regimes comes from lower and middle classes who would benefit under a democratic regime in which they would have more power. Occasionally, these classes can threaten to launch a revolution against the elites in power. This revolution, however, will be costly, with part of the economy destroyed. As such, in making this decision, the citizens have to evaluate how well off they are in an authoritarian regime compared to what would happen if they launched a revolution. Because of this trade-off, elites are sometimes able to withstand threats by spending more on the lower and middle classes, making them indifferent to launching a revolution: "revolution is sufficiently costly that the elites can prevent democratization by redistributing" (Acemoglu and Robinson 2006: 185).

A similar kind of logic underlies the role of spending in the well-known model of Bueno de Mesquita and his colleagues (2003). These authors characterize political systems by their selectorate (the group that has any influence on determining who is leader) and the winning coalition (the subset of the selectorate that causes the leader to come to power). The winning coalition is what keeps leaders in power, and leaders provide the coalition's members with particular benefits for that support. Nevertheless, members of this coalition can decide between continuing to support the leader or switching to back a challenger. The key, however, is that they *know* they are a member of the current leader's winning coalition and will continue to receive benefits, whereas they are less certain of what will happen with the new leader. Therefore, when choosing between the two, they discount the rewards they might receive under a different leader. For this reason, incumbents can always secure their winning coalition if they can promise them enough benefits.

A comparable logic for the positive political effects of spending pervades the literatures on clientelistic and "neopatrimonial" relations between politicians and their citizens (e.g., Scott 1969; Ames 1977), which is prominent in analyses of both the developing and developed world (Kitschelt and Wilkinson 2007; Stokes et al. 2013). As van de Walle (2001: 117) writes of neopatrimonial regimes in Africa, echoing much of the work on clientelism and machine politics, "Political leaders used access to state resources to gain the support they could not gain at the ballot box and dispensed large amounts of patronage." In the model of clientelism developed by Robinson, Torvik, and Verdier (2006), for example, there are different groups in society, and an incumbent can use government spending to create government jobs for people in these groups. Groups reward this spending politically because if the incumbent is not reelected, they will lose the job.

Interestingly, given the message across all these literatures that spending stabilizes governments and leaders, there is surprisingly little cross-national empirical work directly relevant to the topic. The cross-national statistical *rentier* state literature, for example, argues that oil boosts government spending and this leads to stability, but almost all of the work focuses on oil, not spending, as the independent variable. Nevertheless, certainly there are some supportive empirical works in this area (e.g., Bueno de Mesquita et al. 2003; Desai, Olofsgård, and Yousef 2009), and the hypothesis gains additional strength from the work linking political protests around the world to dissatisfaction over levels of public good provision (Finkel, Muller, and Opp 1989; Muller, Dietz, and Finkel 1991; Finkel and Muller 1998). This chapter attempts to add to these empirical studies of the effect of spending on stability.

2.2.2 *Taxation*

While there is little disagreement among scholars about the effects of spending on democracies and dictatorships, the existing work on taxation is less straightforward. The issue is not so much that scholars disagree that taxation should be destabilizing, as argued in this book; it is more that the framing of existing works has blurred the broader lessons from the literature.

The principal framing device causing the problem is the famous link between taxation and representation. It is clearly a powerful framing device – it even appears on license plates in Washington, DC, where residents complain about "taxation without representation."[1] However, as I discuss in this section, by talking about "representation" instead of "regime instability," work in this literature has implicitly suggested that regimes that tax more should be more democratic, and indeed, the empirical work on this topic evaluates exactly that hypothesis (Ross 2004). In contrast, however, the literature on taxation in *democracies* indicates that the link between taxation and the existence of democratic government may not be so positive. To gain a more complete understanding of how taxation relates to political regimes, this section first examines the link between taxation and authoritarian overthrow, and then the link between taxation and democratic overthrow.

As Herb (2003) has explained in an insightful review of the literature on taxation and representation, there are two ways democratization is linked to higher levels of tax revenues in the literature. One is the "bargaining" link, which is implicitly captured in the phrase, "no taxation without representation." As Tilly (1990: 64) argues in discussing the case of England, "representative institutions were the price and outcome of bargaining with different members of the subject population for the wherewithal of state activity, especially the

[1] Washington, DC, as a federal district, does not have voting rights in the U.S. Congress.

means of war. Kings of England did not *want* a Parliament to form and assume ever-greater power; they conceded to barons, and then to clergy, gentry, and bourgeois, in the course of persuading them to raise the money for warfare."[2]

Bates and Lien (1985) explore this bargain hypothesis through the use of a formal model and make some important refinements to it. First, certain aspects of the country's assets may affect how the bargain evolves. Most importantly, the mobility of the economic assets may affect the bargaining power between the state and its citizens, since raising taxes on mobile assets is unlikely to be effective when citizens can simply move them out of the country (a relationship further explored by Boix 2003). And second, the relationship between taxation and representation may be conditional on the amount of spending that citizens receive in return (Ross 2004).

The second mechanism linking democracies to taxation is what Herb (2003) refers to as the "legitimation" model. Especially prominent in the work of Levi (1988), this argument holds that the paying of taxes is motivated partly by a sense of duty, and since representation helps inculcate this sense of duty, the creation of representative institutions helps rulers raise more revenue. Levi herself does not argue that leaders democratize in order to accrue higher revenues (her argument is more that democracies should have higher tax yields compared to dictatorships), and indeed, few scholars have argued that this is a reason why authoritarian leaders democratize.[3] As Herb (2003) notes, however, this legitimation model seems like a reasonable alternative mechanism by which the need for taxation could be linked to the development of representative institutions (also see Guyer 1992). Indeed, there is some support for the idea that democracies are better than autocracies at eliciting tax revenues from their citizens (Timmons 2010).

In any case, the bargaining mechanism has been far more influential in linking taxation and democratization in many parts of the world. This is certainly true of work on Europe (Tilly 1990), where classic studies of political liberalization have argued that this relationship affected the trajectories of several countries, including France (Hoffman 1994) and perhaps most famously England (Stubbs 1896; Mann 1980; North and Weingast 1989). The relationship is also argued to have played a role in the overthrow of colonial government in the United States (Bailyn and others 1977). Although some argue that its contemporary applications are less convincing (Herb 2003), others argue for its continuing relevance (Huntington 1991), and indeed the general framework has been applied to modern political developments in regions as diverse as Africa (Guyer 1992), Asia (Bernstein and Lü 2000), the Middle East (Crystal 1990), and the former Soviet Union (Gehlbach 2008). Supporting the framework's cross-regional utility, Ross (2004) has found in a cross-sectional time-

[2] Emphasis in original.

[3] One exception is Hoffman and Norberg's (1994) argument that France liberalized in 1788 in order to acquire better consent to taxation.

series analysis that a higher ratio of taxation to spending is associated with more democratic political regimes.

Given all of this work suggesting that taxation leads to representation, the hypothesis obviously has significant credibility. However, if one is to account for the *overall* relationship between taxation and the presence of representative government, one should do something that virtually none of the works cited in the previous paragraph do: examine the relationship between taxation and the stability of democratic regimes. That is, it is one thing to argue – as these works do – that rising taxation leads to authoritarian overthrow; it is another to argue – as these works also do – that taxation leads to more representative government. The latter argument implies a relationship between taxation and *democratic* stability – in order for higher levels of taxation to be associated with higher levels of representative government, taxation must at worst have no effect on democratic stability, and at best support it. None of these works, however, examine or test this hypothesis explicitly.

There is a major literature that does, in fact, examine the relationship between taxation and democratic stability, but the scholars in this tradition never (as far as I have seen) engage the literature on taxation and representation. This is the literature mentioned earlier, focused on how redistributional conflicts are central to understanding regime changes (Moore 1966; Rueschemeyer, Stephens, and Stephens 1992; Boix 2003; Acemoglu and Robinson 2006). As I have discussed elsewhere (Morrison 2009), these theories have several defining features. First, they assume that political regimes are essentially a way of allocating resources in society (Kitschelt 1992). As such – almost by definition – conflict over the political regime is conflict about the nature and extent of redistribution in society. Second, these theories tend to assume that conflict over redistribution takes place between wealthy elites and (less wealthy) citizens.[4] Third, they assume that the elites in society are a smaller group than the citizens, a critical step because it leads to the association of dictatorial regimes with elites and democratic regimes with citizens.[5] (Dictatorial regimes are ones in which a minority group – the wealthy elites in society – have decision-making power over resource allocation. Democratic regimes are ones in which the citizens have that power.) Finally, in these theories, redistribution is generally considered to consist of transfers from elites to citizens, and not the other

[4] It may be noted that the central theoretical claims of the work by Acemoglu and Robinson are robust to the presence of other societal divisions (such as ethnic divisions), but it is important for their model that there are elites and citizens *within* these societal groups (see, for example, Acemoglu and Robinson 2006, 203–07).

[5] There is empirical support for the implication of these theories, which is that transitions to democracy should generally involve (1) an incorporation of poorer elements into the country's electorate and (2) an improvement in the government's treatment of those parts of society (Kousser 1974; Bueno de Mesquita and others 2003; Lindert 2004; Jack and Lagunoff 2006). However, it should be noted that some scholars remain skeptical of the approach's explanatory power (e.g., Ansell and Samuels 2010; Timmons 2010; Haggard and Kaufman 2012).

way around.[6] It is a rather quick jump from this final assumption to the critical source of conflict in these models: citizens prefer higher redistribution than elites do. In fact, elites prefer no redistribution at all.

Together, these characteristics lead to specific predictions about the source of threats to dictatorships and democracies. For dictatorships, which elites are assumed to control, the threat is from citizens who are unhappy about the amount of transfers they are receiving. For democracies, in which citizens have more power, the threat is instead from the elites unhappy with the level of taxation imposed on them by those citizens (see, for example, Abente 1990). In Acemoglu and Robinson's (2006) theory, in the transitory moments when the rich can solve their collective action problems and mobilize against the democratic regime, citizens may not be able to credibly promise lower amounts of taxation of elites. In this scenario, the rich overthrow the democracy and impose a dictatorship.

Support for the notion that democracies are overthrown because the rich are concerned about levels of taxation and redistribution can be found in much of the work on democratic stability in Latin America (e.g., O'Donnell 1973; Stepan 1985; Collier 1999b). As Drake (1996: 3–4) writes, "Before the dawn of dictatorships, working-class militance had begun to frighten property owners, who therefore abandoned liberal democracy. Losing profits, power, and legitimacy, the economic elites were rescued by the military. These right-wing, military based governments favored the private over the public, the wealthy over the workers, capital accumulation over redistribution, hierarchy over equity."

While this approach therefore seems to have some explanatory power, it should be noted that it is not only the rich who may find taxation a burden in democracies. Indeed, there are ample cases of tax riots against more democratic regimes (e.g., Kelsall 2000), even in regions where the taxation-leads-to-representation hypothesis has been touted, such as Europe (Mack Smith 1968) and the United States (Lowery and Sigelman 1981). Given the literature cited at the beginning of this chapter regarding the unpopularity of taxation, it seems plausible that any group that saw its taxes raised in a democracy might have less supportive feelings for the regime.

As can be seen, studies of the effects of taxation on democracies have a more pessimistic view of its effect on the presence of representative government than that implied by the taxation-leads-to-representation literature. Indeed, according to these theories, a higher tax burden in democracies may be associated with higher probability of the *overthrow* of democratic regimes. If this is true – if higher tax burdens contribute to the undermining of democratic regimes – a significant reformulation of the conventional wisdom about taxation and

[6] Acemoglu and Robinson (2006: 107–09) do explore the possibility of targeted transfers, which would allow elites in a dictatorship to funnel all tax proceeds to themselves, and the citizens in a democracy to do similarly to themselves. The result is to increase the level of conflict in society, but the comparative statics are generally the same, particularly with regard to inequality.

representation seems needed. It seems more accurate to say that taxation has essentially the opposite effect of spending discussed in the previous section. Whereas spending allows governments to shore up their core supporters and head off threats in all kinds of regimes, taxation upsets supporters and creates threats.

No existing work has analyzed the possibility of this kind of a theoretical relationship between taxation and political stability. The one study analyzing this relationship in a cross-sectional time-series context is that by Ross (2004). Situated in the literature regarding how taxation undermines authoritarian regimes, that article's empirical analysis constrains the effect of taxation to be either "pro-" democracy or "anti-" democracy.[7] As such, there has been no systematic analysis of the possibility that taxation is in fact destabilizing to *all* political regimes, whether authoritarian or democratic.

It is that analysis to which I now turn.

2.3 Taxation, Spending, and Regime Instability

Building off my prior work (Morrison 2009), this section's analysis uses a binary dependent variable (REGIME INSTABILITY) that takes a value of "1" if there is a regime change from one year to the next, and "0" otherwise. Similar to Smith (2004) in his study of regime instability, a regime is considered to have changed if it receives a zero in *Polity IV*'s DURABLE variable (Marshall and Jaggers 2003), which marks the number of years since the most recent regime change. A regime change in *Polity IV* is defined by a change of three points or more in the POLITY2 variable – which ranges from -10 (most authoritarian) to 10 (most democratic) – or the end of a multi-year transition period. By this definition, there are transitions in about five percent of the observations analyzed in this chapter.

The key independent variables in the model are TAX REVENUE PER CAPITA and GOVERNMENT SPENDING PER CAPITA.[8] They are calculated – using the International Monetary Fund's (IMF) *Government Finance Statistics* – by dividing total tax revenue and total government spending (respectively) by total population as

[7] More precisely, the regression is structured with the democracy level of a country as the dependent variable (with higher levels being more democratic), with a lagged value of that indicator as an independent variable. The effect of taxation is therefore measuring whether (and how far) additional taxation pushes a country in a democratic (positive coefficient) or authoritarian direction (negative coefficient). With this structure, the regression cannot analyze whether taxation leads to instability in both kinds of regimes. To be clear, the structure of the regression was perfectly appropriate for Ross's goals, as he was not trying to test the hypothesis offered here.

[8] The standardization by population is suggested directly by formal models relating public finance to regime stability (e.g., Morrison 2007) and is also intuitive: it implies, for example, that a given amount of spending is less useful to regimes if it needs to be distributed among more people.

reported in the World Bank's *World Development Indicators*.[9] In the regressions, I include both the (lagged) level of these variables, as well as their change (Δ) over the previous year.[10] The parameter of the lagged level indicates the permanent effect of a one-off change in that variable, whereas the parameter of the change is a measure of the transitory effect of that one-off change. The coefficient of interest is on the lagged value, which indicates the lasting effect of the variable in the long-term moving equilibrium.

Including both the taxation and spending variables in the same regression echoes other work on the effects of taxation on political regimes, which tends to suggest that citizens make calculated decisions about the burden of taxation. For example, in his study of the effects of taxation on the overthrow of authoritarian regimes, Ross (2004) finds that taxation by itself does not seem to affect transition, but the ratio of taxation to spending does – that is, a higher ratio of taxation to spending leads to more representative government.[11] This is equivalent to saying that taxation and spending have opposite effects, since a higher ratio of taxation to spending can of course be caused by either a cut in spending or a rise in taxation, or both.[12] I prefer to estimate these effects separately, clarifying the analysis, and therefore I have them as separate terms in the regression.

In addition to these key independent variables, it is important to control for other variables that might also be affecting regime stability. I therefore generally use the same control variables as Smith (2004) and Morrison (2009). First, I control for the natural log level of, and growth in, GDP PER CAPITA, following many scholars who have found a relationship between these indicators and regime stability (Lipset 1959; Remmer 1991; Przeworski and others 2000). Second, I control for the change in the percentage of the population that is urban (Δ% POPULATION URBAN) since some scholars have found that urbanization can be destabilizing for regimes (Huntington 1968). Third, I include the level of POPULATION DENSITY to control for the possibility of a relationship

[9] As discussed in the Introduction, the best available data on revenue and spending is from the International Monetary Fund's (IMF) *Government Finance Statistics* (GFS). Unfortunately for researchers interested in revenue over a long time period, in the beginning of the 2000s, the IMF changed the way it categorizes government finance (International Monetary Fund [IMF] 2001). Obviously, this means that the newer categorization is only available for a limited time period. However, the data for the previous coding by the IMF is available over a time period of 1973–2001. Therefore, to analyze a longer time series, I use the previous coding of revenue and spending in this book. The previous coding is detailed in International Monetary Fund (1986).

[10] This echoes the specification common in work on public finance, which will be used in Chapter 3.

[11] A related idea – in the sense of a "relative" tax burden – is found in the literature on the effects of taxation on democratic politics, in which several scholars have found that rising taxation matters in comparison to tax rates in neighboring municipalities (Besley and Case 1995; Bosch and Solé-Ollé 2007).

[12] As Ross points out, this is implied by the formal model that Bates and Lien (1985) discussed earlier regarding the relationship between taxation and representation.

between population, land, and regime stability (Herbst 2000; Fearon and Laitin 2003). All of these variables come from the World Bank. Finally, I include an indicator of whether the country was a DEMOCRACY or not in the year of the observation to account for the fact that during the time period of my sample, democracies fell at a slower rate than dictatorships (Huntington 1991). Following a convention established by prior research (e.g., Rousseau and others 1996; Reiter 2001; Kadera, Crescenzi, and Shannon 2003), the variable is coded as a "1" (democratic) if the country scores seven or above on *Polity IV*'s POLITY2 measure of political regimes (mentioned earlier), whereas countries with a score of six or below are considered to be dictatorships.

The estimation technique used is logistic analysis with errors clustered by country. However, as Beck, Katz, and Tucker (1998) have detailed, cross-sectional time-series data with a binary dependent variable are likely to violate the independence assumption of ordinary logistic analysis. Therefore, as recommended by Beck, Katz, and Tucker and implemented by others (Przeworski and others 2000; Smith 2004), I control for PAST REGIME INSTABILITY in a country, measured as the number of all past regime changes in that country in the sample. In addition, following the advice of Beck Katz, and Tucker, I include cubic splines of the POLITICAL REGIME'S AGE in a given year, to capture temporal dependence in the data.[13]

Model 1 in Table 2.1 presents the initial results of the analysis, which provide strong support for the hypothesis that taxation is destabilizing and spending stabilizing. Both TAX REVENUE PER CAPITA and SPENDING PER CAPITA enter significantly and with coefficients signed appropriately.[14] In substantive terms, a move from the twenty-fifth percentile of TAX REVENUE PER CAPITA to the seventy-fifth percentile would lead to a tripling in the probability of regime change. A move from the seventy-fifth percentile of GOVERNMENT SPENDING PER CAPITA to the twenty-fifth percentile would lead to a seven-fold increase in the probability of change. Many of the other control variables are insignificant, although economic growth has a strongly stabilizing effect and, as expected, democracies fall at a slower rate. The temporal dependence variables are also highly significant.

I submitted these results to a variety of robustness tests.[15] First, I included a measure of whether or not the country was involved in a militarized-interstate

[13] Specifically, the age of a political regime was coded as the lagged value of the DURABLE variable in *Polity IV*, which means that it is the number of years since there was a change of at least three in the POLITY2 score. F-tests revealed that these splines were necessary to include in the regressions. As Beck, Katz, and Tucker (1998) detail, including these splines makes logistic analysis identical to survival analysis techniques.

[14] Ideally, good instruments would exist for these variables, but I have not found one that meets the exclusion restriction. Issues of identification are most directly dealt with in Chapter 5, but most of the results in this chapter and those that follow are robust to country-level fixed effects (Angrist and Pischke 2009).

[15] These additions had little effect on the fit of the statistical model.

TABLE 2.1. *The Effect of Taxation and Spending on Regime Transitions*

Independent Variables	Model 1	Model 2
Δ TAX REVENUE PER CAPITA	0.000726**	0.000899*
	(0.000362)	(0.000495)
TAX REVENUE PER CAPITA (t-1)	0.000542***	0.000513***
	(0.000171)	(0.000162)
Δ GOVERNMENT SPENDING PER CAPITA	−0.000430	−0.000251
	(0.000526)	(0.000572)
GOVERNMENT SPENDING PER CAPITA (t-1)	−0.000608***	−0.000465**
	(0.000173)	(0.000230)
GDP PER CAPITA GROWTH	−0.0614***	−0.0601***
	(0.0206)	(0.0201)
GDP PER CAPITA (ln, t-1)	0.263*	0.210
	(0.149)	(0.173)
Δ% POPULATION URBAN	0.0259	0.0147
	(0.309)	(0.308)
POPULATION DENSITY (t-1)	−0.0422	−0.0548
	(0.0863)	(0.0824)
DEMOCRACY (t-1)	−2.702***	−2.333***
	(0.554)	(0.604)
PAST REGIME INSTABILITY	0.0235	0.0269
	(0.0660)	(0.0648)
AGE OF REGIME	−0.604***	−0.595***
	(0.131)	(0.132)
Δ TAX REVENUE PER CAPITA* DEMOCRACY (t-1)		−0.000846
		(0.00108)
TAX REVENUE PER CAPITA (t-1)* DEMOCRACY (t-1)		0.00171**
		(0.000694)
Δ GOVERNMENT SPENDING PER CAPITA* DEMOCRACY (t-1)		−0.00140
		(0.00209)
GOVERNMENT SPENDING PER CAPITA (t-1)* DEMOCRACY (t-1)		−0.00167**
		(0.000726)
CONSTANT	−1.953*	−1.626
	(1.028)	(1.147)
Observations	1715	1715
Countries	101	101
Prob > χ^2	0.0000	0.0000
Pseudo R^2	0.2593	0.2619

Note: The dependent variable in both regressions is regime transition (where 1 represents a transition), as discussed in the text. Standard errors clustered by country in parentheses. The asterisks denote the following: *** $p<0.01$, ** $p<0.05$, * $p<0.1$. Results for cubic splines of age of regime omitted.

dispute in the prior year (Marinov 2005), since some scholars have argued for war's effects on both taxation and regime instability (e.g., Tilly 1990). Second, I included a variable measuring ethnolinguistic fractionalization, since some scholars have argued that social fragmentation increases regime instability (e.g., Horowitz 1985).[16] Third, I included a dummy variable in the regression that indicated whether the country belonged to the Organization for Economic Co-operation and Development (OECD), to be sure that the dynamics observed were not driven by rich countries (in addition, I also tried running the regression using only non-OECD countries). Fourth, I included dummy variables marking the 1970s and 1980s to control for temporal effects. Fifth, to control for regional effects, I included dummy variables representing the different regions of the world. Sixth, I included a spatial lag of the dependent variable, to account for the possibility that regime transitions are spatially correlated (Gleditsch and Ward 2006). Seventh, I repeated the regression in Model 1 of Table 2.1 using an alternative coding of regime change. I employed the regime coding of Bueno de Mesquita and his colleagues (2003), who focus on the size of the winning coalition in a political regime.[17] Using various indicators from the *Polity* data set, they create a five-point scale to represent coalition size. I considered a regime change as any shift on this five-point scale. And finally, I ran the regression with country-level and year-level fixed effects.[18] None of these modifications had any significant impact on the important results.[19]

While these findings are illuminating, one of the most important ways this chapter differs from previous work is by emphasizing that taxation is destabilizing, and spending stabilizing, for both democracies and dictatorships. In order to evaluate this specific hypothesis, Model 2 in Table 2.1 presents the results of an interaction term between the taxation and spending variables and the DEMOCRACY variable. It might be noted that the model fit improves only slightly, but in any case, the results hold across both kinds of regimes: taxation has a significant and destabilizing effect in both regimes, and spending has a significant and stabilizing effect in both regimes. In fact, contrary to what one

[16] The measure I used is the probability that two randomly chosen individuals in a country do not speak the same language. Roeder's (2001) data set provides observations of this variable for both 1961 and 1985. For all observations prior to and in 1980, I use the 1961 measure, and for all subsequent years I use the 1985 measure.

[17] Using the dichotomous coding of Przeworski and others (2000), the coefficients were in the correct direction and significant on the change term of taxation, and the lagged term of spending, but insignificant on the other taxation and spending terms.

[18] Using country-level fixed effects on regime transition data is problematic, as the many countries that have never had a regime transition simply drop out of the data set. For this reason, Beck and Katz (2001) argue that country-level fixed effects should never be used in this type of analysis. Nevertheless, the stability of the results is encouraging. Note that in this regression I used POLITY2 instead of the dummy variable for democracy, because fixed effects regression causes problems for slowly changing variables.

[19] Results are available from the author as a data archive and Stata do-file.

might expect from the taxation-leads-to-representation hypothesis, democracies seem even more sensitive to government finance effects than dictatorships: the coefficients on the interaction term, representing the additive effect of taxation and spending in democracies, are negative and positive respectively (and significant). The implied size of the coefficients in democracies as opposed to dictatorships suggests that democracies are roughly four times more sensitive to taxation and spending than authoritarian regimes.

2.4 Taxation, Spending, and the Durability of Authoritarian Leaders

While the preceding analysis lends support to the idea that taxation is destabilizing and spending stabilizing for democracies and dictatorships, regime change is clearly only one form of political instability in countries. Regime changes are major events, but leadership transitions take place much more often, both in authoritarian and (by definition) democratic regimes. As mentioned at the beginning of this chapter, research has indicated that taxation and spending affect the fortunes of democratically elected incumbents, but what about authoritarian leaders? For example, after the 1966 coup against Kwame Nkrumah in Ghana, one of the participating members of the military explained that part of the reason for the coup was that "the burden of taxation [under Nkrumah] was heavy" (Afrifa 1966). Is this a common phenomenon: higher levels of taxation raise the probability of transitions between authoritarian leaders?

Addressing this question provides a useful means of differentiating between my hypothesis regarding taxation and authoritarian regimes – that taxation leads to instability – and the conventional wisdom that taxation leads to representation. If higher levels of taxation indeed lead to greater levels of leadership turnover in regimes, then this is not something for which the taxation-leads-to-representation argument can account, unless one believes that increased leadership turnover systematically implies greater representation (which I do not think is credible). The advantage of my framework – which does not explicitly tie taxation to representation – is that it can account for both of these dynamics, whereas the taxation-leads-to-representation approach cannot.

To test the effect of taxation and spending on the durability of leaders in authoritarian regimes, I use the data set originally developed by Chiozza and Goemans (2004) and updated by Goemans, Gleditsch, and Chiozza (2009), containing data on leaders and leadership changes for most countries in the world during the years covered in my sample (in fact, they cover all years between 1875 and 2004). Because of the nature of the data – with the unit of analysis being the leader, not a country in a given year – there can be multiple observations in a country in a given year. This differentiates these data from those on regime transitions and, indeed, from most commonly used economic data for developing countries (such as economic growth, income per capita, and government finance variables), for which there is only one observation per country per year. Therefore, in order to use the leadership data with my other indicators, I follow a strategy used by others (e.g., Marinov 2005). If there are multiple leadership changes in a given year, I code the country-year observation to simply register a leadership change in that year. In other words, there is no difference in my data set between one leadership change in a given year and multiple leadership changes (the leader in power at the end of the year is the one recorded for reference in the following years). Although obviously dropping information is never ideal, this seems a reasonable way to use the leadership data to study the effects of variables measured only on an annual basis.

To examine the effect of taxation and spending on these leadership transitions in authoritarian regimes (as defined earlier using the POLITY2 variable), I use the same taxation and spending variables employed previously, combined with other variables to control for omitted variable bias.[20] In particular, I control for economic growth and income per capita, using the same measures as in the regressions on regime change, as well as the AGE OF THE LEADER (Goemans, Gleditsch, and Chiozza 2009).

Because of the dichotomous dependent variable in this analysis – in which a leadership change is coded as "1" and no leadership change is coded as "0" – I use the same methodology employed earlier: logistic analysis with standard errors clustered by country. And as with those regressions, I again employ a variable to control for the temporal dependence of the observations. While in the earlier regressions I controlled for the age of the regime, here I control for the number of YEARS IN OFFICE a leader has had. As earlier, I supplement this variable with cubic splines of the number of years, to account for how the probability of staying in power rises or falls over time (Beck, Katz, and Tucker 1998).

Table 2.2 presents the results of the regression and shows that taxation and spending have effects similar to the ones they had in the regime change regressions: higher levels of taxation make the ousting of authoritarian leaders more likely, while higher levels of spending make their ouster less likely. Substantively, a move from the twenty-fifth percentile to the seventy-fifth percentile of TAX REVENUE PER CAPITA is associated with a 19 percent increase in the probability of a leadership change. A move from the seventy-fifth percentile to the twenty-fifth percentile of GOVERNMENT SPENDING PER CAPITA is associated with a 31 percent increase in the probability of a leadership change.

Many of these authoritarian leader changes did not lead to democratic transition, and therefore, this finding is difficult to explain with the existing conventional wisdom that "taxation leads to representation." However, it should be noted that this framework would gain support if the positive and significant coefficient on taxation in these regressions were driven primarily by instances in which authoritarian leaders fell to democratic ones. To ensure that these instances

[20] I also analyzed the relationship in those countries Przeworski and his colleagues (2000) code as dictatorships, and the results were similar.

TABLE 2.2. *The Effect of Taxation and Spending on Authoritarian Leader Transitions*

Independent Variables	Dependent Variable: Leadership Transition
Δ TAX REVENUE PER CAPITA	0.000835
	(0.000512)
TAX REVENUE PER CAPITA (t-1)	0.000539***
	(0.000159)
Δ GOVERNMENT SPENDING PER CAPITA	-5.79e-05
	(0.000669)
GOVERNMENT SPENDING PER CAPITA (t-1)	-0.000570***
	(0.000210)
GDP PER CAPITA GROWTH	-0.0760***
	(0.0208)
GDP PER CAPITA (ln, t-1)	0.188
	(0.202)
AGE OF LEADER	0.0108
	(0.0132)
YEARS IN OFFICE	-0.786**
	(0.337)
CONSTANT	-2.831**
	(1.318)
Observations	854
Countries	64
Prob > χ^2	0.0000
Pseudo R^2	0.10

Note: The dependent variable equals "1" when a leadership transition takes place. Results for cubic splines of years in office omitted. Standard errors clustered by country in parentheses. The asterisks denote the following: *** p<0.01, ** p<0.05, * p<0.1.

were not driving these results, I ran the same regression in Table 2.2 without the observations in which a regime change happened in a given year. That is, if a regime change happened in one of these authoritarian countries in a given year, it was excluded from the regression. The results were substantively identical – taxation destabilizes authoritarian leaders, even if no regime change is happening. The results for spending also do not change: in all of the regressions, higher spending leads to less probability of an authoritarian leader exiting office.[21]

To ensure that these results were robust to other operationalizations, I included other control variables from the earlier regressions on regime stability

[21] In addition, I ran an additional regression including only those observations for which the current level of POLITY2 was equal to or less than the previous year's level of POLITY2 – that is, only countries that either maintained the same level of authoritarian regime or became more authoritarian. Again, the results were substantively identical – taxation destabilized leaders and spending stabilized them.

(whether the state was involved in a militarized-interstate dispute in the prior year, growth in urban population, population density, and past regime changes) and found that the results did not change.[22] Similar results were also attained running the regression only with developing countries or including an OECD dummy variable, decade dummies, year dummies, or a Middle East dummy variable.[23]

In combination with existing works on the effects of taxation and spending on democratically elected leaders, these results suggest that taxation and spending have similar effects on leaders as they do on political regimes.[24] Taxation destabilizes them, while spending stabilizes them.

2.5 Conclusion

This chapter has revisited one of the most well-known theories relating an aspect of government finance to an aspect of political regimes: the hypothesis that taxation leads to representation. It has not argued that this approach is wrong as much as it has argued that the approach is misleading. Higher levels of taxation do tend to lead to a higher probability of the overthrow of authoritarian regimes, which is exactly what the conventional literature has argued. However, these higher levels of taxation also lead to a higher probability of overthrow of democratic regimes, as well as to a higher probability of turnover among authoritarian and democratic leaders. None of these latter phenomena can be explained by the traditional taxation-leads-to-representation approach. Instead, they are consistent with an argument that higher levels of taxation lead to political instability, not representation.

I have made this argument by considering the literature on taxation-leads-to-representation alongside several other bodies of work that have linked aspects

[22] These additions had little effect on the fit of the statistical model. Results are available from the author as a data archive and Stata do-file.

[23] Including country-level fixed effects resulted in twenty-seven countries and about a third of my observations dropping from the sample. With this smaller sample, the coefficients on taxation and spending, in fact, almost double in absolute terms (that is, the one on taxation is about 0.001 and the one on spending is about – 0.001), but the standard errors also increase, resulting in insignificant coefficients. The results in the text are robust to year-level fixed effects.

[24] As reflected by the works cited earlier in the chapter, testing the effects of taxation and spending in democracies is much more common subnationally than it is cross-nationally. In a subnational context, one can compare the results of many subnational elections in the same year. In a cross-national context, elections are rarely in the same year, and the "hazard" of leadership transition is close to zero in democracies in other years. Generating comparable units across countries, and getting over-time comparisons within the same country, is therefore quite difficult. I experimented with the data set on national elections compiled by Hyde and Marinov (2012) and, using data for executive elections, ran a regression with the dependent variable of whether or not the party in power was reelected (Cheibub and Przeworski 1999). There were 103 observations in 29 countries, and taxation and spending were insignificant in various specifications. I am more confident in the effects of spending on elections at the subnational level reported by Litschig and Morrison (2013) and in Chapter 5.

of government finance to dynamics in political regimes. In particular, I considered works arguing that higher levels of government spending should help regimes and leaders stay in power, as well as works arguing that higher levels of taxation may be politically damaging for democratic regimes and leaders. Together, these various bodies of work lend theoretical support to the idea that taxation and spending work in opposite ways in all regimes, with taxation acting as a destabilizing force and spending a stabilizing one.

Consistent with my theory, my empirical analysis found that taxation is destabilizing of both democracies and dictatorships, while spending stabilizes both types of regimes. Similarly, I analyzed the effects of taxation and spending on leadership transitions within authoritarian regimes. I found – as other work has found with regard to democratically elected leaders – that taxation leads to a higher probability of leadership turnover, and spending leads to a lower probability, even if one only examines countries that did not transition to democracy.

Collectively, the results here provide the first synthetic analysis of the effects of taxation and spending on democracies, dictatorships, and their leaders. Whereas previous works have looked at various types of spending, and other works have looked at taxation, no work has considered them together in both democracies and dictatorships.

Nevertheless, from the perspective of government finance, this chapter is incomplete. The reason is that it has ignored the other major form of revenue for governments around the world: nontax revenue. And it is to that revenue I now turn.

3

Nontax Revenue Lowers Taxation and Increases Spending

3.1 Introduction

Chapter 2 provided support for my argument that taxation tends to undermine political stability in both democracies and dictatorships, whereas spending tends to strengthen it. And for many scholars, taxation is where an examination of the relationship between government revenue and political stability would stop (for example, Brennan and Buchanan 1980; Levi 1988). Indeed, when anyone thinks of "revenue," he or she very likely thinks first about taxation.

As discussed in the Introduction, however, taxation makes up only one part of revenue for countries. The rest (indeed, the majority in some countries) comes from *nontax* sources. This chapter and Chapter 4 address this latter kind of revenue. In this chapter, I will build a theory about how it relates to taxation and spending, and in Chapter 4, I will combine the insights from Chapter 2 and this chapter to make an argument about how nontax revenue relates to political stability.

In the next section, I develop a framework for considering the effects of this revenue on taxation and spending. Beginning with a simple model that generates clear predictions – nontax revenue should reduce taxation and increase spending – I proceed to show that these predictions should hold under a wide variety of country circumstances, and for different kinds of nontax revenue. In the following section, I turn to empirical evidence supporting these predictions, reviewing the literatures on various sources of nontax revenue and then providing new statistical evidence of my own, drawing on cross-national time-series analysis. A final section concludes.

3.2 A Theory of Nontax Revenue, Taxation, and Spending

As Chapter 2 indicated, taxation is costly for politicians. But in a basic sense it is also costly for all individuals: taxation means that we give up some part of our income. On the flip side, we benefit from government spending, which is why it is beneficial for politicians. Knowing this, how much would we each prefer a government to tax and spend? Obviously we would like to spend as much as possible, but that spending has to be financed by something, and that financing is usually costly.

How this choice about the levels of taxation and spending is made – and the effect of nontax revenue on it – is the focus of this section. I begin by analyzing how any single person would make this decision. Although this initial model abstracts from considerations of governments and regimes, it is essential and enlightening groundwork for what comes in the following sections. I subsequently demonstrate how the model gives us insight into different political regimes, tax systems, and types of nontax revenue. The presentation is mathematical but not exceptionally technical, and the gain from the mathematics is greater precision and – most importantly – an idea of the range of outcomes for which my argument is likely to hold.[1]

Let us assume that individuals like government spending and also like whatever taxation takes away from them. This latter "good" could be just about anything, but for simplicity, let us say that it is an individual's consumption. That is, when I pay taxes, I can no longer use that money to consume something else. To form a utility function that describes preferences over consumption and public spending, we need to assume some sort of relationship between them, so I will use the following (Stone-Geary) utility function:

$$U_i = (c_i - \overline{c})^{\alpha} S^{1-\alpha}, \qquad (3.1)$$

where U_i is the utility of an individual, c_i is the person's consumption, $\overline{c}$ is the baseline level of consumption (below which a person cannot survive), and S is per capita government spending.[2] Because we do not want to assume that spending and consumption are equally valued by an individual, α is included in the function. It ranges between zero and one and captures the relative effect of consumption and government spending on utility (that is, if α is greater than 0.5, consumption is valued more than spending).[3]

[1] To facilitate understanding by readers not mathematically inclined, I provide verbal explanations of each of the mathematical steps, sometimes in footnotes.

[2] Since S is in per capita terms, the assumption is that the effectiveness of government spending is determined by the number of people using the good. This is true of most government spending: as examples, the utility gained from money spent on schools, hospitals, vaccines, housing, pensions, transportation, assistance for the poor, and even public employment is partly determined by the number of people serviced.

[3] This useful utility function subsumes the Cobb-Douglas utility function, for which $\overline{c}$ would be equal to zero (Mas-Colell, Whinston, and Green 1995). The findings would also hold if the $1-\alpha$ term were replaced with β, as long as $\alpha + \beta \leq 1$. The utility function assumes that both public goods and private consumption are what economists refer to as "normal" goods. This means that

Now, obviously, a person's consumption is going to be affected by his or her income, but we are less interested in that relationship, so let us assume we are in a society of individuals who have exactly the same income. This is a gross simplification, but it can easily be relaxed with no effect on the important results of the model. The gain from making the simplification here is that it will help us to focus strictly on the relationship between nontax revenue, taxation, and spending.

With this setup, the consumption of each individual can be represented as:

$$c_i = (1-\tau)y \ , \tag{3.2}$$

where τ is a proportional income tax levied on all citizens and y is everyone's individual income. That is, an individual consumes what is left of one's income after the taxes have been paid.

To finalize the setup of our model, we just need an expression for per capita government spending. This spending is assumed to be financed by tax revenues and nontax revenues (the budget is assumed to be balanced once nontax revenues are included).[4] Thus, per capita government expenditures are equal to

$$S = \frac{1}{n}\left[\sum_{i=1}^{n} \tau y\right] + N = \tau y + N, \tag{3.3}$$

where n is the number of people in the society and N is the per capita amount of nontax revenue.[5]

To derive the tax rate that any given individual would choose (which, in combination with nontax revenue, determines the amount of spending), we need to plug equations (3.2) and (3.3) into (3.1), yielding:[6]

$$V_i = [(1-\tau)y - \bar{c}]^{\alpha}(\tau y + N)^{1-\alpha}. \tag{3.4}$$

This equation enables us to find the ideal tax rate of any given citizen because it tells us precisely how the tax rate affects the utility of the individual, taking

if income increases, the citizen spends some of the increase on each of them. This seems uncontroversial, but it should be noted that if this were not true, some of the predictions in this chapter would not hold.

4 Although nontax revenues are assumed to finance spending on public goods, a decision maker could choose to divert this revenue into consumption by a uniform transfer to citizens. In this model, this would be the equivalent of reducing the tax rate. These relative preferences of consumption and public spending are captured by α.

5 Alternatively, the right-most expression could be $\tau\bar{y} + N$, with $\bar{y}$ equal to the average level of income. However, in this particular setup, everyone has the same income, so $\bar{y}$ is equal to y.

6 As this is an indirect utility function, U_i changes to V_i.

into account that rate's effect on both consumption (the costs) and government spending (the benefits).[7] That ideal tax rate is:

$$\tau = \frac{(1-\alpha)(y-\bar{c})-\alpha N}{y}. \tag{3.5}$$

This expression of the individual's optimal tax rate shows us that this rate will diminish as nontax revenues increase (since N on the right-hand side has a minus sign in front of it).[8] This equation is the foundation for one of the predictions of this chapter: nontax revenue reduces taxation.

To find the implications of nontax revenue for government spending, we simply need to take the optimal level of taxation indicated by equation (3.5) and plug it into equation (3.3), yielding:

$$S = (1-\alpha)(y-\bar{c}+N). \tag{3.6}$$

As can be seen, unless α is equal to one (which would be the very unlikely case in which government spending has no value), the equation indicates that as nontax revenue goes up, spending will go up as well. This equation therefore provides the foundation of the other prediction of this chapter: nontax revenue increases government spending.

This is obviously the simplest of setups. However, even in its simplicity, it captures something essential about decisions regarding taxation and spending. Let us for the moment assume that N is equal to zero: that is, there is no nontax revenue in the society. Any individual making this decision will not choose to spend indiscriminately, because the person will reach a point at which the costs of spending (in terms of taxation) outweigh the benefits. Similarly, the individual will not set the tax rate to zero, because there is some level of government spending that is worth the cost. In the language of economists, individuals making this decision will arrive at their optimal level of taxation by equating the marginal cost of taxation with the marginal benefit of government spending. The exact choice will depend on the levels of the other parameters in equations (3.5) and (3.6), such as how much they like consumption in comparison to public spending (α).

Indeed, because of these various characteristics, the model is able to accommodate the types of rulers described in canonical treatments of revenue and rulers. Although the rulers in theories by Levi (1988), Olson (1993) and others are often called "revenue-maximizing," they, in fact, are not. They raise revenue

[7] One must simply solve equation (3.4) through unconstrained optimization of the tax rate, taking the derivative of (3.4) with respect to τ.

[8] The equation also indicates that the preferred level of public spending increases with income: a common claim is that taste for public goods such as education and healthcare increase with income. I am grateful to an anonymous reviewer for pointing this out.

subject to the costs and benefits of such revenue. As Levi (1988: 13) writes, "It is trivial to say that rulers consider the costs and benefits and choose the policy that gives them the most advantage. Certainly, they are not always choosing the policy that produces the most revenue." Therefore, this simple setup is in line with the essence of these foundational approaches to revenue. The difference is that these approaches generally have not considered the effects of nontax revenue.

Let us now see what will happen if nontax revenue enters the equation. As N increases, two things happen simultaneously. The first might be termed a "substitution" effect: because nontax revenues can be used in place of tax revenues, the individual can diminish the level of taxation. The second dynamic might be termed a "wealth" effect: the citizen is essentially richer, in that her overall budget constraint has expanded, and this will lead to more government spending as well. This is not particularly surprising; these sorts of substitution and wealth effects are commonly seen in the examination of consumer choice (Mas-Colell, Whinston, and Green 1995). However, the overall result is central for the endeavor here: as nontax revenue increases, the preferred level of taxation will decrease, and the preferred level of spending will increase. And these overall negative and positive relationships will hold regardless of the person's income or particular preferences regarding consumption or public spending.[9]

Despite the insight this model yields into how an individual would make this decision, the reader may justifiably be wondering what this could tell us about how nontax revenue affects taxation and spending in modern polities, where decision making is obviously more complicated. This is a critical issue for this chapter: the extent to which this relationship is likely to hold across different leaders, countries, and time. I want to make a broad argument that, in general, higher nontax revenue should be associated with the sorts of dynamics just illustrated: diminished taxation and increased spending. But is there a reason to believe that this would be true across different kinds of political regimes and tax systems? And what about differences inherent in the sources of nontax revenue, such as the differences between foreign aid and natural resource revenues? Let me discuss these in order.

3.2.1 *Different Political Regimes*

When examining whether the approach outlined in the previous section would apply to various political regimes, it is useful to consider what the utility function of a government looks like. This requires trying to represent a government's preferences mathematically. The most straightforward way of doing this is to conceive of a government making decisions by putting different "weights" or levels of importance on each of its citizens. Consider, for example, two

[9] The *extent* of the negative or positive relationship would change with these parameters. For example, the effect of nontax revenue on taxation and spending will change as α changes. But it will be positive no matter what the particular value of α is.

extreme weighting schemes. We would arguably be in a perfectly democratic government (or a benevolent authoritarian one) if the utility of each of the citizens received the same weight in a regime's decision making.[10] In other words, every person's well-being counted equally in the government's decision. At the other extreme, we would be in a perfectly (selfish) authoritarian government if the utility of the dictator received a weight of one, and the utility of everyone else received a weight of zero. In other words, only the dictator's well-being counted in the government's decision. All other regimes lie on the continuum between these extremes.

We can account for this continuum by assuming that every government has a utility function that looks like this:

$$R = \sum_{i=1}^{n} \lambda_i U_i, \tag{3.7}$$

where R is the utility of the government, λ_i is the weight given by the government to person i's utility (the sum of all λ_i's is equal to one), and U_i is as defined in equation (3.1). All this expression means is that, as just discussed, it is possible for certain citizens to have more importance for the government than others (or not, if all λ_i's have the same value). When a government makes a decision, it does so in a way that maximizes equation (3.7).

Representing governments in this way is quite useful, because we can solve equation (3.7) in a way very similar to that in the previous section and find that the optimal taxation and spending rates for a given government are exactly equal to the expressions in equations (3.5) and (3.6), no matter which various weights are assigned. This is true because we are not allowing income to vary across citizens in this simple setup. However, the same comparative statics with regard to nontax revenue would hold if we allowed incomes to vary across citizens. In other words, this analysis indicates that the finding regarding nontax revenue is robust no matter what weighting scheme a government entails. Nontax revenue should decrease taxation and increase spending.

This is an important finding because it turns out that a variety of different approaches to decision making in democracies and dictatorships can be incorporated into the "weights" approach considered here. For example, with regard to democracies, the most famous model for predicting decision making is the median voter theorem (Bowen 1943; Black 1948; Downs 1957). This model has been used to explain not only certain aspects of public finance, such as levels of redistribution (Meltzer and Richard 1981), but also to explain transitions between democracies and dictatorships (Boix 2003; Acemoglu and Robinson 2006). The framework predicts that, given certain assumptions about voters, majority rule should produce the policy that maximizes the utility of

[10] Dahl (1971: 2) writes that one of the hallmarks of contestation is when citizens have their "preferences weighted equally in the conduct of the government."

the median voter.[11] As such, empirical predictions can be generated simply by looking at the preferences of that voter (Barr and Davis 1966; Borcherding and Deacon 1972; Bergstrom and Goodman 1973; Inman 1978). In the framework of equation (3.7), this means that the median voter receives a weight of one, and other citizens receive a weight of zero.

Although the median voter model is the most famous of them, it turns out that many models of democratic decision making can be incorporated within the approach encapsulated in equation (3.7). Models of probabilistic voting, for example, incorporate the possibility that candidates or parties differ in ideology or some other personal characteristic that matters to voters (Enelow and Hinich 1982; Lindbeck and Weibull 1987). In these models, the key citizens are "swing voters," who have weak partisan biases. The same holds true for models of lobbying and influence by interest groups (Olson 1965; Becker 1983; Grossman and Helpman 1994), in which certain groups have more power than others. In all of these approaches, the utility of decision makers can be represented as a weighted sum of the utilities of voters.[12]

This is also true of more complex models of democratic decision making. For example, in the models discussed so far, the politicians themselves do not particularly care about the policies enacted. If they did, any promises they made that were different from their own preferences would not be credible, and people would not vote for them. If this were the case – if politicians did, indeed, have their own preferences over policy – would the implemented policy still resemble the one preferred by certain voters? This is, indeed, one of the results of the so-called "citizen-candidate" models (Osborne and Slivinski 1996; Besley and Coate 1997), in which citizens put themselves forth as candidates. Since their only credible policy position is their own preference, only the citizen with preferences supported by a majority in the population will win the majority rule competition. While the equilibria in these models include the traditional median voter equilibrium, in which the median voter is elected, they also include equilibria in which the median voter is not elected. But regardless of the identity of the actual individual (that is, median voter or otherwise), the important aspect of these models from the perspective of this chapter is that the policy outcome can be captured by the sort of weighted utility function discussed earlier. In this case, the utility of the winner would receive a weight of one, and all other citizens would receive a weight of zero.

In sum, many foundational models of democratic politics boil down to the assumption used in my model: decisions result as if the regime were maximizing a weighted sum of its citizens' utilities. Not surprisingly, models of authoritarian regimes work somewhat differently, but their decision making process can also usually be incorporated into equation (3.7). As I mentioned earlier, this is true in the extreme case where one unconstrained leader makes all of the

[11] The principal assumption about voters is that their preferences are single-peaked.
[12] See Persson and Tabellini (2000), Chapter 3.

decisions. However, research on authoritarian regimes continually emphasizes how leaders in these regimes rely on coalitions and supporters, just as democratic leaders do (Geddes 1999; Pepinsky 2008; Weeks 2008; Wright 2008a; Svolik 2009; Magaloni and Kricheli 2010). For this reason, many scholars model decision making in authoritarian regimes by focusing principally on the decision making of a single leader constrained by the preferences of his or her supporters (Olson 1993; Svolik 2009; Debs and Goemans 2010). The framework here would incorporate these theories by assigning positive weights to those supporters and zero weights to other citizens.

One principal example of this kind of approach is the "selectorate" model of Bueno de Mesquita and his colleagues (2003). As discussed in Chapter 2, these authors characterize political systems by their selectorate (the group that has any influence on who is leader) and the winning coalition (the subset of the selectorate that causes the leader to come to power). In majoritarian democracies, for example, the selectorate would be the group of eligible voters, and the winning coalition would be a majority of voters. These would, of course, be different in an authoritarian regime. However, in both types of regimes, the influence of the winning coalition could be captured by the sort of weighted sum represented in equation (3.7).

In conclusion, many of the most important benchmark models for considering decision making in democracies and dictatorships can be incorporated into equation (3.7). And if equation (3.7) captures decision making in a polity, then the hypothesized effect of nontax revenue should be as previously argued: it should diminish taxation and increase spending.

3.2.2 *Different Government Finance Systems*

We have established that scholars from many traditions and approaches have found it useful to generate predictions about decisions in both democracies and dictatorships by a weighted sum of citizens' utilities. However, even if we assume that decision making in a given country can be plausibly represented by an equation such as (3.7), how robust is the prediction about nontax revenue to making reasonable changes in the model regarding how government finance operates?

For example, tax systems are clearly different around the world, so we would not want the predictions about nontax revenue to change dramatically if we were to change the model in some way to reflect this. Consider an authoritarian leader: Would that leader really, as the model implies, tax herself? After all, the linear tax rate in equation (3.1) falls even on the leader. Although this may seem plausible in models of democracies, it seems more unlikely in the case of, for example, personalist dictatorships. Are the results robust to reasonable changes in the way tax systems are assumed to be structured in the model?

We can answer this question by altering equation (3.1) a bit and exploring the implications. Let us assume that there are two individuals in society, A and B, and that individual A is in power (A and B could just as easily be groups instead of individuals). Individual A can implement a tax on individual B – call this τ_B – in order to fund some public good that has the same utility as that in equation (3.1). In order to generate the prediction that nontax revenue will diminish taxation and increase spending, the only assumption one has to make is that imposing this tax on individual B is – even in some minimal way – costly to individual A. This assumption is, for example, supported by the evidence presented in Chapter 2, as well as the theoretical and empirical literature (e.g., Levi 1988) that points to costs associated with the enforcement and processing of taxes. If these costs exist, then individual A's consumption can be represented as:

$$c_A = y - d(\tau_B), \tag{3.8}$$

where $d(\cdot)$ is an increasing function that captures the costs of taxation. This simply means that as τ_B increases, so do the costs of imposing this tax for person A. Using this equation instead of (3.1), equation (3.4) would then change to

$$V_A = [y - d(\tau_B) - \bar{c}]^{\alpha}(\tau_B y + N)^{1-\alpha}, \tag{3.9}$$

and optimizing this expression with regard to τ_B again yields the prediction that nontax revenue should diminish taxation and increase spending (that is, an increase in nontax revenue diminishes the optimal level of τ_B from individual A's perspective). In other words, the general prediction about nontax revenue is robust to this sort of adjustment to the taxation process.[13]

Although I will not go through the analysis here, using the same sort of technique, one could show that the nontax revenue prediction would also hold if spending could be allocated differently among two different groups in society. The key, as in the taxation analysis, is that as long as there is some cost to taxation and some benefit to spending, nontax revenue should reduce taxation and increase spending.[14]

[13] It is true that the magnitude of the change that results from an additional dollar of nontax revenue in this scenario might be different from the earlier setup, but for my purposes, I am interested in whether the effect is positive or negative for taxation and spending, not the exact point prediction of an effect. Relatedly, I am not so concerned with the literature on the "flypaper effect" (Hines and Thaler 1995), which finds that subnational governments receiving grants often allocate this money more to spending (as opposed to tax breaks) than economic theory would predict. That literature finds similar effects to those posited here – positive effects on spending and negative effects on taxation – but simply finds higher effects on spending and lower effects on taxation than scholars would otherwise predict. As Inman (2008) discusses, the differences can likely be accounted for by greater attention to political factors that differ across countries and levels of government.

[14] Whereas this prediction would hold with many standard government-finance models (e.g., Meltzer and Richard 1981), it is possible to find situations in which it would not hold. For example, Battaglini and Coate (2011) develop a model examining the relationship between fiscal policy and unemployment. In the model, jobs can be created either by cutting taxes or

3.2.3 Different Kinds of Nontax Revenue

The third potential issue with the model developed earlier is whether different kinds of nontax revenue can be expected to act similarly. For example, might foreign aid act differently than state-owned enterprise revenue, intergovernmental grants, or borrowing? In order to address this issue, it is first necessary to highlight why, exactly, nontax revenue leads to lower taxes and higher spending in the model. I will first discuss the two key characteristics of nontax revenue and then turn to a discussion of whether various possible sources of nontax revenue have these characteristics.

The first key aspect of nontax revenue is essentially definitional: it is positive revenue that does not accrue from taxing citizens of the recipient government (as represented by equation [3.7]). This does not mean that acquiring it is necessarily costless. For example, revenues that accrue from state-owned enterprises require investment, paying employees, managing volatility, managing environmental costs, and so forth. Revenues from foreign aid require time and travel spent on negotiations with donors. Almost every type of nontax revenue entails at least some cost to attain it. However, the important aspect of nontax revenue sources is that, net of these costs, they provide revenue that does not come from taxes of the recipient government.[15]

increasing government spending, and jobs respond to taxation and spending at different rates in different economies. While in some scenarios the prediction given in this chapter holds (nontax revenue leads to less taxation and more spending), in other scenarios different predictions are generated. Principally this occurs in bad economic times, when the government introduces distortions into the economy by taxing and spending "too much" in order to maintain full employment (or "too little" if the effect of taxation on employment is relatively strong). In this scenario (the "too much" scenario), a decrease in nontax revenue might cause the government to raise *both* taxation and spending – the former to meet financing needs and the latter to hire the workers displaced by taxation.

[15] To see this, assume that there is an exogenously determined cost per person x associated with a certain amount of per capita nontax revenue N. In other words, we can rewrite equation (3.4) as: $V_i = [(1-\tau)y - x - \bar{c}]^{\alpha}(\tau y + N)^{1-\alpha}$. In this case, the equilibrium tax rate is

$$\tau = \frac{(1-\alpha)(y - x - \bar{c}) - \alpha N}{y}.$$

It is straightforward to see that the presence of positive N and x (compared to a situation in which they are both zero) has a negative effect on taxation. Indeed, both costs and the nontax revenue have a negative effect, the result of both income and substitution effects. The equilibrium level of spending will be

$$S = (1-\alpha)(y - x - \bar{c} + N).$$

Unlike the taxation equation, the relationship between nontax revenue and costs matters here. The presence of positive N and x (compared to a situation in which they are both zero) has a positive effect on spending if $N > x$. It is straightforward to show that these same results obtain if one models the cost x as a percentage of income. In this case, the important condition is that N is greater than xy.

The second key characteristic of nontax revenue in the model is that it is not associated with a change in the weighting scheme used by the government (that is, a change in the weights assigned to citizens in equation [3.7]).[16] This aspect becomes theoretically important as soon as we allow incomes to vary across citizens in society. When incomes vary, individuals have different preferred tax and spending rates. Because of this, changing the weights assigned to different individuals in society could result in different tax and spending rates. The desired result – that an increase in nontax revenue for any particular government would lead to less taxation and more spending – is therefore contingent on nontax revenue not changing the weighting scheme itself. If the influx of nontax revenue changed the weighting scheme, one could potentially get offsetting impacts, with nontax revenue pushing the tax rate down, but the change in weighting scheme tilting the tax rate in the other direction. Therefore, the neutrality of nontax revenue with regard to the weighting scheme is important to the theory.

In order to consider the effects of different possible sources of nontax revenue, we thus need to examine whether they meet these two conditions: 1) they do not change the weights given to different citizens in a government's utility function, and 2) they generate positive revenue that does not accrue from taxing citizens. In this light, let us consider four main types of nontax revenue: natural resource rents, foreign aid, intergovernmental grants, and borrowing.

NATURAL RESOURCE RENTS. It seems relatively uncontroversial that revenues flowing into the coffers of state-owned natural resource enterprises generate positive revenue that does not accrue from taxation. Indeed, on this point, this book is in line with much of the large literature on the *rentier* state, which has primarily focused on the various ways in which large natural resource revenues increase spending and diminish the need for taxation (Mahdavy 1970; Beblawi and Luciani 1987; Karl 1997; Ross 2001). The one point of qualification is that the only oil that accrues as nontax revenue is that which comes through state-owned enterprises.

Indeed, this distinction is important in understanding how this book relates to recent empirical and theoretical scholarship on the resource curse. On the empirical side, it suggests that the important variable of interest is not oil, per se, but the nontax revenue that the oil generates. Important recent work by Haber and Menaldo (2011) has questioned the hypothesis that oil causes countries to become more authoritarian, but their measure of interest does not distinguish between state-owned and privately owned oil. Andersen and Ross (2014) have responded by using Haber and Menaldo's techniques and showing that oil's effects have changed since the 1980s. Andersen and Ross mention that this is the period right after oil industries were nationalized, which is directly in line with my argument (Morrison 2009) and others' (Jones Luong

[16] I am grateful to Stephen Coate for this point and related conversations.

and Weinthal 2006), that natural resources only have certain effects when they are in the hands of state-owned enterprises.[17]

The exclusive focus on nontax revenue also distinguishes this book from work on the resource curse that attributes oil's effects to information problems or other factors. For example, Ross (2012) has recently highlighted four different factors that lead to oil revenue's ostensibly negative effects: its scale, its source (largely state-owned), its volatility, and its secrecy. The argument in this chapter and Chapter 4 demonstrate that secrecy and volatility are not necessary to generate stabilizing effects, which can be attributed to the fact that they do not come from taxes.[18] This is why the book treats them as part of the broader phenomenon of nontax revenues, rather than considering them on their own.

The second key characteristic of nontax revenue highlighted earlier – regarding the effect of nontax revenue on the relative weight given to certain citizens – is useful in drawing one more distinction between the approach of this book and much existing work on natural resources and democracy. Because most of that literature is situated in the traditional "taxation leads to representation" literature, authors in the *rentier* tradition have assumed that lowering taxes and increasing spending will lead to more authoritarian regimes. In contrast, I have shown here that lowering taxes and increasing spending should stabilize whatever regime is in place – I have essentially shown that the *rentier* mechanism should apply in democracies, too. Without this mechanism, it is still possible that oil could have negative effects on democracy (although I am not sure what the mechanism would be). In the language of this chapter, this would mean that oil would have some independent effect on the weighting scheme of the existing regime, leading more weight to be put on fewer people (that is, a more authoritarian regime). If this were the case, it would generate quite different predictions than the ones made in this chapter and Chapter 4. For example, in Chapter 4, oil would be predicted to destabilize democratic regimes, instead

[17] This raises an interesting issue, which is how a government decides whether natural resource revenue will be tax revenue or nontax revenue – equivalently, privately owned or state owned. This issue has not received enough scholarly attention, although important works exist that emphasize the roles of international oil prices, the availability of other revenue sources, domestic politics, and the cost of nationalization (Jones Luong and Weinthal 2010; Guriev, Kolotilin, and Sonin 2011; Stroebel and van Benthem 2013). In very rough terms, the argument in this book would seem to suggest that we would see nationalization (which, in a sense, is a very large tax) only when a government was exceptionally stable and willing to trade-off a short-term increase in instability for the longer term benefits of nontax revenue. I leave detailed investigation of this issue for future work.

[18] This is certainly not to say that international efforts to improve the transparency of oil revenues are not worthwhile. Citizens should by all means know the state of their country's budget, and budget transparency seems to have important effects on people's willingness to hold their governments accountable (Paler 2013). It is also true that secrecy and volatility may determine other effects of oil (such as on economic growth). The point here is simply that these are not necessary for oil to affect the stability of oil-rich regimes and their leaders.

of my argument that these oil revenues should stabilize democracies as well as dictatorships. Or, if applied to this chapter, the effect of oil revenues on taxation and spending would be indeterminate: the oil revenues would change taxation and spending directly through the mechanism I describe here, but then have additional, indirect effects on taxation and spending through their alteration of the weighting function. Without knowing the latter, it would be impossible to predict the overall effects on taxation and spending. I will therefore try to adjudicate between these hypotheses and mine empirically in this chapter and next.

FOREIGN AID. The main reason that foreign aid's effects might differ from those of natural resource revenues is that aid is delivered by donors who presumably have some control over the way the money is used. In fact, however – as I will explain here – there are good theoretical reasons to suspect that these revenues act similarly to natural resource rents and other nontax revenues (Bräutigam 2000; Svensson 2000; Moore 2001; Therkildsen 2002; Collier 2006; Morrison 2007; Smith 2008). The upshot, as Collier (2006, 1483) notes, is that both foreign aid and natural resource revenues are "sovereign rents." Again, I will focus on the two key conditions under which nontax revenues would reduce taxes and increase spending: 1) they accrue to the government without taxation, and 2) they have no effect on the weights given to citizens' utility in the government's decision making.

There are two principal reasons aid might not accrue to the government without taxation.[19] One is that it actually may not even accrue to the government because it is often delivered in the form of projects that bypass the recipient government's normal budgetary process (Dietrich 2013). Many of these aid-financed projects are designed by donors in cooperation with the government, but there is little doubt that project-based aid is meant to reduce the discretion of recipient countries in terms of how to spend the money. Indeed, standard principal-agent theory suggests that as preferences between a donor (the principal) and the recipient country (the agent) increasingly differ, the donor should augment its control of how the money is spent (Winters 2010), such as by implementing projects on its own. Not surprisingly, policy prescriptions in this regard are not difficult to find: Radelet (2004: 13) writes, for example, that "in weak, failing, and poorly governed countries, donors should retain a strong role in setting priorities and designing programs."

Nevertheless, donors face a problem with project funding: it is largely fungible, in the sense that it simply enables a government to take money it would have spent on that item (for example, a school) and spend it on another item

[19] The focus here is on the flow of money. As such, one aid modality that may be different than natural resource revenue is "technical assistance," which is often provided by donors in the form of people (that is, experts), not money (Collier 2006; Gibson and Hoffman 2007). However, this kind of aid makes up a clear minority of global aid flows.

(Feyzioglu, Swaroop, and Zhu 1998; Farag and others 2009). In this way, while donors may fund a school, their money may simply free the government to spend its money on other priorities (arms, for example). From the perspective of equation (3.1), what this means is that donors are simply financing some part of the overall *S*. If they specify that they themselves are going to actually build and run the school, for example, it makes little difference to the government. It is still just *S*.

The second reason aid might not accrue to the government without taxation is that donors sometimes put policy conditions on the receipt of their aid, saying that the government needs to cut spending or raise taxes. This practice – attempting to change a government's policies in exchange for money – has been one of the more controversial aspects of foreign aid practice over the past few decades. Underlying the ideas of both the practitioners of it (many donors) and its critics (many nongovernmental organizations) has been the assumption that these conditionalities actually work – that is, the assumption that governments actually implement the policies required by foreign donors. In fact, while there are certain instances in which these conditions have probably influenced a government to act in a specific way, studies have largely concluded that these conditions have no systematic influence on policy (World Bank 1992; Mosley, Harrigan, and Toye 1995; Collier 1997; Alesina and Dollar 2000; Burnside and Dollar 2000; van de Walle 2001; Easterly 2005; Heckelman and Knack 2008). For example, in a particularly detailed analysis of ten African countries, a study by the World Bank found that "[l]arge amounts of aid to countries with bad policy sustained those bad policies. The funding allowed the delay of reform. Attaching conditions to the aid in these cases has not successfully led to policy change, nor has it delayed the disbursement of funds" (Devarajan, Dollar, and Holmgren 2001: 6).

There are two principal reasons why conditionality has not worked in general. The first is on the recipient side – simply put, there are strong political forces in place that are opposed to the policy conditions. If this were not true, conditionalities would, of course, usually be unnecessary: the policy would already be in place (Coate and Morris 2005). Opposition may exist in the executive branch or outside it, but either way it is likely to continue even if the policy is instituted at first. As such, policies adopted because of conditionalities are often reversed or simply ignored in practice.

This raises the second reason conditionality has not worked, this one on the donor side: donors have strong incentives to continue to disburse funds even if conditionalities are not met. These incentives can be political – such as the need to support a government for strategic reasons – or they can be economic – such as the need not to disrupt strong trade or investment relationships with the country. The incentives can even be bureaucratic, such as the need for aid agencies to disburse all their funds in order to get the same amount of funds the following year. Regardless of their origin, these incentives often mean that aid is disbursed regardless of whether or not conditions are met (World Bank

1992). It is therefore not surprising that the conditionalities have little systematic effect.

This issue of conditionality is also relevant to the second condition needed for my theory to apply: nontax revenue cannot affect the weights given to citizens in decision making by the regime. After all, donors could, in principle, put democratic governance conditions on their aid (although this is not true of the World Bank and IMF, which are prohibited from intervening in such matters).[20] However, these sorts of conditionalities are subject to exactly the same problems just discussed – perhaps even to a greater degree than economic conditionalities. In a detailed analysis of donors' attempts (or lack thereof) to influence political reform, Crawford (2001: 185) has argued, "[I]n general, there appears more hesitation by donors in prescribing specific political reform measures to be undertaken, in contrast to economic reform where there are no such qualms.... Taking into account these differences, particularly political conditionality's lack of specificity, commentators have anticipated an even lower rate of effectiveness than that for economic reform." And indeed, in Crawford's own study, he finds that such conditionalities are, in general, ineffective.

Some scholars have argued that the apparent ineffectiveness of conditionalities is likely to have been mainly an artifact of the Cold War (for example, Dunning 2004; Wright 2011; Bermeo 2013). According to these arguments, aid is likely to have worked differently after the Cold War than it did during the Cold War because political interests during the Cold War made it difficult for donors to hold countries to the conditions put on aid. When the Cold War ended, so the argument goes, donors became more development oriented and less hamstrung by political exigencies. Particularly important to the argument here (specifically the condition earlier regarding the weights put on citizens' utility in regimes), some scholars have made the argument that donors are more concerned about democracy in the post-Cold War world (Dunning 2004; Wright 2011). I will therefore check to make sure aid does not have different effects in the Cold War and post-Cold War periods.

Nevertheless, I am skeptical of these arguments. For one, it is not clear that donors are giving aid to democracies in the post-Cold War period any more than they did in the Cold War (Wright and Winters 2010). This is not particularly surprising, given the tensions often seen in the foreign policy establishment between promoting democracy and fighting terrorism (Carothers 2003). But arguably more importantly, the arguments about the political effects of the Cold War on conditionality ignore the fact that, as just discussed, there are many reasons that donor conditionalities are not met – only one of which is the pressure that results from political relationships (Crawford 2001).

[20] Many donors also allocate some aid directly to building democracy in developing countries. However, this sort of aid makes up a tiny fraction of foreign aid (Crawford 2001; Finkel, Pérez-Liñán, and Seligson 2007).

As mentioned earlier, one of the main pressures is for donor agencies to "move the money," in the sense that they need to disburse funds or they will not receive the same amount the following year (Kapur, Lewis, and Webb 1997; World Bank 1998). One of the reasons for this emphasis on money moved is that aid is often "tied" to the recipient country's use of donor-country service providers to conduct the project. As such, there is a strong commercial interest on the part of the donor countries to keep the money flowing (van de Walle and Johnston 1996). Another reason for the emphasis is that oftentimes the money must be moved to cover previous donor loans in danger of default (Boyce 2002; Easterly 2002b; Birdsall, Claessens, and Diwan 2003; Morrison 2011a). As Easterly (2002a: 228) catalogs, donors have tended to "define their output as money disbursed rather than service delivered.... The emphasis on moving money led to IFIs [international financial institutions] allocating too little effort to two important activities: (1) insuring that loan conditions were actually observed, and (2) ex-post evaluation of loan effectiveness."

It is easy to see how this pressure would undermine conditionalities. Countries can institute (or promise to institute) a policy on the basis of conditionality, receive the money, and then retract the policy. One might think that in this scenario the donor would no longer give money to this country. However, because of the reasons just stated, donors do indeed continue to give the countries conditional loans. Collier (1999a: F645) reports, for example, that "the government of Kenya 'sold' the same agricultural reform to the IFIs five times in fifteen years, while the same commitment to reform was agreed to seven times by governments of Malawi." Easterly (2002a: 228) reports that "The World Bank and IMF gave Argentina 33 adjustment loans over 1980–2001 during repeated macroeconomic crises, yet at the end Argentina went into an even more severe macroeconomic crisis than the previous ones (complicated by the huge debt now owed to multilateral institutions)." The Cold War – or the end thereof – had no effect on these essentially bureaucratic incentives, and their importance suggests that we should expect less of a change across time periods than some scholars have suggested.[21]

To be clear, however, the two conditions specified in my model for nontax revenue also identify the conditions under which foreign aid would *not* work like natural resource rents and other nontax revenue. If donors could credibly impose conditions on taxing and spending, and/or were to become serious about democratic reform, then foreign aid might indeed work differently. My argument is that these conditions have not been present, however, and that foreign aid therefore tends to reduce taxation and increase spending.

INTERGOVERNMENTAL TRANSFERS. Although my focus thus far in this section has generally been on nontax revenues at the national level, as mentioned in the

[21] The same is true about the economic incentives driving aid. Indeed, largely because donor countries have little political incentive to reform the incentives of aid agencies, aid effectiveness problems continue to the present day (van de Walle and Johnston 1996; Lancaster 1999, 2007).

Introduction, another major source of nontax revenue throughout the world is intergovernmental grants to subnational governments. If a central government were to get its own revenues exclusively from nontax sources, then these would obviously be nontax revenues for local governments, too. But people do pay central government taxes in most countries, part of which then gets disbursed as transfers to lower governments. How can we thus consider these as nontax revenues for subnational governments?

The answer lies again in one of the conditions detailed earlier: nontax revenue is positive revenue that does not accrue from taxing citizens of the recipient government. As discussed in the Introduction, the majority of local jurisdictions around the world receive much more in grants than they pay out in taxes that fund the grants because the systems are highly redistributive. As Broadway (2008: 355) has written, "transfers to subnational governments are ... typically highly redistributive horizontally in the sense that they compensate for differences in fiscal capacity of the recipient jurisdictions." For example, "transfers that are equal per capita to all jurisdictions are none the less implicitly redistributive if financed out of federal general revenues, because the latter come disproportionately from jurisdictions with higher per capita tax bases."

In other words, from the perspective of most subnational governments (that is, the ones in which recipients are receiving more than they are paying out), the large majority of an intergovernmental transfer is nontax revenue. As such, this transfer should also be associated with lower taxes and higher spending. Although the empirical analysis in this chapter is at the national level, I will discuss the relevant effects found in the literature at the subnational level and return to evaluating this hypothesis empirically in Chapter 5.

BORROWING. Although it may seem reasonable that borrowing does not change the decision-making weights of a government, it may seem odd initially to think that borrowing accrues to a government without taxation. After all, we usually assume that borrowing must be paid back in the future, and if there is no additional input of nontax revenue, this would require raising taxes.

Nevertheless, I will make the argument in this section that borrowing – at the national and subnational levels – acts very much like other nontax revenues. A government that borrows money is receiving revenue that does not accrue from taxation in that same time period. And as a result, borrowing should lead to lower taxes and higher spending, even though the government will pay back the loan in the future. That is, it will have the same effects as other nontax revenue in the period when the loan is taken.

Consider a variant of my initial model in which we assume that the source of nontax revenue is a loan. Since the loan will be paid back in the future, we need to develop a simple two-period model in which, for tractability, I use the log-transformed version of the Stone-Geary function employed earlier. In this case,

$$U_t = \alpha ln(c_t - \bar{c}) + (1 - \alpha) lnS_t.$$

Following standard practice, assume that a citizen lives for two periods t = 1, 2. Total utility is additively separable over time, so that

$$W = U_1 + \delta U_2,$$

where δ captures how much the citizen values the future, and $0 < \delta \leq 1$.

In each period, the citizen sets a preferred tax rate as shown previously, so that

$$c_t = (1 - \tau_t)y.$$

We also assume that a loan $L > 0$ taken in period 1 must be paid back in period 2, so that

$$S_1 = \tau_1 y + L \text{ and}$$

$$S_2 = \tau_2 y - rL,$$

where r captures the interest rate on the loan (generally, $r \geq 1$).

Maximizing the indirect utility yields that

$$\tau_1 = \frac{(1-\alpha)(y-\bar{c}) - \alpha L}{y} \tag{3.10}$$

$$\tau_2 = \frac{(1-\alpha)(y-\bar{c}) + \alpha r L}{y}.$$

These expressions indicate that even though it needs to be paid back in period 2, a loan taken in period 1 acts exactly like other forms of nontax revenue (compare equation [3.10] with equation [3.5] earlier): it diminishes the tax rate. It similarly increases spending in the same period, as the expressions for spending are:

$$S_1 = (1-\alpha)(y - \bar{c} + L) \text{ and}$$

$$S_2 = (1-\alpha)(y - \bar{c} - rL).$$

The main difference between a loan and other kinds of nontax revenue is that in future periods, the loan must be paid back. But this turns out to be not as important for my theory as one might think. My argument in this chapter is about the effect of nontax revenue when it accrues: What does such revenue do to taxing and spending in that period? These equations indicate that the effects of borrowing on public finance should be very similar to other kinds of nontax revenue: when it increases, it should lower taxes and increase spending compared to a situation in which there is no borrowing.[22]

This is of course not to say that paying the loan back in future periods is unimportant. I will address the issue of how borrowing affects stability in Chapter 4, but a relevant question there will be when a regime would actually want to borrow, since the loan will have to be paid back. For example, if the loan (and paying it back) reduced overall regime utility over the two periods, then it would mean that it would prefer for L to be equal to zero. This decision depends on the relationship between the interest rate and how the regime values the future. Specifically, the ideal amount of borrowing for the citizen is:[23]

$$L^* = \frac{(1-\delta r)(y-\bar{c})}{r(1+\delta)}.$$

This will be positive if $\delta r < 1$. That is, if the regime faces a relatively low interest rate (r), or sufficiently values the present more than the future (low δ), then borrowing will take place.

Most importantly from the perspective of this chapter, if borrowing does take place, then this section shows that lower taxes and higher spending should result.

3.2.4 *Summary*

In sum, this section has offered a broad theoretical approach arguing that in most circumstances – including different kinds of political systems and tax systems – nontax revenues of all types are likely to have two effects: they are likely to diminish taxation and increase spending. I now turn to interpreting existing relevant empirical literature in light of this approach, as well as conducting my own original analysis of the hypotheses.

3.3 Nontax Revenue, Taxation, and Spending: The Empirics

The theory offered here provides a way to understand a variety of existing empirical work within a common framework. In particular, many studies of

[22] This prediction is not in contrast to the "tax smoothing" model of public finance (Barro 1979), which argues that taxation and spending should remain relatively constant over time, as governments take loans during bad times and pay them back in good times, to avoid the economic costs of raising taxes. Indeed, the intuition of that model is that governments borrow precisely to avoid having to cut spending and raise taxes in bad times. If they did not borrow, taxes would go up and spending would go down. This is exactly the argument here.

[23] This is found by finding the condition for optimal borrowing, which is $\delta r(\tau_1 y + L) = \tau_2 y - rL$, and solving for L.

both a qualitative and quantitative nature have provided evidence of the types of dynamics predicted by the theory, although they have all generally been focused on a particular kind of nontax revenue.

On the oil side, for example, Crystal (1990) studies Qatar and Kuwait before and after oil entered their economies. She finds that both regimes relied on taxation of merchants before the influx of oil revenues in the 1950s and 1960s, a practice that had costs for the rulers in terms of the bargains they needed to strike with the merchants in return for taxation. Oil revenues changed the fiscal relationship dramatically. "The most important impact of oil and the rentier economy it produced was that it gave rulers direct access to external revenues, revenues generated outside the economy.... The external nature of oil rents, the enclave nature of the industry, and the size of the boom spared rulers the need to extract, through taxation and repression, economic and social resources" (Crystal 1990: 6–7). As a result, Crystal finds, taxation went down while spending went up.

Another example is Smith's (2007) study of Iran, in which he finds that prior to the 1950s, when significant oil revenues began to accrue to the country, Iran had a reasonably strong state and an effective tax bureaucracy (Banani 1961; Cronin 1997). After a decade of reliance on oil revenues, however, the extractive capacity of the state began to atrophy, mainly as a result of a "lack of fiscal necessity" (Smith 2007: 113). While the economy boomed from 1963–69, direct tax revenues were essentially stagnant, reflecting diminished effective tax rates. In contrast, spending on development and industrial projects skyrocketed: "[N]early all of the incoming oil wealth was channeled out to industrial projects and to various incentives for private investment" (Smith 2007: 112).

Finally, a similar example is provided by Chaudhry in her studies of Iraq and Saudi Arabia. She finds that prior to the 1980s, "[o]il revenues, like state controlled loans and aid, saved the government from having to tax its population directly and enhanced the ease with which the state could ameliorate political conflict through directly distributing resources through gifts, subsidies, loans, and state contracts" (Chaudhry 1992: 149). In contrast, when oil revenues fell in the 1980s and economic crisis hit, the government attempted to cut spending and raise taxes (Chaudhry 1994).

Whereas these examples come from authoritarian regimes, similar dynamics are also evident in democracies. Take, for example, Norway, which has been oil rich since the 1970s.[24] Eifert, Gelb, and Tallroth (2003: 98) recount how the boom in oil prices in 2000 created pressures on political parties in the parliamentary elections of 2001:

As oil markets bounced back in 2000 and the Petroleum Fund grew, political pressures to boost public spending resumed, especially by local governments, which are

[24] For another democratic example, see Acemoglu, Johnson, and Robinson's (2003) discussion of Botswana.

> responsible for the bulk of spending on health and education. The governing Social Democratic Party ran on a platform favoring an expansion of expenditures only, but the elections paved the way for a new government, formed by parties favoring both an expansion of the welfare state and a redirection of policy toward reducing Norway's high tax burden.

Again, increasing oil led to increased spending and decreased taxation.

With these examples from democracies and dictatorships, it is not surprising that recent studies using data from both kinds of regimes have found a statistically significant negative relationship between resource revenues and domestic revenue effort. For example, in a panel of thirty hydrocarbon-producing countries, Bornhorst, Gupta, and Thornton (2009) find that revenues from oil and gas activities are offset by reductions in other domestic revenue sources. Similar results have been found looking only at Latin American countries (Ossowski and Gonzáles 2012) or African countries (Treviño and Thomas 2013). Most recently, studying thirty-five resource-rich democracies and dictatorships, Crivelli and Gupta (2014) find that increasing resource revenues tended to diminish goods and services taxes as well as corporate income and trade taxes.

Dynamics akin to those observed in these natural-resource revenue examples have also been seen by scholars studying countries receiving foreign aid. Perhaps the most detailed and insightful analysis of the effects of aid on developing countries remains that by van de Walle (2001). Studying the period of 1979–99, a period he calls one of "permanent crisis" for African economies, he shows how inflows of aid actually increased government consumption in the context of fiscal crisis. "Thanks in part to substantial donor support to state structures, twenty years of crisis have resulted in a bigger state that does less for its citizens" (van de Walle 2001: 66). At the same time, and in direct contrast to donor conditions, he finds that tax revenues stagnated or declined.

The results are not restricted to Africa. In her study of Jordan, for example, Brand calls the country a *rentier* state because of its dependence on foreign aid and remittances. Very similar to the patterns observed by Chaudhry with regard to oil in Iraq and Saudi Arabia, Brand finds that while Jordan was flush with these revenues, it was able to spend significantly without taxation. However, when an economic crisis hit its donors in the 1980s and nontax revenues dried up, "the state increasingly found itself in dire need of both cutting expenditures and expanding its [tax] revenue base" (Brand 1992: 169).

Indeed, this overall pattern with aid has shown up in cross-national statistical studies. In perhaps the first work of this kind, Heller (1975) studied eleven countries for about a ten-year period, finding that aid led to increased public spending (consumption or investment) as well as decreased taxation. Similar results were found by Feyzioglu, Swaroop, and Zhu (1998), studying thirty-eight countries for a twenty-year period, as well as Remmer (2004), studying more than 100 middle- and low-income countries over the period 1970–99. Other works have found one result and not the other. For example, Khilji and

Zampelli (1994) examined eight aid recipients over a fifteen-year period and found that aid was mainly funneled into tax relief, with little impact on public spending. Boone (1996), in contrast, found that aid is associated with increased public spending but has no effect on taxation.[25]

Considering the literatures on aid and natural resource revenue together, as this section has, demonstrates how similar many of the findings are across the two bodies of work. They are also similar to the effects of nontax revenue found at the subnational level, in the form of intergovernmental grants, which studies show also tend to reduce taxation and increase spending (e.g., Brollo et al. 2013).[26] This literature has given rise to a work on the "flypaper effect" (Hines and Thaler 1995), based on many studies that find that the percentage of a dollar of grants received that is allocated to government spending is higher than one would expect. As Inman (2008) discusses in a review of this literature, the difference can likely be accounted for by greater attention to political factors that differ across countries and levels of government. Nevertheless, the overall pattern is still the one argued for here: grants are associated with lower taxes and higher spending.

Despite the apparent similarities across these various literatures, little empirical work has focused on examining these similarities explicitly. An important exception is work by Knack (2009), showing that foreign aid and natural resource rents are both associated with diminishing quality of the tax system, as measured by the World Bank's Country Policy and Institutional Assessment. In contrast, I focus here on actual tax revenues and government spending at the national level, and establish that nontax revenue in general has these effects (I consider subnational nontax revenue in Chapter 5).

To test the hypothesis that nontax revenue diminishes taxation and increases spending, I draw on a fixed-effects error-correction model that has become standard in recent research on government finance (for example, Iversen and Cusack 2000; Kaufman and Segura-Ubiergo 2001; Rodden 2003; Wibbels 2006).[27] The equation estimated is as follows:

$$\Delta Y_{i,t} = \beta_0 + Y_{i,t-1}\beta_1 + X_{i,t-1}\beta_2 + \Delta X_{i,t}\,\beta_3 + \varepsilon_{i,t},$$

in which $Y_{i,t}$ is tax revenue or spending in country i in time t, X is a matrix of independent variables (including country-level fixed effects), and Δ is the first difference operator. Therefore, the dependent variable is the change in tax revenue or spending per capita from one year to the next.

As other authors have discussed (for example, Beck 1991), this type of model assumes a moving equilibrium relationship between variables, allowing

[25] Some works examine why certain governments would want to funnel aid into either tax breaks or spending (Mosley, Hudson, and Horrell 1987; Cashel-Cordo and Craig 1990; Pack and Pack 1993).

[26] I know of no empirical work on the effect of being able to borrow on taxes and spending.

[27] Also see Beck (2001).

for the estimation of both permanent and transitory relationships. The coefficient on the lagged level of the dependent variable (β_1) is an indicator of equilibrium properties – that is, it should be between -1 and 0 so that the effects of shocks in an exogenous variable are reduced over time and the system returns to equilibrium. The parameter of the lagged level of an independent variable (β_2) indicates the permanent effect of a one-off change in that variable, while the parameter of the change variable (β_3) is a measure of the transitory effect of that one-off change. In general, as has been noted elsewhere (Rodden 2003; Remmer 2004), the coefficient of interest is on the lagged value, which indicates the lasting effect of the variable in the long-term moving equilibrium. As is standard in the literature, the equation is estimated using ordinary least squares (OLS) with panel-corrected standard errors with panel-specific patterns of first-order autocorrelation to accommodate the problems that plague cross-sectional time-series research designs, notably heteroskedasticity and serial correlation (Beck and Katz 1995).

The principal variable of interest is the NONTAX REVENUE PER CAPITA variable defined in the Introduction. However, since my objective is to estimate the impact of nontax revenue on taxation and spending, I must also control for other factors whose omission might cause omitted variable bias. Based on previous studies, I include four other control variables in each regression. Perhaps the most important is GDP PER CAPITA, to account for the effect of economic development on the size of the public sector (for example, Boix 2001). Second, I include the percentage of the population that is sixty-five years and older (% POPULATION OVER 65), since this tends to drive pensions and thereby social spending (for example, Perotti 1996). Third, I include trade dependence, measured as exports plus imports as a percentage of GDP (TRADE/GDP), building off work that asserts a relationship between trade openness and the size of the public sector (for example, Rodrik 1998). Fourth, in the regressions with taxation as the dependent variable, I include SOCIAL SPENDING PER CAPITA as an independent variable, to isolate the effect of nontax revenue from increases or decreases in taxation simply caused by changes in spending needs (for example, Remmer 2004). Similarly, in the spending regressions, I include INCOME TAX PER CAPITA. All of these variables are attained from the World Bank. Finally, as is standard in this research area, I include country dummies (fixed effects) in all of the regressions, to avoid bias owing to omitted variables that help determine long-term cross-country differences in government activity (for example, Beck 2001; Hsiao 2003; Rodden 2003).

In conducting the analysis, I first made sure that combining the nontax revenue categories into one variable was justified in both the tax revenue and spending regressions. If some kinds of nontax revenue have different effects on taxation and spending, then it would be difficult to find a significant result for the aggregate variable (for example, variables with both negative and positive effects would be aggregated into one variable). However, to be sure that combining them into one indicator is justified, I began my analyses by including various components of nontax revenue separately in the regressions. Specifically, three categories of nontax revenue were entered: foreign aid, an indicator of state-owned enterprise revenue, and a residual indicator consisting of the aggregate nontax revenue variable minus these two components. An important part of this third category is borrowing, to finance deficit spending for example (definitions for each indicator are presented in Figure 1.2 in Chapter 1). These disaggregated components are available for a smaller set of observations than the aggregate nontax revenue variable, which is calculated using two more widely available indicators (tax revenue and total spending). However, before using the aggregate indicator to achieve greater data coverage, one should be sure the different elements belong together. Supporting the approach here, a t-test could not reject the hypothesis that these components had the same coefficient for either the taxation or the spending regression.[28] In other words, aggregating the different nontax revenue variables is justified.

Using this aggregate nontax revenue variable, Table 3.1 presents the results for both taxation and spending, indicating a significant negative relationship between nontax revenue and taxation, and a significant positive effect between nontax revenue and spending. In line with the theory advanced earlier, as nontax revenue goes up, tax revenue goes down and spending goes up. In substantive terms, a move from the twenty-fifth percentile level to the seventy-fifth percentile of nontax revenue is associated with a long-term decline of about 17 percent in tax revenue per capita. A move from the seventy-fifth percentile to the twenty-fifth percentile in nontax revenue is associated with about a 20 percent decline in government spending per capita.[29]

To ensure the result was robust, I subjected it to a number of robustness checks.[30] Including dummy variables for geographic regions, decades, or whether or not a country is a member of the OECD made no difference in the results. Neither did running the regression for developing countries only.

I also ran several robustness tests to explicitly account for the potential concerns noted earlier with regard to my theoretical approach, in terms of whether it applied to different regimes, tax systems, and types of nontax revenue. In order to explore whether the theory shed light on different kinds of regimes, I included a term that interacted nontax revenue with democracy (as well as the democracy term separately) in both regressions.[31] This interaction term was insignificant, so that the predicted relationship held in both: as the level

[28] The p-values were 0.36 and 0.10, respectively. Whereas the p-value for the t-test in the spending regressions was close to significance, all of the coefficients for the nontax revenue components were positive and highly significant.

[29] These are roughly similar to the effects of foreign aid found by Remmer (2004).

[30] None of these specifications had a significant impact on the fit of the model.

[31] In line with convention, democracy was defined as having a POLITY2 score equal to or greater than seven.

TABLE 3.1. *The Effect of Nontax Revenue on Taxation and Spending*

Variables	Change in Tax Revenue Per Capita	Change in spending Per Capita
Δ NONTAX REVENUE PER CAPITA	−0.459***	0.871***
	(0.0340)	(0.0225)
NONTAX REVENUE PER CAPITA (t-1)	−0.177***	0.115***
	(0.0301)	(0.0375)
Δ INCOME PER CAPITA	0.0759***	0.0857***
	(0.0196)	(0.0160)
INCOME PER CAPITA (t-1)	0.0494***	0.0504***
	(0.0106)	(0.0103)
Δ SHARE OF POPULATION OVER 65	−14.57	−16.80
	(68.94)	(41.87)
SHARE OF POPULATION OVER 65 (t-1)	11.38	−2.084
	(11.79)	(7.300)
Δ TRADE/GDP	0.302	−0.602*
	(0.391)	(0.339)
TRADE/GDP (t-1)	1.126***	0.131
	(0.387)	(0.275)
TAX REVENUE PER CAPITA (t-1)	−0.311***	
	(0.0406)	
SPENDING PER CAPITA (t-1)		−0.145***
		(0.0324)
Δ SOCIAL SPENDING PER CAPITA	0.712***	
	(0.0595)	
SOCIAL SPENDING PER CAPITA (t-1)	0.241***	
	(0.0396)	
Δ INCOME TAX PER CAPITA		0.956***
		(0.0510)
INCOME TAX PER CAPITA (t-1)		0.0833*
		(0.0446)
CONSTANT	−1110***	−726.2***
	(221.7)	(195.9)
Observations	1356	1775
R-squared	0.711	0.843
Countries	100	107

Notes: Panel corrected standard errors (AR1) in parentheses. Country-level fixed effects not shown. The asterisks denote the following: *** $p<0.01$, ** $p<0.05$, * $p<0.1$.

of nontax revenue rose, tax revenue went down in both regimes, and spending went up in both regimes. I interpret this as evidence that the *rentier* mechanism is at work in both democracies and dictatorships, in contrast to most work on the resource curse.

To explore whether the approach shed light on dynamics in different kinds of taxation and spending schemes, I investigated how nontax revenue affected different subsets of taxation and spending. Specifically, I examined nontax revenue's effects on income tax and taxes on goods and services, and on social spending and spending on the military. In these regressions, nontax revenue had a significant and negative effect on both kinds of taxes, and a positive and significant effect on both kinds of spending.

Finally, I tested the hypothesis that foreign aid had different effects during the Cold War than it did afterward, as some authors have argued (for example, Dunning 2004; Wright 2011; Bermeo 2013). In the regressions for taxation and spending in which I included the disaggregated components of nontax revenue, I included a dummy variable for the post-Cold War period (that is, after 1990) as well as an interaction term between this variable and the aid variables (that is, the change and lagged level of aid received). In the spending regressions, the coefficient on the interaction term was insignificant (p-value of 0.478). In the taxation regressions, the coefficient on the interaction term was significant but *negative*, suggesting that if anything, aid has had a worse effect on tax revenue in the post-Cold War period than previously, contrary to the hypothesis that conditionality has been more effective.[32]

3.4 Conclusion

This chapter has developed and provided empirical support for the argument that nontax revenue, of various forms, lowers taxation and increases government spending. It is very much a "lumping" type of argument as opposed to a "splitting" one (Hexter 1979; Gerring 2001): I am arguing that we gain much insight from considering the various kinds of nontax revenue as a whole, similar to the work that has been done with regard to aggregate tax revenue and aggregate government spending. The argument is that this nontax revenue should have similar effects across a wide variety of circumstances. In support of this theory, the chapter has provided the first systematic evidence that across different political regimes, and across different time periods, nontax revenue of various kinds leads to diminished taxation and increased spending.

While this chapter can hopefully be seen as a theoretical and empirical contribution by itself, I obviously mean it to be seen in light of Chapter 2, in which I showed that increased taxation is associated with greater rates of regime and leadership transition, and increased spending is associated with lower rates of such transitions. The implication of these two chapters together seems to be that nontax revenue should lead to lower rates of transition in democracies and dictatorships. And that is the hypothesis Chapter 4 explores.

[32] All robustness checks are available from the author as a data archive and Stata do-file.

4

Nontax Revenue (Therefore) Leads to Stability

4.1 Introduction

Chapters 2 and 3 have shown that taxation leads to political instability, government spending has the opposite effect, and nontax revenue diminishes taxation and increases spending. This chapter turns to examining the hypothesis that results from the combination of these findings: nontax revenue should lead to greater political stability.

While my hope is that, given the preceding chapters, this hypothesis will seem intuitive to the reader, it should be noted that conventional wisdom about two major kinds of nontax revenue – natural resource revenues and foreign aid – often seems to imply opposite predictions about their effects on political regimes. Consider the contrasting titles of two important works: Ross (2001) asks "Does Oil Hinder Democracy?" whereas Knack (2004) asks "Does Foreign Aid Promote Democracy?" Often, the prevailing assumption is that oil generally has negative (that is, antidemocratic) implications for political regimes, while aid has positive ones.

Instead, in this book, I am arguing that these revenues do not have antidemocratic properties, or even "pro-democratic" properties. What they have are stabilizing properties, in the sense that their presence reduces the probability of a regime transition and leadership changes in both democracies and dictatorships. These revenues enable a government to stay in power by whatever fiscal means are best for it, and this is true in democracies as well as dictatorships.

To make this argument, this chapter returns to the discussion in Chapter 2 to show the effects nontax revenue has in the theoretical approaches discussed there, and it illustrates these effects with two case studies of Mexico and Kenya. Finally, I present statistical analyses that echo those in Chapter 2, investigating nontax revenue's effects on regime transitions in democracies and dictatorships, and on leadership transitions in authoritarian regimes. These will show, as expected, that higher levels of nontax revenue are associated with less regime transition and less leadership turnover.

This chapter, therefore, brings to a close the theoretical argument of the book: taxation hurts stability, spending helps it, and nontax revenue helps stability because it allows regimes and leaders to diminish taxation and increase spending. However, even after this chapter, there will remain some outstanding empirical issues, particularly with regard to nontax revenue's effects in democracies, and I will discuss these in a concluding section, leading into Chapter 5.

4.2 Nontax Revenue and Political Stability

In Chapter 2, I argued and showed that taxation hurts regimes and leaders, and spending helps them. In Chapter 3, I showed that nontax revenue leads to lower taxation and greater spending. Nontax revenue should therefore lead to greater stability for regimes and leaders as long as – and this is the key condition – tax reductions and spending increases financed by nontax revenue do not have different effects on stability than other kinds of tax reductions and spending increases.

To consider whether this condition holds, I return in this section to three seminal approaches that linked taxation and spending to political stability in Chapter 2 and examine how scholars approach nontax revenue within those approaches. I show that they tend to think the tax breaks and spending increases funded by these revenues work similarly to other tax breaks and spending increases. Then, in the subsequent section, I illustrate the effects of nontax revenue in two of these theoretical approaches with case studies of Kenya and Mexico.

TAXATION LEADS TO REPRESENTATION. As discussed in Chapter 2, the theory that taxation leads to representation has been perhaps the most influential framework for scholarship on the effect of natural resources on politics. As such, to get a sense of how nontax revenues would work within this framework, it is useful to turn to *rentier* literature. And the main argument of this literature is exactly that tax breaks and spending increases financed by nontax revenues work the same way as "normal" tax breaks and spending increases. The argument is that natural resource revenues keep leaders and regimes in power precisely by giving them inordinate amounts of money with which to lower taxes and raise spending (Entelis 1976; Vandewalle 1998). Indeed, in a quotation that nicely sums up the similarity between "normal" politics and politics with nontax revenues, Ross (2001: 333–34) writes, "While all authoritarian governments may use their fiscal powers to reduce dissent, these scholars [in the *rentier* literature] imply that oil wealth provides Middle East governments with budgets that are exceptionally large and unconstrained."

The only difference between this approach and mine is that, as I found in Chapter 2, it is not only dictatorships that find taxation politically challenging;

democracies do, too. As such, one would expect *rentier* effects in democracies as well, with nontax revenue having a similar kind of stabilizing effect.

REDISTRIBUTIONAL APPROACHES TO REGIME CHANGE. In the theories of Acemoglu and Robinson (2006), Boix (2003), and others discussed in Chapter 2, transitions between political regimes are driven by groups unhappy with the level of redistribution in society. Coups, in this framework, are launched against democracies by rich elites concerned about the level of taxation in a society. When the elites can solve their collective-action problems and mobilize against the democratic regime, citizens may not be able to credibly promise a level of taxation sufficiently low enough to satisfy the elites. In this scenario, the rich overthrow the democracy and impose a dictatorship.

Although Acemoglu and Robinson (2006) did not consider the possibility that some revenue could come from nontax sources, I have examined the effect of such revenue within their framework in prior work (Morrison 2007, 2009).[1] Importantly, it turns out that if there are diminishing marginal returns to government spending, then the presence of nontax revenue will reduce the desire of the median voter in a democracy to tax, exactly as it did in Chapter 3. This is critical in a redistributional approach to regime change because with this lower tax burden, elites have less dissatisfaction with democracy, and the probability of a coup will diminish. In other words, nontax revenue stabilizes democracies because it facilitates the lowering of taxes.

The effect works slightly differently in authoritarian regimes. In these redistributional theories, the threat to authoritarian regimes comes from lower and middle classes who would benefit under a democratic regime in which they would have more power. As such, these classes can occasionally threaten to launch a revolution against the elites in power. Under certain conditions, elites can redistribute enough money to ward off this threat, but under other conditions, they cannot because they cannot spend enough to satiate the rebellious citizens. In order to head off revolution, the elites democratize. However, as I have shown in the earlier work just mentioned (Morrison 2007), the presence of nontax revenue in these circumstances expands the range of conditions under which the elites can withstand a rebellious threat because they can promise more to the unhappy lower- and middle-class citizens. Nontax revenue therefore stabilizes authoritarian regimes, too.

SPENDING APPROACHES. Finally, in Chapter 2 I also examined important theories in which leaders are rewarded for spending on their groups of supporters. This mechanism underlies the logic of selectorate theory (Bueno de Mesquita et al. 2003), in which coalition members reward their leaders for private and public goods, and it also underlies theories of clientelism (Kitschelt and Wilkinson 2007; Stokes 2007), in which citizens reward leaders for spending on their group. In many of these theories, supporters reward the incum-

[1] Dunning's (2008a) important work has a similar model.

bent because there is a risk that they would not benefit under the rule of the incumbent's challenger.

Nontax revenue in this sort of a framework simply strengthens the incumbent's hand (Smith 2008). Consider, for example, the model of clientelism developed by Robinson, Torvik, and Verdier (2006). There are different groups in society, and an incumbent can use revenues to create government jobs for his supporters. In turn, the supporters reward this spending politically because if the incumbent is not reelected, there is a risk they will lose their job. Nontax revenue in this theory provides a way to deliver more of these jobs, thereby ensuring greater stability for the incumbent. And indeed, using their model, Robinson, Torvik, and Verdier (2006) show that natural resource revenue results in greater spending on citizens, who reward the incumbent with reelection.

This kind of approach is also useful for examining the particular effect of borrowing, the one kind of nontax revenue that might work differently from the others. As I discussed in Chapter 3, like all nontax revenues, borrowing diminishes taxation and increases spending in the period in which the loan is taken. However, these tax decreases and spending increases might indeed work differently than "normal" tax decreases and spending increases in terms of stability, because everyone knows that the loan will need to be paid back.

A key consideration for the stabilizing effects of borrowing is who needs to do this paying back. If some of the loan is paid back without taxing citizens of the recipient government, then borrowing should work fairly similarly to other kinds of nontax revenue. This is more common than one might expect. For example, some debt in the developing world is never paid back by people from the recipient country, either being forgiven or simply rolled over into new loans over the years (Easterly 2002b; Birdsall, Claessens, and Diwan 2003; Morrison 2011a). In addition, many subnational governments around the world have the ability to borrow, assured that these debts will be covered by other parts of the country (Rodden 2004). The debts, therefore, act quite similar to intergovernmental grants. Under these circumstances, subnational jurisdictions receive the full benefit of the spending without internalizing the full cost.[2] The result is widespread borrowing by subnational governments and leaders that rewards their constituencies.[3]

Things are different, however, if the loans must be paid back by taxing citizens of the recipient government. In this case, the effects of borrowing on stability are likely to be more complex. For insight, it is useful to turn to the

[2] This is essentially captured in Chapter 3 by a lower interest rate for the government in power.

[3] Knowing this, national governments can try to limit the ability of subnational governments to borrow, but in general, the political commitment required to limit subnational governments in this way is difficult to achieve (Treisman 2000; Wibbels 2000). Borrowing autonomy at the subnational level is therefore reasonably common (Rodden 2004), and as the dynamics described here would predict, that autonomy is generally associated with deficits (Rodden 2002). For relevant theoretical discussions, see chapter 7 in Persson and Tabellini (2000).

literature on the strategic use of debt in democracies, which has considered why democratic governments would run a deficit. Consider any government that is in power and spending money on its coalition of choice. If it knew for sure that it would be in power in the future, under normal circumstances it may not want to borrow, as borrowing now would mean lower spending in the future. However, every government – whether democratic or authoritarian – ends, and this affects the desirability of borrowing.

In particular, if another group were to come to power in the next period, the people in the current coalition would unlikely benefit from spending in that period. One can see very clearly the parallels of this situation and the spending and clientelistic models just discussed. If the next ruling coalition will not spend on goods the current coalition values, there is no incentive for the current coalition to protect future spending.[4] They might as well borrow more now, since spending that benefits them in the future will not be affected by the need to pay back the loans (since spending on their coalition in the future will already be zero). This is the intuition behind the benchmark models of deficit spending in democracies (Persson and Svensson 1989; Alesina and Tabellini 1990; Tabellini and Alesina 1990). As Persson and Tabellini (2000: 353) write, "Whereas the incumbent government fully internalizes the benefits of borrowing associated with spending in the public good benefiting its constituency, it does not fully internalize the cost of lower public spending in the future, since it bears this cost only if the government is reelected."[5]

To see how this dynamic could lead to reelection of the incumbent group, consider someone who would benefit from the opposition group's spending. Under normal circumstances, a citizen's preferences over public finance would push the individual to vote for the opposition group. However, the fact that the incumbent has borrowed money in the current period means that in the period after the election, spending will be less, in order to pay back the loan. In other words, this particular factor in the election does not push the voter as much in favor of the opposition group. If there are other factors that determine an individual's vote, and one's position on these is closer to the incumbent group with respect to those factors, the individual will now support the incumbent group. Therefore, under certain conditions in the selectorate, borrowing can push swing voters in the direction of the incumbent, leading to the incumbent's reelection (Persson and Tabellini 2000).

The effect of borrowing on political stability is a surprisingly understudied area, and certainly exploring the nuances of this relationship is an important area for future research. Nevertheless, this example gives a sense of how, under certain conditions, it can have stabilizing effects for governments. By

[4] This applies equally to any median voter who might not be a median voter in the future for some reason (Tabellini and Alesina 1990).

[5] This is equivalent to a government's discount rate affecting its incentive to borrow, which was shown in Chapter 3.

considering the flip side of the conditions just discussed, it is certainly possible to identify conditions under which borrowing would not lead to stability. However, under these conditions, it would be difficult to understand why leaders would engage in it. It would therefore make sense that although borrowing under all conditions is not stabilizing, the borrowing we observe is.

SUMMARY. By revisiting important theoretical approaches reviewed in Chapter 2, and demonstrating how nontax revenue works within them, this section has argued that the tax breaks and spending increases financed by nontax revenue will generally work exactly like other tax breaks and spending increases. In other words, they will stabilize the existing political regime and its leaders.

What the section also suggests, however, is that the particular ways in which nontax revenue's effect plays out will likely differ by case. That is, the groups supported and rewarded by governments and regimes will likely differ markedly across different countries and time periods. For example, some countries may be characterized by redistributional cleavages while others will not be (Haggard and Kaufman 2012). In clientelistic countries, the group in power may change over time, with accompanying implications for patterns of taxation and spending. It is an advantage of my theory that it can accommodate these differences, as illustrated by the discussion of regime weighting functions in Chapter 3.[6]

To further illustrate these different dynamics, and show how my theory applies in a variety of settings, the next section turns to two case studies, each illustrating a different theoretical approach at work from Chapter 2.

4.3 Illustrating the Mechanisms: Mexico and Kenya

To demonstrate nontax revenue's effects in different contexts, it is useful to hold many things constant. Upon embarking on the case study analysis, I therefore sought two countries that had both wide within-country variations in nontax revenue and yet were reasonably comparable along other dimensions (King, Keohane, and Verba 1994). I chose Mexico and Kenya for the following reasons: from 1984–89, Kenya's nontax revenue per capita jumped 96 percent, largely because of increased foreign aid – a percentage increase close to the 105 percent increase in Mexico's per capita nontax revenue over the period 1977–82 that was largely caused by rising oil income. Over the next nine years in each country, nontax revenue dropped dramatically, and by approximately the same amount (66 percent in Kenya; 63 percent in Mexico). During these rises and falls, Kenya had a single-party authoritarian regime very similar to Mexico's (e.g., Magaloni 2006; Friedman and Wong 2008) and resistance to

[6] This is, for example, one reason why this theoretical approach has an advantage over my previous work (Morrison 2007, 2009), which focused exclusively on the redistributional approach to regime change.

the regime was growing in both countries. In addition, during the time under study, these countries had similarly high levels of economic inequality – an important factor in some theories regarding the effects of natural resources (e.g., Boix 2003; Dunning 2008a), as well as theories of the size of government (Meltzer and Richard 1981).

Despite their comparability on a host of dimensions, they obviously varied along others. Most importantly for the purposes here, the regimes had important differences in their sources of support (in terms of the model in Chapter 3, different weighting functions in equation [3.7]). The Mexico case study largely accords with the kind of story that Acemoglu and Robinson (2006), Boix (2001), and others tell about redistributional cleavages, whereas the Kenya case study is more akin to theories of clientelism (Morrison 2011b). These differences enable the countries to illustrate the different "versions" of the causal mechanism discussed earlier.

Essential to this endeavor will be an understanding of the different regimes into which nontax revenue was flowing in these countries, and the threats the groups in power faced. Therefore, each of the case studies follows a similar pattern. A first part broadly explores the nature of the political regimes in each country, giving an historical overview of the country's modern political history, so that the reader understands the context in which nontax revenue rose and fell. The second part in each case study addresses the nature of threats to the particular regime in question, the responses by the regime, and the role of nontax revenue in these responses.

4.3.1 *Mexico*

In 1938, President Lázaro Cárdenas reorganized Mexico's *Partido Nacional Revolucionario* (PNR) into a new official party – the *Partido de la Revolución Mexicana* – which replaced the geographic organization of the PNR with a representation based on sectors: labor, peasant, military, and popular. This reorganization, apparently an effort to provide a check on elite manipulation of the masses by giving the masses themselves a role in the party (Córdova 1974), ironically seems to have provided the foundation for conservative dictatorial rule after Cárdenas. The organization not only separated laborers and peasants – thereby hindering their cooperation – but also funneled their demands into party-managed confederations that by all accounts were essentially authoritarian in nature.[7]

As conservative strength grew within the party through the military and popular wings (the latter being principally middle-class groups such as teachers and state employees), and the voices of laborers and peasants were managed by their respective confederations, the party turned to the right. Its first president, Luis Rodríguez, whose goal was the eventual socialization of production, was

[7] For example, Fidel Velázquez was head of the major labor confederation – the *Confederación de Trabajadores de México* – from the early 1940s until he died in 1997 (Minns 2006).

forced to resign by conservative elements in the party. When the election to succeed Cárdenas took place, the choice was between two conservative candidates (Manuel Avila Camacho and General Juan Andréu Almazán), and the stage for the next several decades was set. In the hands of the winner (Camacho) was a party apparatus almost ideally constructed for elite manipulation of the populace. As Hamilton wrote in 1982, "In the 1930's, the state was still sufficiently dynamic for progressive groups within it to respond to peasant and worker mobilization. Since that time, conservative groups within the state have become consolidated, structures uniting the state and dominant class interests at various levels have been considerably strengthened, and progressive groups and individuals brought into positions within the state apparatus have been easily isolated" (Hamilton 1982: 279–80). In 1946, Camacho would give the party a new name, the *Partido Revolucionario Institucional* (PRI).

The responsiveness of the PRI to the rich elite in society – essential to authoritarian regimes in redistributional theories of regime change – was reflected in the composition of the party as well as its policies. Specific data on the elitist nature of the authoritarian regime are, of course, hard to come by, but work by Centeno and Maxfield (1992: 66) is indicative. They examined the personal backgrounds of the Mexican bureaucratic elite and concluded:

> As previous analysts have noted, the elite is becoming even less representative of the classes for which the Mexican Revolution was supposedly fought, and is increasingly monopolized by those born in Mexico City. If we analyse the data by either generational cohorts or date of entry into the bureaucracy, we note that both trends have been increasing since the 1950s. These findings lend some support to the contention that the educational criteria used for the entry into the public bureaucracy, and its meritocratic legitimation, are merely political veneers for the continuing inequality which pervades Mexican society.

A variety of other scholars – including Reynolds (1970) and Knight (1986) – have interpreted the PRI principally as "an alliance among elites for the distribution rather than the *re*distribution of wealth" (Purcell and Purcell 1980).

Not surprisingly, given this interpretation of the PRI regime, policies by the PRI generally contributed to a small portion of Mexican society, along the lines of the theories of Boix (2001), Acemoglu and Robinson (2006), and others. It has been estimated that about 70 percent of the population experienced a diminished share of national income between 1950–70 (de Navarrete 1967; Banco de México 1973; Gollás 1980; Cockcroft 1983). There is little doubt that much of this was a result of policy. For example, while Cárdenas had conducted major land reform and provided some government credit to 30 percent of those receiving land, by 1960, only 14 percent of these *ejidatarios* had access to credit. By the early 1980s, 85 percent of credit provided to agriculturalists was received by the wealthiest 0.5 percent of landowners (Cockcroft 1983). In the working class, unions (such as the *Confederación General de Trabajadores* and the *Confederación de Trabajadores de México*, or CTM) were corrupted by the PRI and worked to undermine serious resistance and militant movements (Minns 2006).

In 1950, the average income of the top five percent of Mexico's households was 22 times greater than that of the poorest 40 percent, and that of the next richest five percent was 5.2 times greater than the poorest 40 percent. Two decades later, the multiples had increased to 34 and 10.7, respectively (Felix 1977). By 1970, two percent of farms accounted for 76 percent of arable land (Cockcroft 1983).

Throughout the 1960s, as inequality rose, unrest among lower and middle classes was growing in the country, and cracks began to appear in the PRI's hold on power (Brachet-Márquez 1994). Peasants began to seize land in the countryside and form independent organizations (such as the *Central Campesina Independiente* in 1963), and workers began to break away from the PRI's unions such as the CTM (e.g., workers for the state-run diesel truck manufacturer in 1961). The PRI was increasingly under attack from urban workers, intellectuals, teachers, and students, and when hundreds of protesters were killed in Mexico City in 1968 before the Summer Olympics were to be held there, the regime had essentially lost all legitimacy. In 1970, the new president – Luis Echeverría – was elected by only 37 percent of the electorate, and 25 percent of those who had voted had turned in blank ballots (Spalding 1981).

Echeverría's response to this pressure was to dramatically increase spending on the lower and middle classes in a variety of ways. The number of civil service jobs was doubled during the 1970–76 period, half of which was a result of the expansion of basic education and technical education. In addition, the government created a "Social Solidarity" program to partially include the rural population and urban poor in the social security system. As Figure 4.1 shows, social spending per capita in Mexico continued to rise until the early 1980s. And most importantly from the perspective of this book, the figure also shows that this spending was made possible by a boom in nontax revenue, caused by a spike in international oil prices and extensive international borrowing.

Certainly the figures presented here raise the question of whether the PRI would have survived without the rise in nontax revenue (Philip 1980). It is remarkable that between 1977–94 – the period when Mexico was most flush with nontax revenue – there was not a single major democratic electoral reform by the PRI.[8] When social spending began to fall along with nontax revenue in the 1980s (and as the economic crisis hit), citizens increasingly took to protest (for example, Williams 2001). However, it was not until 1994, when oil prices had fallen and Mexico's nontax revenue per capita had dropped to its early

[8] In 1977, the PRI introduced proportional representation and legalized the Communist Party.

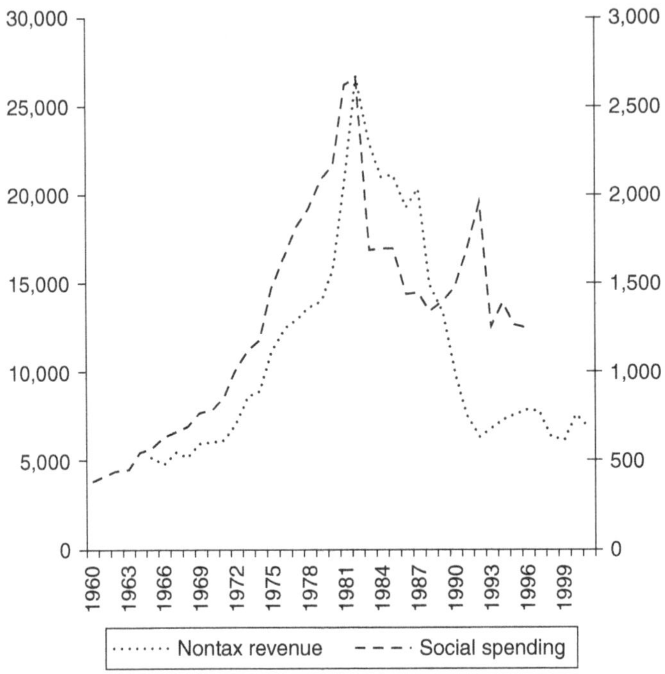

FIGURE 4.1. Nontax revenue and social spending per capita in Mexico.
Note: Numbers are in 2003 pesos. Author's calculations using data from INEGI (1999) and http://www.inegi.gob.mx).

1970s level, that the PRI again implemented a major electoral reform, making the Federal Electoral Institute independent.[9]

In this context, it is illuminating how the PRI acted with regard to social spending as the party faced increased pressure and declining resources. Beginning with López Portillo (1976–82) and culminating with Salinas (1988–94), presidents tried to gain some autonomy from the PRI unions who had come to control social spending. As Trejo and Jones (1998: 74) write,

> These two trends – growing union control of social policy and shrinking presidential power over welfare policy – were not problematic as long as the country enjoyed the longest economic expansion of the twentieth century and authoritarian rule was accepted. However, when the legitimacy of the regime was shattered by the 1968 student massacre and the 'Mexican miracle' came to an end, the constraints that the presidency faced in managing welfare policy autonomously became a fundamental problem for the sustainability of authoritarian rule.

[9] Other reforms were made between 1977–94, such as the introduction of a voter identification card in 1990, but these reforms were seen as much less important a blow to the dominance of the PRI than making the Federal Electoral Institute independent (Scherlen 1998; Trejo 2004).

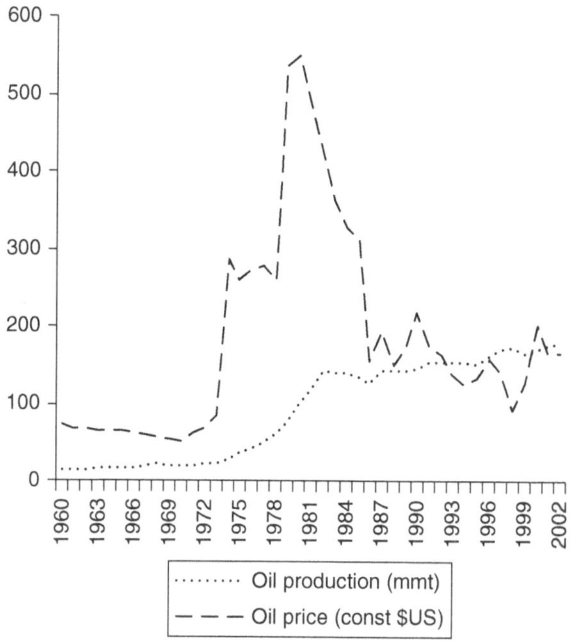

FIGURE 4.2. The international oil price and oil production in Mexico.
Note: Oil production in millions of metric tons. Data from Ross (2008).

It is therefore neither surprising that oil money was used by López Portillo directly to fund poverty alleviation projects, nor that Salinas used it to create the National Solidarity Program (PRONASOL) after the 1989 presidential election, one of the most contested in the PRI's history. An antipoverty program that was controlled exclusively by the president, PRONASOL was an erratic force against poverty, but its principal goal was political (e.g., Cornelius, Craig, and Fox 1994). As Dresser (1994: 147) has noted, "PRONASOL's strategy is to build a new coalition of support by denying the concept of class as an organizational factor of political life."

In addition to these efforts at greater "efficiency" in the political use of social spending, it is interesting to note in Figure 4.1 that, beginning in the late 1980s, the PRI seems to have attempted to stop the overall decline in social spending per capita despite the fall in nontax revenue per capita. As predicted by the framework in this book, this was accomplished as a result of an increase in the share of government spending financed by tax revenue. Despite the large fluctuations in the international price of oil shown in Figure 4.2, the share of spending financed by nontax revenue was fairly stable until the late 1980s; nontax revenue financed 70–80 percent of spending by the PRI. However, as regime pressures increased, and nontax revenue fell, the PRI attempted to compensate with increased tax revenue. Using data from Mexico's statistical agency (INEGI 1999), it is possible to show that by the early 1990s, tax revenue financed about 50 percent of spending. In other words, as nontax revenue fell, fiscal pressures increased, and the PRI's distributional regime came to an end. The PRI increasingly lost control as nontax revenue fell, and eventually the presidency was lost in 2000 (Magaloni 2006; Greene 2007).

4.3.2 *Kenya*

Kenya achieved its independence from Britain in 1963 and was subsequently ruled for forty years by just two leaders: Jomo Kenyatta (until 1978) and Daniel arap Moi (until 2002). Their party – the Kenya Africa National Union, or KANU – was similar to Mexico's PRI in that both were "hegemonic parties" using the distribution of resources to stay in power (Magaloni 2006). As I discussed earlier, they were also similar in that they relied particularly on nontax revenue – Mexico on oil, Kenya on foreign aid – and experienced similar dynamics in that revenue. As I discuss in this section, however, one of the more important differences between Kenya and Mexico is the extent to which ethnic politics played a role in the regime. This led to different patterns of tax and spending, but the same overall pattern of stability associated with nontax revenue.

Even though the Kenyan government unfortunately stopped reporting ethnicity information in their recent censuses, ostensibly for fear of political manipulation (Makoloo 2005), we know that Kenya's population consists of more than forty different ethno-linguistic groups. Around the time of independence, the five largest groups were the Kikuyu (21 percent of the population), the Luo (14 percent), the Luhya (14 percent), the Kamba (11 percent), and the Kalenjin (11 percent).[10] These groups were – and are – spread throughout the country's eight provinces, although they tend to concentrate in certain areas. For example, the Kikuyu are associated with Central Province, the Luo with Nyanza Province, and the Luhya with Western Province (see Figure 4.3 for reference). The Kikuyu's numbers and concentration in Central Province – next to Nairobi and in one of the best agricultural areas – historically placed them at the center of colonial politics and at a general economic advantage over other ethnic groups.

Upon independence, Kenyatta moved to diffuse potential divisions by incorporating different groups into his coalition. In addition to stabilizing his Kikuyu-centered coalition against threats from other groups, the incorporation of various ethnic groups had the critical function of diminishing the chances for any class-based threat to the regime. As Widner (1992: 41–42) describes, "At independence, class division and the leaders of class-based organization held greater power than they did only a few years later. The new government moved quickly and successfully to attenuate horizontal divisions, so that by the

[10] These figures are from the population census in 1969, the first I know of that surveyed information about tribes. The source is Republic of Kenya (1979).

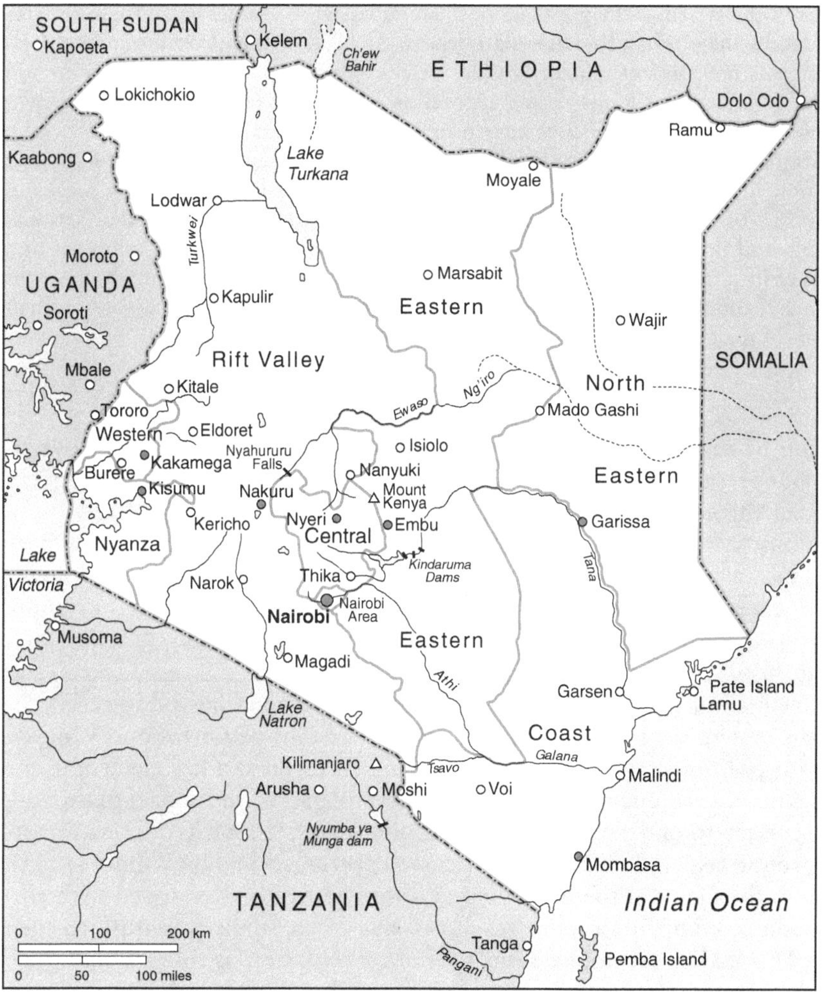

FIGURE 4.3. Map of Kenya's provinces.

time it entered its second or third year, patron-client ties had become stronger elements in defining personal identities than incipient classes." In other words, the dynamic at work seemed to approximate the spending and clientelistic theories in Chapter 2 more than the redistributional theories of regime change.

These clientelistic ties were to be an essential part of the regime throughout Kenyatta's and Moi's rule, largely working through the legislature. As Barkan (1979: 72) described,

> The linkage chains through which members of the Kenya National Assembly connect their constituencies to the center usually consist of a hierarchy of patron-client linkages.... In most cases, these linkage chains embrace four tiers of patron-client relationships. At

the apex of the system is the president of the republic who, as chief patron, coordinates and balances the claims of competing lineages. As head of the government, the president awards government ministries (and the resources of patronage they command) to senior politicians of longstanding reputation who wield power beyond their own parliamentary districts. Ministries have usually been awarded to regional leaders who have demonstrated their ability to "bring in their ethnic base," or region in support of the government. These regional leaders are simultaneously clients of the president and patrons of aspiring younger politicians, including backbenchers in the National Assembly and potential backbenchers. The latter are in turn clients of ministers and patrons of local notables in their constituencies. These notables, some of whom might hold elective office themselves as members of town councils, are in turn patrons of small segments of the general public.

Given this extensive dynamic of clientelism, money was "the mother's milk of politics," as Barkan (1979: 74) put it. Elites were bought into the KANU coalition by providing them land or through postings in the central government (Sanger and Nottingham 1964). With these postings, legislators were rewarded through the extensive use of patronage, which helped them win reelection. "Ministers and Assistant Ministers, with greater access to state patronage, were far more successful at securing re-election than ordinary backbenchers. Three quarters of Cabinet Ministers were re-elected in 1969, and in 1983 the proportion rose to more than four fifths" (Throup and Hornsby 1998: 40).

As mentioned earlier, a massive amount of foreign aid flowed into this clientelistic system over the course of the 1980s, as international donors played Cold War politics in Africa and Kenya, which was seen as a key element in the fight against Communism (Clough 1992). To understand the impact of this aid, it is necessary to understand that the clientelistic system of KANU was organized around regional divisions, as discussed previously and by Widner (1992). Owing to the fact that these regional divisions generally overlapped with ethnic divisions, competition over resources was often ethnic in nature (Bienen 1974). This had major implications when Moi took over as ruler, as his ethnic base of Kalenjin differed from that of Kenyatta's Kikuyu (Barkan and Chege 1989; Hornsby and Throup 1992).

As a result of the transition to Moi, many Kikuyu feared losing access to the clientelistic system of KANU politics. As Throup and Hornsby (1998: 27) write, Moi's "attempt to restructure Kenya's political economy, to broaden the development base, and to reward his allies in the Rift Valley and in Western and Coast Provinces undermined the regime's political stability by alienating Kikuyu businessmen and civil servants ... who found that their influence had declined and that they were losing contracts to Asians and their Kalenjin front-men." Indeed, in August 1982, just before the boom of nontax revenue studied in this section (1984–89), Moi had to withstand an attempted coup d'etat with links to Kikuyu politicians and officers in the army, police, and air force.

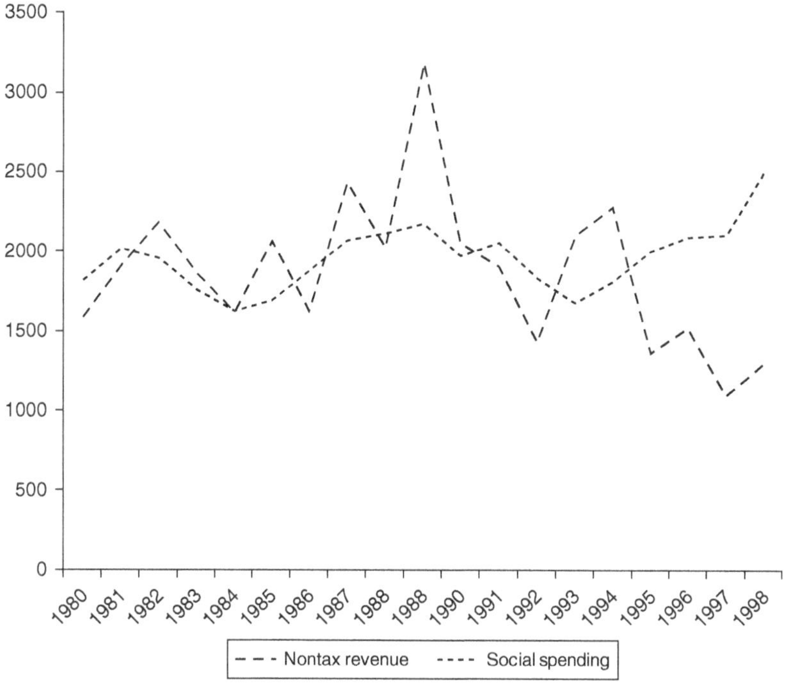

FIGURE 4.4. Per capita social spending and nontax revenue in Kenya.
Note: Numbers are in constant shillings.

It is interesting to note that when the boom in nontax revenue occurred, it had virtually no effect on social spending in Kenya, as Figure 4.4 shows.[11] The figure is strikingly unlike the one for Mexico (Figure 4.1), in which social spending followed nontax revenue closely. In fact, social spending in Kenya did not vary much at all over the time period in question. Simple correlational analysis confirms the visual impression: the correlation coefficient between nontax

[11] It is worthwhile to consider the possibility that the different primary sources of nontax revenue – oil for Mexico and foreign aid for Kenya – may have caused the different usage in these two countries. However, as discussed in Chapter 3, this is unlikely. There is no theoretical reason to expect systematic differences in the effects of foreign aid and natural resource rents. Although foreign aid is often funneled into projects or delivered with conditions in an effort to change government behavior, these mechanisms are undermined by the problems of fungibility and an ineffectiveness of conditionalities. Indeed, there is evidence that both of these have been problems in the particular case of Kenya. James Njeru (2003), for example, has documented the issue of fungibility in the country. And a study by the World Bank concluded that all of the institution's structural adjustment programs to Kenya actually resulted in *worse* policies from the Bank's perspective, because the money from the programs financed the government's inefficiencies (O'Brien and Ryan 2001).

TABLE 4.1. *Per Capita Curative Health Spending in Kenya*

	1985/86	1988/89	1992/93
Kenyatta (Kikuyu) stronghold	1,746	2,974	1,057
Moi (Kalenjin) stronghold	905	3,038	2,690
Rest of country	2,105	7,606	6,811

Note: Numbers are in constant shillings. Own calculations using data from Kenya's Central Bureau of Statistics.

revenue per capita and social spending per capita in Mexico in Figure 4.1 is 0.73, whereas the correlation coefficient for Kenya in Figure 4.4 is -0.05.

Instead of being funneled into social spending, the allocation of nontax revenue in Kenya followed more ethnically delineated lines in an attempt to diffuse tensions with the Kikuyu. Using government data, I analyzed per capita curative health spending during this time period to see where Moi chose to spend his resources. These data are line-item projects that are listed by region, and although curative health spending is only one area of the total health budget, it constitutes the majority of spending in most years. Using the overlap between ethnic groups and regions, Barkan and Chege (1989) demonstrated how it was possible to analyze which ethnic groups were benefiting from government spending in Kenya. Using their same methodology (in terms of which groups and regions were part of which stronghold), Table 4.1 indicates that as nontax revenue rose in the late 1980s, Moi paid careful attention to spreading the wealth around, particularly to the Kikuyu regions where he was feeling particularly threatened.

It should be noted that it is unlikely that this spending benefited all of the Kikuyu. In particular, Moi's response to the coup was to simultaneously expunge the old guard of Kikuyu elites from KANU and court new Kikuyu leaders, using a strategy of divide-and-rule. For example, he recruited former leaders of the Mau Mau anticolonial movement, such as Kariuki Chotara, who saw directly the benefits of the nontax revenue boom. "During the mid-1980s, development resources poured into Naivasha, Chotara's base, transforming the sleepy market town into a hive of business activity with a host of plush new government offices, banks and businesses" (Throup and Hornsby 1998: 36). Such resources were obviously not available to government critics, or even to certain members of the Kikuyu who were not necessary for Moi to placate. All of this money enabled Moi to stay in power: "Throughout Moi's first decade in power ... the use of coercion was rare. The President preferred to use cash to cement his alliances" (Throup and Hornsby 1998: 42).

However, by the beginning of the 1990s, a series of factors had conspired against Moi. The economic crisis of the 1980s – when industrial production stalled and earnings from coffee, tea, and tourism fell – combined with a population growth rate of more than four percent to put great pressure on state resources. In much the same way that Mexico's drop in nontax revenue was borne by the lower and middle income classes, Moi seems to have put most of this fall on Kikuyu strongholds instead of his own Kalenjin strongholds. The severity of the declines also hints that an even further decline in nontax revenue almost certainly would have cut into Moi's spending on the citizens within his own base.

This no doubt helps explain why many scholars point to aid donors as having played an important role in Moi's 1991 decision to allow the political opposition to participate in democratic elections (e.g., Grosh and Orvis 1996). Although Moi would win the 1992 and 1997 elections, this move is often seen as the beginning of Kenya's long transition to democracy, which most scholars say was completed with the 2002 election. As Figure 4.4 indicates, Moi's decision was made when nontax revenue levels were low, and in fact, the date of his decision was only weeks after Kenya's donors decided to suspend $350 million of new aid until corruption was alleviated and the political system liberalized. The fact that donors reinstated their aid soon afterward is reasonably thought to have prolonged Moi's rule (Brown 2001).

4.4 Nontax Revenue and Political Regimes: Cross-National Statistical Analysis

Building on Chapters 2 and 3, the preceding sections have argued that across different theoretical approaches, country contexts, and time periods, nontax revenue should have a similar effect: it should stabilize political regimes and their leaders. In this section, I begin the statistical analysis of this hypothesis by focusing on regime transitions. I use the same binary dependent variable as in Chapter 2 (REGIME INSTABILITY), which takes a value of "1" if there is a regime change from one year to the next, and "0" otherwise. Again, a regime is considered to have changed if it receives a zero in *Polity IV*'s DURABLE variable, which counts the number of years since the most recent regime change (Marshall and Jaggers 2003). A regime change in *Polity IV* is defined by a change of three points or more in the POLITY2 variable – which ranges from -10 (most authoritarian) to 10 (most democratic) – or the end of a transition period.

The key independent variables in the model are the change and level of NONTAX REVENUE PER CAPITA as defined in the Introduction. As I noted in Chapter 3, if different kinds of nontax revenue had different effects on regime stability, it would be difficult to find a significant result for this variable (for example, nontax revenues with both negative and positive effects would be aggregated into one variable). However, as I discuss in this section, I conducted tests to be sure that combining them into one indicator is justifiable, as in Chapter 3.

A simple logit regression of the REGIME INSTABILITY dependent variable on the lagged level of NONTAX REVENUE PER CAPITA yields a negative and significant coefficient (indicating that nontax revenue has a stabilizing effect), with a p-value of 0.024. However, it is important to control for other variables that might also be affecting regime stability, to ensure confidence in the results. I therefore use the same control variables as in Chapter 2. First, I control for the natural log level of, and growth in, GDP PER CAPITA, following many scholars who have found a relationship between these indicators and regime stability (Lipset 1959; Remmer 1991; Przeworski et al. 2000). Second, I control for the change in the percentage of the population that is urban (Δ% POPULATION URBAN), since some scholars have found that urbanization can be destabilizing for regimes (Huntington 1968). Third, I include the level of POPULATION DENSITY, to control for the possibility of a relationship between population, land, and regime stability (Herbst 2000; Fearon and Laitin 2003). All of these variables come from the World Bank. Finally, I include an indicator of whether the country was a DEMOCRACY or not, to account for the fact that during the time period of my sample, democracies have fallen at a slower rate than dictatorships (Huntington 1991). Following a convention established by prior research (e.g., Rousseau et al. 1996; Reiter 2001; Kadera, Crescenzi, and Shannon 2003), the variable is coded as a "1" (democratic) if the country scores seven or above on *Polity IV*'s POLITY2 measure of political regimes (mentioned earlier), whereas dictatorships are considered those countries with a score of six or below.

The estimation technique used is logistic analysis with errors clustered by country. However, as discussed in Chapter 2, cross-sectional time-series data with a binary dependent variable are likely to violate the independence assumption of ordinary logistic analysis (Beck, Katz, and Tucker 1998). Therefore, I control for PAST REGIME INSTABILITY in a country, measured as the number of all past regime changes in that country in the sample. In addition, following the advice of Beck Katz, and Tucker (1998), I include cubic splines of the POLITICAL REGIME'S AGE in a given year to capture temporal dependence in the data.[12]

In conducting the analysis, I first made sure that combining the nontax revenue categories into one variable was justified, as in Chapter 3. Specifically, three categories of nontax revenue were entered into the regression separately: foreign aid, an indicator of state-owned enterprise revenue, and a residual indicator consisting of the aggregate nontax revenue variable minus these two components. An important part of this third category is borrowing; for example, to finance deficit spending (definitions for each indicator are presented in Figure 1.2). In the regression, all three nontax variables entered with negative coefficients, but a t-test rejected the hypothesis that the coefficients were exactly the same because of a larger (i.e., more negative) coefficient on foreign aid.[13] Nevertheless, a linear combination of the coefficients was negative and

[12] Specifically, the age of a political regime was coded as the lagged value of the DURABLE variable in *Polity IV*, which means that it is the number of years since there was a change of at least three in the Polity score. F-tests revealed that these splines were necessary to include in the regressions. As Beck, Katz, and Tucker (1998) detail, including these splines makes logistic analysis identical to survival analysis techniques.

[13] The p-value was 0.007.

significant, suggesting that aggregating the different nontax revenue variables is justified.[14]

Model 1 of Table 4.2 reports the results with the aggregated nontax revenue variable. Nontax revenue is negative and significant, indicating that nontax revenue reduces regime instability as predicted. Substantively, the results indicate that a move from the twenty-fifth percentile of nontax revenue per capita to the seventy-fifth percentile would decrease the probability of regime change by about 27 percent.

With respect to the other independent variables, there is strong evidence that economic growth is stabilizing to political regimes and, as expected, democracies have fallen at a lower rate than dictatorships during the period under study.

I submitted these results to a variety of robustness tests.[15] First, I included a measure of whether or not the country was involved in a militarized-interstate dispute in the prior year (Marinov 2005) since some scholars have argued for war's effects on both taxation and regime stability (e.g., Tilly 1990). Second, I included a variable measuring ethnolinguistic fractionalization since some scholars have argued that social fragmentation increases regime instability (e.g., Horowitz 1985).[16] Third, I included a dummy variable in the regression that indicated whether the country belonged to the OECD to be sure that the dynamics observed were not driven by rich countries (in addition, I also tried running the regression using only non-OECD countries). Fourth, I included dummy variables marking the 1970s and 1980s to control for temporal effects. Fifth, to control for regional effects, I included dummy variables representing the different regions of the world. Sixth, I included a spatial lag of the dependent variable to account for the possibility that regime transitions are spatially correlated (Gleditsch and Ward 2006). Seventh, I repeated the regression in Model 2 of Table 4.2 using an alternative coding of regime change. I used the regime coding of Bueno de Mesquita and his colleagues (2003), who focus on the size of the winning coalition in a political regime.[17] Using various indicators from the *Polity* data set, they create a five-point scale to represent coalition size. I considered a regime change any shift on this five-point scale. And finally,

[14] As discussed earlier, this is highly desirable because the disaggregated components are available for a smaller set of observations than the aggregate nontax revenue variable, which is calculated using two widely available indicators (tax revenue and total spending). The p-value of the linear combination was 0.009.

[15] None of these specifications greatly improved the fit of the model. All robustness checks are available from the author as a data archive and Stata do-file.

[16] The measure I used is the probability that two randomly chosen individuals in a country do not speak the same language. Roeder's (2001) data set provides observations of this variable for both 1961 and 1985. For all observations prior to and in 1980, I use the 1961 measure and for all subsequent years, I use the 1985 measure.

[17] I also used the dichotomous measure of regime change from Przeworski and others (2000), and the effect of nontax revenue was significant and stabilizing (p-value = 0.008).

TABLE 4.2. *The Effect of Nontax Revenue on Regime transitions*

Independent Variables	Model 1	Model 2
Δ NONTAX REVENUE PER CAPITA	−0.000664**	−0.000591
	(0.000330)	(0.000372)
NONTAX REVENUE PER CAPITA (t-1)	−0.000564***	−0.000481***
	(0.000149)	(0.000141)
GDP PER CAPITA GROWTH	−0.0586***	−0.0581***
	(0.0205)	(0.0201)
GDP PER CAPITA (ln, t-1)	0.221*	0.235*
	(0.129)	(0.126)
Δ% POPULATION URBAN	0.0180	0.0272
	(0.307)	(0.303)
POPULATION DENSITY (T-1)	−0.0464	−0.0480
	(0.0865)	(0.0864)
DEMOCRACY (t-1)	−2.759***	−2.326***
	(0.524)	(0.525)
PAST REGIME INSTABILITY	0.0235	0.0259
	(0.0656)	(0.0647)
AGE OF REGIME	−0.604***	−0.602***
	(0.131)	(0.130)
Δ NONTAX REVENUE PER CAPITA* DEMOCRACY (t-1)		−0.000076
		(0.00202)
NONTAX REVENUE PER CAPITA (t-1)* DEMOCRACY (t-1)		−0.00150
		(0.000945)
CONSTANT	−1.675*	−1.789**
	(0.917)	(0.912)
Observations	1715	1715
Countries	101	101
Prob > χ^2	0.0000	0.0000
Pseudo R^2	0.2587	0.2609

Notes: The dependent variable = 1 if regime changes in current year (0 otherwise). Cubic splines of AGE OF REGIME not reported. Table entries are logistic regression estimates with standard errors (in parentheses) clustered by country. The asterisks denote the following: *p<0.10; **p<0.05; ***p < 0.01.

I ran the regression with country-level and year-level fixed effects.[18] None of these modifications had any significant impact on the important results.

[18] Using country-level fixed effects on regime transition data is problematic, as the many countries that have never had a regime transition simply drop out of the data set. For this reason, Beck and Katz (2001) argue that country-level fixed effects should never be used in this type of analysis. Nevertheless, the stability of the results is encouraging. Note that in this regression, I used POLITY2 instead of the dummy variable for democracy because fixed-effects regression causes problems for slowly changing variables.

I also explored whether the results were different for different types of regimes. Given that the existing literature on oil and aid has focused on transitions to democracy, one might expect the effect of nontax revenue to be much stronger in dictatorships. I therefore included interaction terms consisting of DEMOCRACY (as defined earlier) and a country's change and level of nontax revenue. The results of this regression are included in Model 2 of Table 4.2. They indicate that nontax revenue has a stabilizing effect in both dictatorships and democracies – the interaction term is not significant (p-value of 0.112).

Finally, to address the scholarship discussed in Chapter 3, arguing that aid's effects after the Cold War may have been different than those during the Cold War, I followed a strategy similar to that in Chapter 3. In the regression with the disaggregated components of nontax revenue, I included an interaction term between foreign aid and a dummy variable equaling 1 if the year was equal to or later than 1990. This interaction term was insignificant (p-value = 0.217) and foreign aid's effects were negative (stabilizing) and significant in both periods. Foreign aid has the same effect in the Cold War and afterward.

4.5 Nontax Revenue and the Durability of Authoritarian Leaders

As discussed in Chapter 2, regime change is only one form of political change in countries. Regime changes are major events, but leadership transitions within political regimes take place much more often, both in authoritarian and (by definition) democratic countries. And as I showed in Chapter 2, tax breaks and spending increases affect leadership stability the same way they affect regime stability: they lead to longer-lasting leaders. As such, we should also expect that nontax revenue has similar effects on leaders as it does on regimes. Similar to the literature on regime stability, there have been separate studies of the effects of oil and aid on leadership duration (Omgba 2009; Licht 2010; Crespo Cuaresma, Oberhofer, and Raschky 2011), but not generally of nontax revenue as an aggregate category. The one exception is Bueno de Mesquita and Smith (2010), who use my measure of nontax revenue (Morrison 2009) to show that it stabilizes authoritarian leaders. This section therefore supplements their work.

To test the effect of nontax revenue on the durability of leaders in authoritarian regimes, I again use the data set originally developed by Chiozza and Goemans (2004) and updated by Goemans, Gleditsch, and Chiozza (2009), containing data on leaders and leadership changes for most countries in the world during the years covered in my sample. As discussed in Chapter 2, because of the nature of the data – with the unit of analysis being the leader, not a country-year – there can be multiple observations in a given country-year. This differentiates these data from those on regime transitions, and indeed from most commonly used economic data for developing countries (such as economic growth, income per capita, and government finance variables), for which there is only one observation per country per year. Therefore, in order to use the leadership data with my other data, as in Chapter 2, I follow a strategy used by others (e.g., Marinov 2005). If there are multiple leadership changes in a given year, I code the country-year observation to simply register a leadership change in that year. In other words, there is no difference in my data set between one leadership change in a given year and multiple leadership changes (the leader in power at the end of the year is the one recorded for reference in the following years). While obviously dropping information is never ideal, this seems a reasonable way to use the leadership data to study the effects of variables measured only on an annual basis.

To examine the effect of nontax revenue on these leadership transitions in authoritarian regimes (defined earlier using the POLITY2 variable), I use the same nontax revenue variables employed previously, combined with other variables to control for omitted variable bias.[19] In particular, as in Chapter 2, I control for economic growth and income per capita, using the same measures as in the regressions on regime change, as well as the AGE OF THE LEADER (Goemans, Gleditsch, and Chiozza 2009). I also use the same methodology employed earlier, logistic analysis with clustered standard errors, and as with those regressions, I again employ a variable to control for the temporal dependence of the observations. I control for the number of YEARS IN OFFICE a leader has had, and I supplement this variable with cubic splines of the number of years to account for how the probability of staying in power rises or falls over time, without imposing any particular functional form on this relationship (Beck, Katz, and Tucker 1998).

Table 4.3 presents the results of the regression and shows that nontax revenue has effects similar to the ones it had in the regime change regressions: higher levels of nontax revenue make the ousting of authoritarian leaders less likely. Substantively, the results suggest that a move from the twenty-fifth percentile of nontax revenue to the seventy-fifth percentile of nontax revenue would diminish the probability of a leadership transition by about seven percent.

To ensure that these results were robust to other operationalizations, I included the other control variables from the earlier regressions on regime stability (growth in urban population, population density, and past regime changes) and found that the results did not change.[20] Similar results were also attained when running the regression only with developing countries or excluding countries that underwent regime change in the current year, as well as when including an OECD dummy variable, decade dummies, year dummies, or regional dummies.[21]

[19] I also analyzed the relationship in those countries Przeworski and his colleagues (2000) code as dictatorships, and the results were similar.

[20] None of these had a significant impact on model fit. Results are available from the author as a data archive and Stata do-file.

[21] Including fixed-country effects resulted in twenty-seven countries and about a third of my observations dropping from the sample. With this smaller sample, the coefficient on the level of nontax revenue increased 70 percent in absolute terms, to approximately -0.0085, but the standard errors also increased, resulting in insignificant coefficients.

TABLE 4.3. *The Effect of Nontax Revenue on Authoritarian Leader Transitions*

Independent Variable	
Δ NONTAX REVENUE PER CAPITA	−0.000560
	(0.000414)
NONTAX REVENUE PER CAPITA (t-1)	−0.000505***
	(0.000113)
GDP PER CAPITA GROWTH	−0.0705***
	(0.0202)
GDP PER CAPITA (ln, t-1)	0.160
	(0.128)
AGE OF LEADER	0.0111
	(0.0129)
YEARS IN OFFICE	−0.785**
	(0.333)
CONSTANT	−2.678***
	(0.977)
Observations	854
Countries	64
Prob > χ^2	0.0000
Pseudo R^2	0.0947

Notes: The dependent variable = 1 when a leadership transition takes place (0 otherwise). Cubic splines of YEARS IN OFFICE are not reported. Table entries are logistic regression estimates with standard errors (in parentheses) clustered by country. The asterisks denote the following: *$p<0.10$; **$p<0.05$; ***$p<0.01$.

In sum, there is robust statistical evidence that higher levels of nontax revenue are associated with lower rates of regime transition in both democracies and dictatorships, as well as lower rates of leadership transition in authoritarian regimes.

The final piece of helpful statistical evidence would be nontax revenue's effects on leaders in democratic regimes. This is not a hypothesis that can be tested with the data and empirical strategy used so far in this chapter because leadership transitions are regulated in democracies, which means that not every democratic observation in the data set has an equal probability of a leadership transition (for example, an observation of the United States in 1992 would have an extremely high probability of a leadership transition because it was an election year, whereas 1993 would not).[22] For this reason, Chapter 5 uses a subnational research design to examine this effect.

[22] Nevertheless, I experimented with the data set on national elections compiled by Hyde and Marinov (2012) and, using data for executive elections, ran a regression with the dependent

4.6 Conclusion

This chapter brings to a close the theoretical argument of this book, making the case that tax decreases and spending increases financed by nontax revenue should not generally have different effects in terms of stability than "normal" tax decreases and spending increases. In other words, nontax revenue, by allowing regimes and leaders to lower taxes and raise spending, should stabilize countries. I returned to Chapter 2 and examined the role of nontax revenue in important theoretical approaches considered there, showing how nontax revenue would stabilize regimes and leaders, and I illustrated these mechanisms with case studies of Mexico and Kenya. I also provided cross-national time-series statistical support for the regime transition hypothesis and the leadership transition hypothesis for authoritarian regimes.

Three empirical issues remain, however. First, although I have made predictions about the effect of nontax revenue on democratic leaders, I have not analyzed this hypothesis yet. For the reasons mentioned earlier – the regularized transition of power in democracies – testing the leader-transition hypothesis in democracies cannot be done with the sort of national-level data employed in this chapter and Chapter 2. It would therefore be desirable to analyze this hypothesis in a rigorous way.

The second empirical issue is that the empirical analyses of the last three chapters have focused on national-level revenue, spending, and stability, while throughout the book's theoretical sections I have highlighted the presence of similar dynamics at the subnational level. Clearly it would be appropriate, then, to examine these hypotheses at the subnational level, too.

Finally, the third remaining empirical issue concerns whether the type of analysis employed in the book up until now is credible for establishing causation. Although the majority of works on which this book builds have used this kind of "model-based" analysis, much emphasis has recently been placed in political science and economics on issues of causal "identification" (Sekhon 2009; Dunning 2010). For adherents to this approach, the results in this chapter, as well as Chapters 2 and 3, will be interesting but less convincing than if they had been produced using a different research strategy.

Chapter 5 attempts to address all of these issues.

variable of whether or not the party in power was reelected (Cheibub and Przeworski 1999). There were 103 observations in 29 countries, and higher levels of nontax revenue were associated with less electoral losses by the party in power (p-value = 0.083), controlling for economic growth. This finding also held in elections more broadly (i.e., not just executive elections).

5

This Happens at Subnational Levels of Governments, Too

With Stephan Litschig

5.1 Introduction

In 2008, Goldberg, Wibbels, and Mvukiyehe published an important article on the political effects of oil entitled, "Lessons from Strange Cases: Democracy, Development, and the Resource Curse in the U.S. States." The "strange" in the title referred to the fact that the cases examined in the paper were not the standard ones associated with the resource curse, such as those discussed in Chapter 2, but rather certain oil-rich states in the United States of America. This research design provided the authors with several advantages over the normal nation-state focus in the resource curse literature, such as controlling for the potentially confounding but unobserved variables that can plague cross-country research. And one of the most important lessons gained from this design was that *rentier* dynamics could be present at lower levels of government. The key insight was that at the subnational level, just as at the national level, "state revenues derived from oil had a profound impact on the nature of domestic political institutions" (Goldberg, Wibbels, and Mvukiyehe 2008: 497). In line with the argument in this book, the authors found that influxes of oil revenues were associated with lower taxes, higher spending, and a greater margin of victory by incumbents in gubernatorial elections.

The argument that Goldberg and his colleagues made – that these sorts of dynamics might also be present at lower levels of government – expanded the geographic extension of work on the resource curse, from national capitals to the outlying areas around them that gain revenues from natural resources or other nontax sources. Subsequent work has demonstrated the utility of this approach (Monteiro and Ferraz 2010; Caselli and Michaels 2013), and this book is very much in the same spirit. The broadening of focus from natural resources to nontax revenue, as this book attempts to do, greatly expands the geographic extension of traditional *rentier* state theories, from oil-rich countries clustered in certain regions to a large cross-section of national governments spanning the globe, and to an even wider set of subnational governments around the world.

Indeed, while there are many subnational areas with access to natural resource revenues around the world, there are even more with access to other nontax revenues, as discussed in the Introduction. Subnational governments around the world rely on intergovernmental transfers from their central government for much, if not most, of their revenue (Ter-Minassian 1997; Rodden 2004). These intergovernmental transfers are the subnational equivalent of foreign aid, in the sense that they are resource transfers from one governmental entity to another. And in fact, a couple of years after the article by Goldberg and his colleagues, a paper was published by Gervasoni (2010) documenting patterns in democratic Argentina very similar to the ones observed in the United States by Goldberg and his colleagues. However, in the case of Argentina, the larger margins of incumbent victory were associated with greater federal transfers, not oil. Gervasoni found that provinces that receive more transfers from the federal government tax less, spend more, and have gubernatorial incumbents more likely to win by a large margin and control the state legislature. Subsequent work has also documented *rentier* effects at the subnational level owing to such transfers, as discussed in this section.

This chapter adds to this literature on subnational nontax revenue, but more broadly it demonstrates that the theory developed in this book is relevant not only at the national level, but also at the subnational level. Taxation is destabilizing, spending is stabilizing, and nontax revenue is stabilizing because it enables governments to lower taxes and increase spending.

In particular, this chapter reports the results of research I have done with Stephan Litschig of the Department of Economics and Business at Universitat Pompeu Fabra in Barcelona (Litschig and Morrison 2013). For reasons that will be explained shortly, our work focuses on a particular federal transfer in Brazil that made up a substantial share of municipal revenues in the 1980s. If the theory in this book is correct, then receipt of this nontax revenue should have been associated with lower taxes, higher spending, and higher reelection rates of incumbent parties in mayoral elections. We find that this was generally the case.

Empirically, there are both advantages and disadvantages to moving to a subnational level of analysis. One primary disadvantage is, of course, that one always wonders about external validity when only looking at one country. For example, Gervasoni's analysis revealed interesting patterns about Argentina, but how can we know if similar patterns regarding transfers would hold in other federal countries, such as India or Mexico? A second disadvantage is that analysis at the subnational level do not necessarily reveal anything about other levels of analysis. The article by Goldberg, Wibbels, and Mvukiyehe, for example, illustrated important patterns with regard to natural resources and political dynamics at the subnational level, but without other research (of which there is, of course, much), it is impossible to know if similar patterns exist at the level of nation-states.

Both of these disadvantages are diminished in this case, given the other chapters in this book. The previous chapters have shown that similar patterns regarding taxation, spending, and nontax revenue exist at the level of the nation-state for countries around the world. And this chapter will discuss why we consider Brazil to be a "least likely" case, in the sense that if these dynamics were observed at the subnational level there, then they are likely to be observed in many places. It is, however, true that there will be no other subnational evidence offered in the book, and so the reader will have to judge whether the dynamics revealed here in the Brazilian case are likely to hold in other countries as well.

Compensating for these disadvantages is a major advantage of studying this Brazilian case: clear identification of causality. Whereas the prior chapters in this book have taken various measures to rule out alternative explanations and address issues of endogeneity, they have nevertheless presented statistical correlations. These correlations, in the context of a compelling theory, are significant and hopefully have convinced the reader to some degree of the validity of the argument. However, it is well known that correlations do not establish causality, and so the reader may remain somewhat skeptical of the empirical results.

This case study of Brazil addresses this problem by using a quasi-experimental research design (Shadish, Cook, and Campbell 2002). In Brazil from 1982–85, the transfer we study was allocated according to population thresholds. That is, if a municipality's population was just below a certain population threshold, then it received a certain amount of transfer, but if it was just above that population threshold, it received a higher amount. The municipalities clustered around these thresholds should not have been systematically different from one another (which we verify in this chapter); for example, there is no reason a municipality with 9,990 people should be systematically different than a municipality with 10,010 people. However, in our case, if the allocation threshold was 10,000 people, then the latter municipality would have received substantially more in per capita transfers than the former municipality. This means that, of the municipalities whose populations were close to the threshold, extra transfers were "as good as" randomly assigned. And this random assignment enables us to examine the causal effect of these extra transfers on taxation, spending, and reelection rates. In particular, we study the effect of transfers allocated from 1982–85 on reelection rates in the 1988 municipal elections.

This quasi-experimental design sets this chapter apart from the other works that have studied the reelection effects of nontax revenue at the subnational level (and indeed, at the national level).[1] Other than the work by Goldberg and his colleagues and Gervasoni, there are only two other relevant works of which we are aware.[2] The first is by Solé-Ollé and Sorribas-Navarro (2008), who analyzed how intergovernmental grants in Spain affected local re-election prospects. They found that grants allocated to local governments politically aligned with the central government had more of an effect than grants allocated to non-aligned local governments. And the second is by Monteiro and Ferraz (2010), who study the effect of oil royalty payments in Brazil's democracy, finding that they strongly benefit incumbents.[3]

However, none of these works can be said to have clearly identified a causal impact of the subnational nontax revenue on political stability. They all rely on what may be called "model-based" research strategies, as opposed to "design-based" research strategies (Sekhon 2009; Dunning 2010). The principal objective in much research is to identify the causal effect of some variable, but this is, of course, quite difficult. Confounding factors (omitted variables) and nonrandom assignment of the treatment can cause mistaken inferences about the effects of some variable of interest. In model-based research designs, researchers rely on statistical methods to handle these problems, as in previous chapters in this book.[4] With any model-based strategy, true conditional independence – that is, confidence that one is estimating the causal effect correctly – is difficult to achieve (Brady 2010). In design-based strategies, by contrast, there is some treatment that can be considered "as if" it was randomly assigned to subgroups of the population. If this research design is believable, then one can often simply analyze the difference in means between the treatment and control group, as with a laboratory experiment, for example.

Although design-based research can be quite powerful, such research is only as good as it is "plausible," in the sense that the researcher must show that the treatment can really be considered "as if" it were randomly assigned (Dunning 2008b, 2010). Simply put, some designs are more believable than others. For

[1] Other works have focused on subnational resource effects on corruption (Caselli and Michaels 2013; Brollo et al. 2013). Caselli and Michaels (2013) find results for spending similar to those in this chapter: oil abundance causes spending to increase.

[2] A third work is that by Brollo et al. (2013), who also find that reelection prospects are enhanced by subnational transfers. However, as they acknowledge, they use the research design employed in this chapter and developed in our previous work (Litschig 2010; Litschig and Morrison 2013).

[3] Although it does not look at actual nontax revenue or voting behavior, an important related work is that by Paler (2013), who conducts a field experiment simulating how taxes and nontax revenue affect citizens' likelihood of sanctioning an incumbent. She finds, consistent with the theory here, that the tax treatment leads to more sanctioning of the incumbent than the windfall treatment, although her explanation of this is different than the theory offered here.

[4] For example, the paper by Solé-Ollé and Sorribas-Navarro (2008) uses the instrumental variables strategy of Levitt and Snyder (1997), instrumenting for local spending in one district with the spending in a neighboring district. Monteiro and Ferraz (2010), for their part, instrument for royalties with the level of oil production in a municipality (Caselli and Michaels 2013).

this reason, much of this chapter focuses on establishing the validity of our particular research design. Indeed, once this validity is established, the "results section" is extremely straightforward. Robustness checks, and the similar other procedures one often sees in model-based research, are essentially unnecessary since the assignment of the treatment is random (we will, nevertheless, provide some robustness checks to ensure that our design is valid).

The chapter will therefore proceed as follows. The next section provides some background on the Brazilian case we examine. It gives some information on the political situation during the time we study, particularly focusing on the clientelistic mechanism discussed in Chapter 4. It also introduces the key federal transfer we study, and the important details about it. The third section is the most important: it establishes why we think this transfer can be considered a plausible quasi-experiment, analyzing in detail the potential threats to the validity of the design. The fourth section discusses how we study the effects of this transfer, detailing the estimation approach. The fifth section provides the results, and a final section concludes. Two Appendices, referred to in the text when necessary, contain some technical details of the analysis.

By the end of the chapter, the reader will hopefully have gained three important insights relevant to the rest of the book. First, the results here complement the results with regard to nontax revenue and authoritarian leaders in Chapter 4, providing evidence that nontax revenue stabilizes democratic leaders as well. Second, this chapter indicates that the theory advanced in this book about revenue, spending, and stability applies at the subnational level in addition to the national one. And third, the chapter shows that it is possible to observe these effects with a design-based research strategy in addition to a model-based one. In all, the chapter not only suggests the robustness of the findings in the previous chapters of the book, but also expands their empirical domain.

5.2 Brazil: The Details of a Least-Likely Case

As mentioned previously, the natural experiment examined in this chapter is the "as if" random assignment of extra federal transfers to local municipalities in Brazil, with which we can observe the effects of these transfers on taxation, spending, and reelection rates. We will discuss the particular details of this design in a moment, but first it will be helpful for the reader to have some background on Brazil during the period we study. In particular, we believe that the political setting in Brazil during this time – 1982–88 – represents a difficult one in which to observe the sorts of effects we predict: that is, extra transfers will result in a higher probability of reelection. In this sense, we think of this study as a "least likely" case, in that the conditions are challenging for observing support for the hypothesis (Eckstein 1975). As such, finding support for the hypothesis here raises confidence that we might observe a similar (or even stronger) relationship in other settings, although, of course, this remains speculative.

Why do we think it would a priori be difficult to observe an effect of transfers allocated in 1982–85 on the municipal elections in 1988? Most importantly, because of term-limit rules, incumbent mayors during this time could not be individually reelected to serve consecutive terms (although they could be elected again after skipping one term). In a consecutive term, which is what we study, citizens could only reelect the party of the mayor. Although this may not have diminished reelection prospects in some settings, satisfaction with parties in Brazil was particularly low during this time.[5] In fact, public opinion surveys showed that the percentage of the population agreeing that "the candidate's party is the decisive factor" in their vote had declined from 43 percent in 1982 to 24 percent in 1986, and to 18 percent in 1988 (Muszynski and Teixera Mendes 1990; Ames 1994). Perhaps not surprisingly, party switching by politicians in Brazil was rampant around this time: Mainwaring (1991) reports that during the 1987–90 Congress, about one-third of the 559 representatives switched parties.

In addition to these institutional challenges, politics in Brazil during this time was anything but "normal": it was a period of great political change in the country. Most importantly, the 1988 local elections were some of the culminating events of Brazil's extended transition to democracy. The military had ruled the country since 1964 and over the course of the 1980s gradually loosened its power and eventually lost control. In 1985, the party of the dictatorship, the *Partido Democrático Social* (PDS), lost the presidency to the major opposition party, the *Partido do Movimento Democrático Brasileiro* (PMDB).[6] The 1988 elections were thus the first in more than two decades in which the PDS was not in control of the central government.

Importantly for the analysis here, change at the national level was reflected at the local level. As Table 5.1 shows, the PDS won mayoral elections in almost two-thirds of the municipalities in 1982, to go along with its control of the central government. However, when mayoral elections were held in the state capitals and other select municipalities in 1985, the party essentially disappeared from major urban areas – the result of a party split (in which the *Partido da Frente Liberal*, or PFL, was formed) and widespread popular rejection of conservative parties. Smith (1986) reports that the conservative PDS, PFL, and *Partido Trabalhista Brasileiro* (PTB) parties only won 28.2 percent of the vote in the 1985 mayoral elections. This decline would continue in 1988, when PDS candidates would be elected to the mayor's office in a mere 10 percent of municipalities, leaving a void that was filled by an explosion of new parties (see Table 5.1). Whereas the period of the dictatorship had seen electoral "competition" limited to only a few parties, voters in 1988 chose from thirty-one political parties – sixteen of which

[5] Party identification in Brazil faces particularly strong challenges in general (Kinzo 1993; Shidlo 1998). As Moisés (1993: 577) puts it, "Brazilians don't vote for parties, they vote for people."

[6] This loss, however, was in an election by Parliament, not a popular election.

TABLE 5.1. *Brazilian Mayoral Party Affiliations in 1982 and 1988*

Party	Party type	1982		1988	
		N	%	N	%
PDS	Right	2,537	64.5	444	10.4
PFL	Right			1,054	24.7
PTB	Right	7	0.2	333	7.8
PMB	Right			58	1.4
PL	Right			237	5.5
PDC	Right			231	5.4
PRN	Right			4	0.1
PSC	Right			26	0.6
PRTB	Right			8	0.2
PSD	Right			2	0.1
PMDB	Left	1,366	34.7	1,593	37.3
PDT	Left	20	0.5	192	4.5
PT	Left	2	0.1	38	0.9
PSB	Left			37	0.9
PSDB	Left			18	0.4
PSTU	Left			1	0.0
Total	Left	3,936	100	4,276	100

Source: Tribunal Superior Eleitoral do Brasil.

were winners somewhere in the country – to elect mayors in about 4,000 municipalities.

In sum, for a variety of reasons, one may have expected that the record of the previous mayoral incumbent would not have played a great role in the municipal elections of 1988. If true, this would diminish our ability to observe an effect of nontax revenue. Nevertheless, despite this difficult context in which to test the hypothesis, there are three reasons to think that transfers might have had an effect. Those reasons are that spending at the local level was significant, was almost certainly subject to the clientelistic dynamics discussed in Chapters 2 and 4, and was funded primarily by these intergovernmental transfers.

Consider that during our study period of 1982–85, local governments managed about 17 percent of public resources in Brazil (Shah 1990) – about four percent of GDP – with 20 percent of local budgets going to education, and similar shares to housing and urban infrastructure, as well as transportation spending (Litschig and Morrison 2013).[7] This spending was vital to education,

[7] Local governments also provided some primary health care services (about 10 percent of local budgets). Local welfare assistance was close to negligible.

TABLE 5.2. *Gross Tax Revenues Collected by Jurisdiction in Brazil, 1960–88*

	1960	1980	1988
Percent of GDP			
Total	17.4	24.6	22.5
Federal government	11.1	18.5	15.8
States	5.5	5.4	6.0
Municipalities	0.8	0.7	0.7
Percent of total revenues			
Total	100	100	100
Federal government	64	75.1	70.6
States	31.2	22	26.5
Municipalities	4.8	2.9	2.9

Source: Afonso and de Mello (2000).

among other public services, as public provision of elementary education in the early 1980s was, for the most part, a joint responsibility of state and local governments (the federal government was primarily involved in financing and standard setting). In 1980, 55 percent of all elementary school students in Brazil were enrolled in state administered schools, 31 percent in municipality schools, and the remaining 14 percent in private schools. In small and rural municipalities, which constitute the focus of the analysis below, the proportion of students in schools managed by local governments was 74 percent, while the proportions in state-run and private schools were 24 percent and 2 percent respectively (World Bank 1985).

Almost certainly this spending was subject to the kinds of clientelistic dynamics discussed in Chapters 2 and 4, underlying the link between spending and political success. Indeed, the extent of patronage and clientelistic politics in Brazil has been widely documented (e.g., Geddes 1994). As Ames (2001: 24) has written, "Without question, political support is exchanged for government jobs and public works in every society, but Brazil is unique in the pervasiveness of these exchanges." Municipal politics are no exception to this, as we know from much monographic and statistical work (Leal 1977; Ames 1994; Bezerra 1999; Lyne 2007). In other words, the mechanism was in place for parties to derive political benefit from extra spending.

Table 5.2 shows that this municipal spending was not funded by local taxes; municipalities in Brazil have never collected much in the way of tax revenues despite taking on more and more responsibilities. In 1988, municipal taxation was only 0.7 percent of GDP, and so the municipalities relied almost exclusively on grants from the state and federal governments.[8] The most important among these transfers was the federal *Fundo de Participacao dos Municípios* (FPM), a largely unconditional revenue-sharing grant funded by federal income taxes and industrial products taxes.[9] Indeed, this grant accounted for about 52 percent of the total revenue of the municipalities in our analysis (58 percent in rural areas). Therefore, if the record of the previous mayoral incumbent mattered *at all*, it is very likely that transfers mattered.

If municipalities were paying out as much in income taxes and industrial products taxes as they received through the FPM financed by them, then the FPM could clearly not be called nontax revenue. However, consistent with the discussion in Chapter 4, federal grants like the FPM in Brazil are "strongly redistributive" (Shah 1990: 19), similar to federal grants in most countries (Broadway 2008). There is no data on federal taxes paid at the municipal level during this time, but Haddad (1999: 13) has analyzed the flows of revenue and expenditure at the regional level in Brazil and found that "the redistributive role of the government played through the federal fiscal system was a common practice in the 1970s and 1980s." Given the level of regional inequality in Brazil at the time, and that the FPM was financed by income and industrial taxes, it is virtually certain that the vast majority of municipalities were receiving far more in grants than they were paying out in federal taxes. In other words, much, if not most, of this transfer was nontax revenue for municipal governments.

Apart from being nontax revenue, the FPM transfer suits our purposes here perfectly. In addition to being vital for the financing of local municipalities in Brazil, this transfer had a unique feature: as mentioned earlier, it was allocated in discontinuous fashion on the basis of population thresholds. The exact formula for the allocation is given in Appendix 5A, but the most important aspect for our purposes is that municipal population estimates – only available for census years or years when a national population count was conducted – should have been the *only* determinant of cross-municipality variation in FPM funding. If this were in fact true, then the discontinuities in the allocation mechanism would provide us with an ideal research design for studying the effects of nontax revenue, using what is called regression discontinuity (RD)

[8] In fact, even as late as 2001, federal and state government transfers made up 80 percent of local revenue for counties with a population below 50,000. Overall, in 2002, local governments were in charge of 16.6 percent of total public revenue (Banco Nacional de Desenvolvimento Econômico e Social 2003).

[9] The one condition over our study period was that municipalities must spend 20 percent of the transfers on education and culture (Decree No. 83.556, Art. 5, I). This constraint is usually considered nonbinding, in that municipalities typically spend about 20 percent of their total revenue on education anyway. It is also not clear how this provision was enforced in practice since there is no clear definition of education and cultural expenditures, and audits were weak or nonexistent.

analysis. Unless municipalities just over the population threshold systematically paid more in income and industrial taxes – which is improbable (particularly because we find in this chapter that treatment municipalities were not systematically more developed than control municipalities) – the allocation mechanism enables us to study an exogenous jump in nontax revenue. Therefore, establishing that the transfer was actually allocated in this way will be a critical part of our analysis.

Before moving on to that analysis, however, two questions that may have occurred to the reader warrant discussion here. First, why would the Brazilian federal government have allocated such a large transfer in this (allegedly) nondiscretionary way? The answer to this question probably lies in the political agenda of the military dictatorship that came to power in 1964 and established this allocation mechanism in 1967. As detailed by Hagopian (1996), two major objectives of the military were to wrest control over resources from the traditional political elite and depoliticize public service provision. The creation of a revenue-sharing fund for the *municípios* based on an objective criterion of need (population) may have been part of this greater agenda. It reflected an attempt to break with the clientelistic practices of the national elite, which manipulated public resources to the benefit of narrowly defined constituencies. Obviously, this did not preclude these resources from being used clientelistically at the local level.

Second, why allocate resources by brackets – that is, in this discontinuous way? The answer to this is less clear. One explanation could be that compared to a linear allocation formula, for example, the bracket design mutes incentives for local officials toward the middle of the bracket to tinker with their population figures, or to contest the accuracy of the estimates in order to get more transfers.[10] However, we do not know for certain the reason behind this allocation strategy.

A related question is where the exact cutoffs come from. Their actual values – 10,188; 13,584; 16,980; and so forth – certainly seem somewhat irregular. Although we are unable to trace the origin of these cutoffs precisely, we know roughly how they came about. The initial legislation from 1967 created cutoffs at multiples of 2,000 up to 10,000 people, then cutoffs at multiples of 4,000 up to 30,000 people, and so forth. The legislation also stipulated that these cutoffs should be updated proportionally with population growth in Brazil.[11] The cutoffs were thus presumably updated twice, once with the census of 1970 and then again with the census of 1980, which explains the irregular

[10] That is, consider the mayor of a town with a population of 5,000 people. If the transfer were allocated on a strictly linear basis, with each additional member of the population resulting in some extra transfer, mayors would have incentive to raise the reported population as much as credibly possible. If they would only get more money, however, if the population crossed 10,000 people, then they might have less incentive to misreport.

[11] Supplementary Law No. 35, 1967, Art. 1, Paragraphs 2 and 4.

numbers. It is noteworthy that the thresholds during our study period are still equidistant from one another (see Appendix 5A), the distance being 6,792 people for the first seven cutoffs (except for the second cutoff, which lies exactly halfway between the first and the third cutoffs).

In addition to these questions about the thresholds, the reader may wonder why we only study them during this particular time period: examining the effects of transfers from 1982–85 on the election of 1988. The reason is that our research design is only valid during this time period. Transfers were allocated from 1982 until 1985 on the basis of the 1980 census population.[12] From 1986–88, the transfers were based on extrapolations produced by the national statistical agency, Instituto Brasileiro de Geografia e Estatistica (IBGE).[13] As a result of the update in 1986, the funding discontinuities disappeared since municipalities changed brackets because of falls or, more often, increases in their population relative to 1980.[14] The "treatment" in our case – a (presumably) unexpected influx of nontax revenue to the municipal budget – therefore only lasted from 1982–85. We could not find other examples of this sort of treatment in later periods in Brazil.[15]

5.3 Validity of the Design

There are three principal ways in which the validity of our research design might be compromised. First, and perhaps most obviously, it may have been that allocations of the FPM transfer did not, in fact, follow the population-threshold formula. If this were the case, clearly we would have no research design. Fortunately, this is straightforward to examine. Second, the particular population thresholds may have been manipulated by the central government – that is, although the allocation formula was followed strictly, the allocation formula itself had been manipulated in some way, so that the particular population cutoffs benefited certain kinds of municipalities (such as those with certain political characteristics). This would undermine the validity of the design because the allocation would be on some basis other than just population.

[12] The first year the 1980 census figures were used was 1982. Prior to 1980, the population numbers were also updated every five years.

[13] The 1985 official estimates were already based on extrapolations that resulted in minor changes compared to the 1980 census estimates. The methodology used by the statistical agency in principle ensures that population estimates are consistent between municipalities, states, and the updated population estimate for the country as a whole (Instituto Brasileiro de Geografia e Estatistica 2002).

[14] To be clear, there are no economically or statistically significant differences in FPM transfers between our treatment and comparison groups (those around the first three cutoffs based on the 1980 census) from 1986 onward. Results are omitted to save space and are available on request.

[15] Interestingly, over the 1990s, the transfer mechanism was apparently manipulated to benefit municipalities with roughly equal right-wing and non-right-wing vote shares (swing voter municipalities), relative to opposition or conservative core support municipalities (Litschig 2012).

Third, even if the formula itself was not altered for political reasons, municipalities themselves may have manipulated their own population numbers in order to access larger transfers. In this case, an unobserved variable systematically correlated with both the treatment and reelection – for example, political ambition – may cause results to be biased.

In our examination of these threats to validity (as well as in the rest of our analysis), we draw from multiple sources of information from Brazil. Population estimates – ostensibly determining transfer amounts – were taken from successive reports issued by the Federal Court of Accounts. Data on local public budgets, including FPM transfers, were self-reported by municipal officials and were compiled into reports by the Secretariat of Economics and Finance inside the federal Ministry of Finance.[16] Electoral data for the municipal executive 1982 and 1988 elections are from the Supreme Electoral Tribunal (TSE).

In addition to these indicators, we also use a variety of other measures in our analysis, including the 1980 levels of municipal income per capita, average years of schooling for individuals twenty-five years and older, the poverty head-count ratio, illiterate percentage of people older than fifteen, the infant mortality rate, the education enrollment rate of 7–14-year-olds, and the percentage of the municipal population living in urban areas. Data on these municipal characteristics are based on a random sample of 25 percent of each municipality's population taken by the census and have been calculated by the national statistical agency (only a shorter census survey was administered to 100 percent of the population).

Let us now consider the threats to validity in turn. First, the transfers were indeed allocated according to the population formula over the period we study.[17] Figure 5.1 plots cumulative FPM transfers over the period 1982–85 against the official population in 1982. The horizontal lines correspond to the modal levels of cumulative transfers for each bracket in our data. The figure shows that funding jumps by about 1,320,000 Reais (2008 prices) or about $1,000,000 international U.S. dollars at each threshold over this period.[18] Observations that appear above or below the horizontal lines are most likely caused by measurement error because as just mentioned, transfer data in this figure are self-reported by municipalities rather than based on administrative records of the Ministry of Finance (these records are not available for the period considered).[19] The cumulative transfer differential during the period 1982–85 corresponds to about 2.5 percent of annual GDP in rural areas of the country

[16] The data from these reports were entered into spreadsheets using independent double-entry processing (Litschig 2010). All public finance data were converted into 2005 currency units using the GDP deflator for Brazil.

[17] As mentioned in footnote 15, this did not continue to be the case after this period.

[18] The 2005 Real/$ purchasing power parity exchange rate was about 1.36.

[19] For later periods, the data is available from the Ministry of Finance, and in these data there is essentially no variation in FPM transfers for a given state and population bracket.

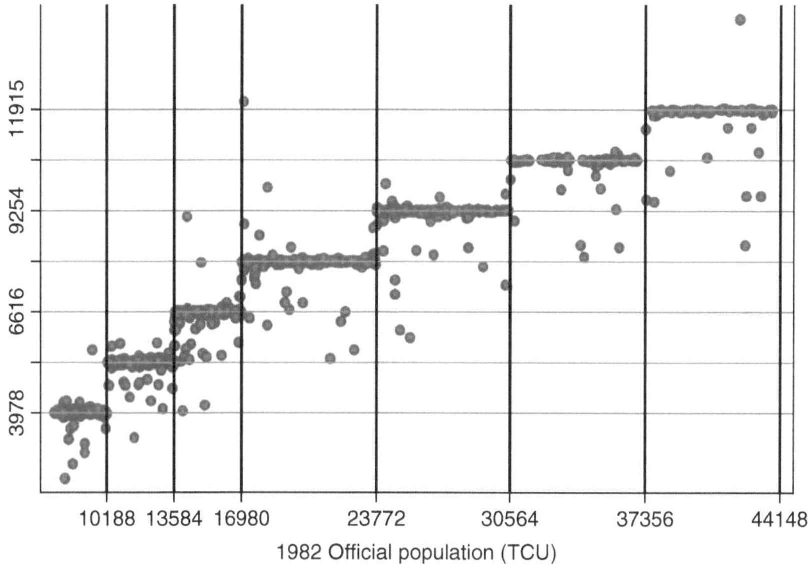

FIGURE 5.1. FPM transfers, 1982–85.
Note: Numbers are in thousands of 2008 Reais. Each dot represents a municipality. The official 1982 population is based on the 1980 census conducted by the national statistical agency, IBGE. The observations that appear off the line in each interval are explained by a few factors. The most important is probably measurement error since the transfers in this table (and in our data) are self-reported by municipalities, rather than based on administrative records of the central government treasury (which are not available for the period considered).

and about 1.4 percent of annual GDP in urban areas for the municipalities in our estimation sample (Litschig and Morrison 2013).

Since every municipality within a given bracket received the same amount of FPM transfer, the per capita FPM transfer declines as one moves higher within a given bracket. Immediately to the left of the first three cutoffs, per capita FPM funding is about R$ 390 (US$ 286). Then, as one crosses the cutoff, there is a major increase in the per capita FPM transfer. This is the "treatment" in this chapter. Although the funding jump is the same in absolute terms at these and other cutoffs, the jump declines in per capita terms at each successive cutoff. That is, as populations increase, a certain funding jump is obviously worth less in per capita terms. Funding jumps by approximately R$130 (US$ 95) per capita at the first threshold, R$ 97 (US$ 70) at the second, R$ 78 (US$ 57) at the third, and declines monotonically for the following cutoffs. For the first three cutoffs, the funding increase per capita is therefore established from the same baseline level and represents about 33 percent at the first, 25 percent at the second, and 20 percent at the third cutoff. Although the differences are not great, this means that the treatment in terms of additional per capita nontax revenue is not exactly the same across these cutoffs. However, since there are likely to be economies of scale, the differences in treatment across cutoffs might be even smaller than what the per capita funding jumps would suggest. It thus seems reasonable to expect similar treatment effects around these cutoffs, as further discussed in the next section.

Therefore, funds were allocated according to the cutoffs established. But might the cutoffs themselves have been designed to benefit certain local leaders? We consider this unlikely. In order for leaders in the central government to have used the cutoffs to benefit subnational leaders of their party, there would have had to have been places along the municipality population distribution where aligned municipalities appeared systematically more often than other municipalities. It is noteworthy in this context that the thresholds are equidistant from one another, making it even less likely that the thresholds were set in order to benefit leaders of a certain type. In support of this contention, we tested whether the cutoffs were associated with any differences in the 1980 values for the municipal-level characteristics mentioned earlier (i.e., income per capita, and so forth). An F-test failed to reject the joint null hypotheses of no discontinuity in any of these characteristics at conventional levels of significance.[20] In other words, from a statistical point of view, there is no evidence that treatment group municipalities (i.e., those who received the extra transfers) were systematically different from municipalities in the comparison group with regard to local development or overall public resources prior to the treatment.[21] In particular, local governments that were run by the PDS – the party of the authoritarian regime that was in control of the central government until 1985 – did not systematically receive higher transfers.[22]

Finally, even if the cutoffs themselves were not systematically adjusted to benefit certain groups in Brazil, local elites clearly had an incentive to manipulate the number of their local residents so that it exceeded a particular threshold. Although the population numbers were produced by the census, they may also have had some control over their numbers, either by influencing census officials or by actually attracting more citizens to their municipality. However, there are two reasons why we are unconcerned by this threat to the validity of the research design.

First, even if local elites had maintained perfect control over the number of residents in their municipality, the legislation specified that thresholds be updated in accordance with population growth in the country as a whole

[20] The test of the joint null hypotheses of no jumps in pretreatment covariates is done by stacking these variables and running a joint estimation of individual discontinuities (Lee and Lemieux 2010).

[21] See Litschig and Morrison (2013) for complete results.

[22] In other words, PDS municipalities were not overrepresented to the right of the cutoffs (the treatment group).

after the release of the 1980 census results. Put differently, local elites were unlikely to know the exact locations of the new thresholds even if they wanted to manipulate their population count. This means that, at best, they had imprecise control over the size of their population and whether or not they received the extra nontax revenue.

Second, it is only *perfect* control of the assignment variable – in this case, population – that would compromise the validity of our regression discontinuity (RD) analysis. This nonobvious result was established by Lee (2008), and its importance is explained in a passage from Lee and Lemieux (2010: 283):

> Intuitively, when individuals have imprecise control over the assignment variable, even if some are especially likely to have values of X [the assignment variable] *near* the cutoff, *every* individual will have approximately the same probability of having an X that is just above (receiving the treatment) or just below (being denied the treatment) the cutoff – similar to a coin-flip experiment. This result clearly differentiates the RD and instrumental variables (IV) approaches. When using IV for causal inference, one must *assume* the instrument is exogenously generated as if by a coin-flip. Such an assumption is often difficult to justify.... By contrast, the variation that RD designs isolate is randomized *as a consequence* of the assumption that individuals have imprecise control over the assignment variable.

In combination, these two reasons give us confidence that municipal alteration of population estimates is not a major threat to the validity of our study. Nevertheless, to strengthen this confidence, we checked for any evidence of this sort of alteration in the distribution of the 1982 municipal population. If alteration was a major problem, we would expect to see clustering (discontinuities) of population estimates around the thresholds determining FPM transfers. Figure 5.2 plots the histogram for official municipality populations in 1982.[23] Visual inspection reveals no discontinuities, except perhaps for a small bump to the right of the third cutoff, which turns out to be statistically insignificant according to the density test suggested by McCrary (2008).

In sum, we are confident that our design is valid, and that within the neighborhood of each population threshold, the assignment of extra per capita nontax revenue can be considered "as if" it were randomly done. This means that we can study revenue, spending, and reelection results in the municipalities close to either side of the threshold and attribute any significant differences to the variation in the level of transfers.[24] Indeed, because of the design's characteristics, the analysis can proceed as if this were actually a

[23] The bin width in these histograms is 283, which ensures that the various cutoffs coincide with bin limits. That is, no bin-counts observations from either side of any cutoff. The histogram for the full support is omitted to save space and available on request.

[24] Obviously, one final potential concern is that other government policies were also related to the cutoffs specified in Decree 1881/81. If so, any differences we observe would reflect the combined causal effects of the transfers and those other policies. To our knowledge, however, there are no other programs that use the same cutoffs (although some government programs and policies do use other local population cutoffs for targeting).

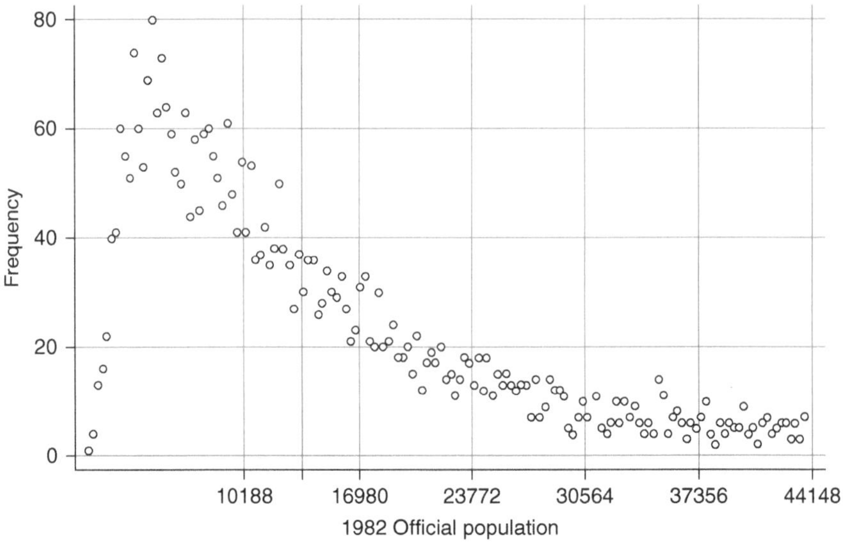

FIGURE 5.2. Histogram for 1982 population in small to medium municipalities.
Note: The bin width is 283. The official 1982 population is based on the 1980 census conducted by the national statistical agency, IBGE. McCrary density test fails to reject the null of no discontinuity in the density at conventional levels of significance for the first six cutoffs.

randomized experiment (Lee and Lemieux 2010), the gold standard of scientific research.

5.4 Estimation Approach

If this research design is essentially like a randomized experiment, why can we not simply compare the revenue, spending, and reelection rates of those municipalities that received the treatment and those who did not? After all, that is generally how researchers proceed in randomized experiments. The reason is that the treatment in this case is a fixed (extra) amount of nontax revenue and its effects may vary slightly with population. As discussed earlier, the per capita amount of this revenue declines over the range of any given bracket, and then at the threshold, it jumps up and begins declining again. Although it may not be immediately obvious, this dynamic could cause biased estimates of the treatment effect at the threshold if we did not somehow account for it.

Consider a stylized example. Let us say we want to analyze the reelection effects of the additional transfer at one particular threshold, and we are going to do so by comparing outcomes in the closest five municipalities of the previous bracket (that is, closest to the threshold) with those in the closest five municipalities of the next bracket. Let us also say that the closest five municipalities of the previous bracket received five, four, three, two, and one dollars of per capita transfer respectively (that is, the municipality closest to the threshold received one dollar of transfer per capita), and that the closest five municipalities of the next bracket received twenty, nineteen, eighteen, seventeen, and sixteen dollars of transfer per capita respectively (that is, the closet municipality on the other side received twenty dollars of transfer per capita). Finally, let us say that the "real" jump at the threshold (that is, the amount whose effect we are actually trying to measure: simply the extra amount of transfer from one bracket to the next) is nineteen dollars. In other words, the difference in the per capita transfers of the two municipalities closest to the threshold (one on either side of it) actually reflects quite accurately the difference in transfers. We could just compare these two municipalities, but we would not have much confidence in the results since they are only two municipalities. As with any experimental research, confidence in our results will increase by looking at a larger number of observations (King, Keohane, and Verba 1994).

However, as we begin to move away from the threshold and include the other eight municipalities in our analysis, the effect of that additional treatment is likely to be less than on those two municipalities closest to the threshold. For example, the average per capita transfer of the five municipalities below the threshold is three, whereas the average per capita transfer of the five municipalities above the threshold is seventeen, a difference of fourteen dollars per capita, not nineteen. Presumably, this smaller difference will be reflected in less difference in the reelection rates. If we use these reelection rates to estimate the effect of an additional nineteen dollars of transfer, then our estimates will therefore be biased downward.

In order to account for this dynamic, we follow Hahn, Todd, and Van der Klaauw (2001), Porter (2003), and Imbens and Lemieux (2008) and use local linear regression in the samples around the thresholds, including population as a variable in the regression. This essentially allows for (potentially different) slopes of the regression function in the neighborhood of the cutoff, enabling the proper estimation of the "jump" in the outcome because of the treatment (i.e., the treatment effect). Specifically, the model we use is

$$Y = \tau D + f(pop) + u$$

$$D = 1[pop > c],$$

where Y denotes the outcome of interest (taxation, spending, or whether or not the party of the previous mayor was reelected), τ the (constant) treatment effect, D the indicator function for treatment (additional resources), pop municipal population, c a particular cutoff, $f(pop)$ a polynomial function of population, and u unobserved factors that affect outcomes.[25]

Although this approach enables us to use observations further away from the threshold in order to increase our statistical power, the disadvantage of the approach is that the specification of the function $f(pop)$, which determines the slopes and curvature of the regression line, becomes particularly important. Our theory gives us no guidance on how population exactly influences the effect of a given transfer amount – for example, it could be that the effectiveness of a transfer declines linearly with population or more gradually or exponentially, and so forth. To ensure that our findings are not driven by odd functional-form assumptions, we present most estimation results from linear specifications in the discontinuity samples. We supplement the local linear estimates with higher order polynomial specifications using a larger sample of municipalities and we choose the order of the polynomial such that it best matches the local linear estimates in the samples of municipalities closer to the thresholds. Our approach thus combines the advantage of the local linear approach – comparing municipalities closest to the threshold, where local randomization of the treatment is most likely to hold – with the main advantage of using a larger neighborhood around the threshold, namely sample size.[26]

With our approach in hand, all that is left to do is choose the thresholds to analyze. This is a choice determined by two competing objectives. If we only choose one of the thresholds, then the external validity of our study will be quite small (i.e., only municipalities in a small population range). If we choose them all, however, then we are making an assertion that the treatment effect is the same across all of the thresholds, which is almost certainly not true since municipalities get larger and larger and the jump in resources stays the same.

To resolve this dilemma, we focus particularly on the first three population cutoffs (10,188; 13,584; and 16,980). We do not choose more than these because at subsequent cutoffs, the variation in FPM transfers is too small to affect municipal budgets.[27] And we do not choose less than these because we

[25] If the potential regression functions $E[Y|D=1, pop]$ and $E[Y|D=0, pop]$ are both continuous in population, or equivalently, if $E[u|pop]$ is continuous, then the difference in conditional expectations identifies the treatment effect at the threshold $\lim_{pop\downarrow c} E[Y|pop] - \lim_{pop\uparrow c} E[Y|pop] = \tau$. As shown in Lee (2008), sufficient for the continuity of the regression functions is the assumption that individual densities of population are smooth. As discussed earlier in this chapter, this assumption thus allows for mayors or other agents in the municipality to have some control over their particular value of population. Lee shows that as long as this control is imprecise, treatment status (extra transfers) will be randomized around the cutoff.

[26] We follow the suggestion of Imbens and Lemieux (2008) and use a rectangular kernel (i.e., equal weight for all observations in the estimation sample).

[27] In other words, there is no "first stage" in terms of overall resources available for the municipality (Litschig and Morrison 2013). Another reason for focusing on the first three population cutoffs is that assuming a common treatment effect across cutoffs becomes less tenable the larger the differences in population, and municipalities around the fourth cutoff (23,772 people) are more than twice as populous as those at the first cutoff (10,188).

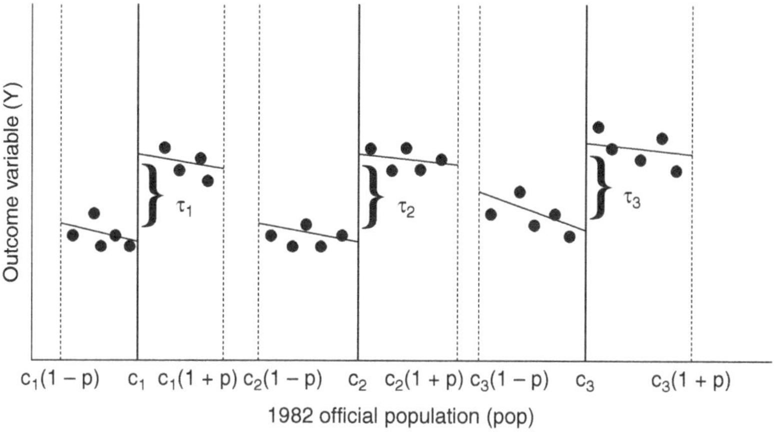

FIGURE 5.3. Estimation approach.

are reasonably confident that the treatment effect is similar across these three thresholds. And indeed, we explicitly test for this hypothesis of similar effects and find support for it.

In sum, we estimate the treatment effects using an approach represented by Figure 5.3. In that figure, there are three cutoffs, and the effect at each is denoted by τ_1, τ_2, and τ_3. Theoretically, these effects could differ from one another, but an F-test cannot reject the hypothesis that they are the same across the three thresholds. Therefore, in order to increase our statistical power, we pool the municipalities near each of the three thresholds and study the overall effect of the additional resources. These pooled results will be the focus in the next section, although readers interested in the more detailed results of each of the individual thresholds can refer to Litschig and Morrison (2013). Appendix 5B discusses the particular methods and equations we use to study both the individual and pooled cutoffs, and test whether or not the effects are the same across different cutoffs.

5.5 Estimation Results

Finally, we are ready to present our results. When we interpret the results, we focus on those that control for the municipal-level characteristics discussed earlier (i.e., income per capita, etc.), as well as pretreatment outcomes, because these results are the most reliable and also the most precisely estimated (results without these are also presented in the tables). This simply means that there is some correlation between these and municipal reelection and thus, including them helps to reduce standard errors in the regression.

We first examine the effects of additional resources on spending and taxation. Table 5.3 gives estimates of the jump in total local public spending per

TABLE 5.3. *The Effect of Extra Transfers on Municipal Public Spending (1982–85)*

Specification	Linear	Linear	Linear	Linear	Quadratic
Neighborhood (percent)	2	2	4	4	15
Pretreatment covariates	No	Yes	No	Yes	Yes
$I[X_{ms}>0]$	0.158** (0.076)	0.191*** (0.063)	0.197*** (0.054)	0.167*** (0.046)	0.156*** (0.036)
Observations	198	195	384	380	1235
R-squared	0.75	0.85	0.66	0.77	0.75

Note: Dependent variable is log municipal public spending per capita (1982–85). These results are for the pooled sample of the first three population thresholds. The F-statistic tests the null hypothesis of a common spending increase at the first three thresholds. The numbers in parentheses are heteroskedasticity-robust standard errors. Neighborhood (percent) is the distance from the respective threshold (in terms of population) from which municipalities were drawn for the sample. $I[X_{ms}>0]$ is the function indicating whether the municipality received the treatment (i.e., extra transfers). All specifications include state-level fixed effects. Pretreatment covariates (1980 census) include county income per capita, average years of schooling for individuals twenty-five years and older, poverty headcount ratio, illiterate percentage of people older than fifteen years, infant mortality, enrollment of seven- to fourteen-year olds, and percent of population living in urban areas. All specifications allow for differential slopes or curvature by segment and on each side of the cutoff. The asterisks (***, **, and *) denote significance at the 1 percent, 5 percent and 10 percent levels, respectively.

capita over the 1982–85 period. The pooled estimates suggest that per capita public spending increased by about 20 percent at the thresholds.[28] An F-test indicates that there is little statistical evidence against the null hypothesis of a common spending jump across the first three cutoffs and essentially no evidence against it for the first two cutoffs. The magnitude of the jump is roughly consistent with the size of FPM transfers in local budgets (about 50 percent) and the jump in per capita FPM transfers at the cutoffs (about 33 percent for the 10,188 cutoff and less for subsequent cutoffs).

Panel B of Figure 5.4 presents this result graphically. Each dot represents the average residual from a regression of per capita spending on state and bracket dummy variables. These dummy variables are included to absorb some of the variation in per capita spending and make the jump at the cutoff more easily visible. For example, the first dot to the left of zero represents the residual spending per capita for all municipalities within one percentage point (in terms of population) to the left of one of the first three population thresholds.[29] If

[28] Results were similar across different spending categories – that is, the share of spending in individual categories did not change (Litschig and Morrison 2013). The null hypothesis of a proportional, 20 percent per capita increase cannot be rejected in any of the specifications.

[29] We fail to reject the null hypothesis that population means are different for two sub-bins within each bin, suggesting that the graph does not overly smooth the data (Lee and Lemieux 2010).

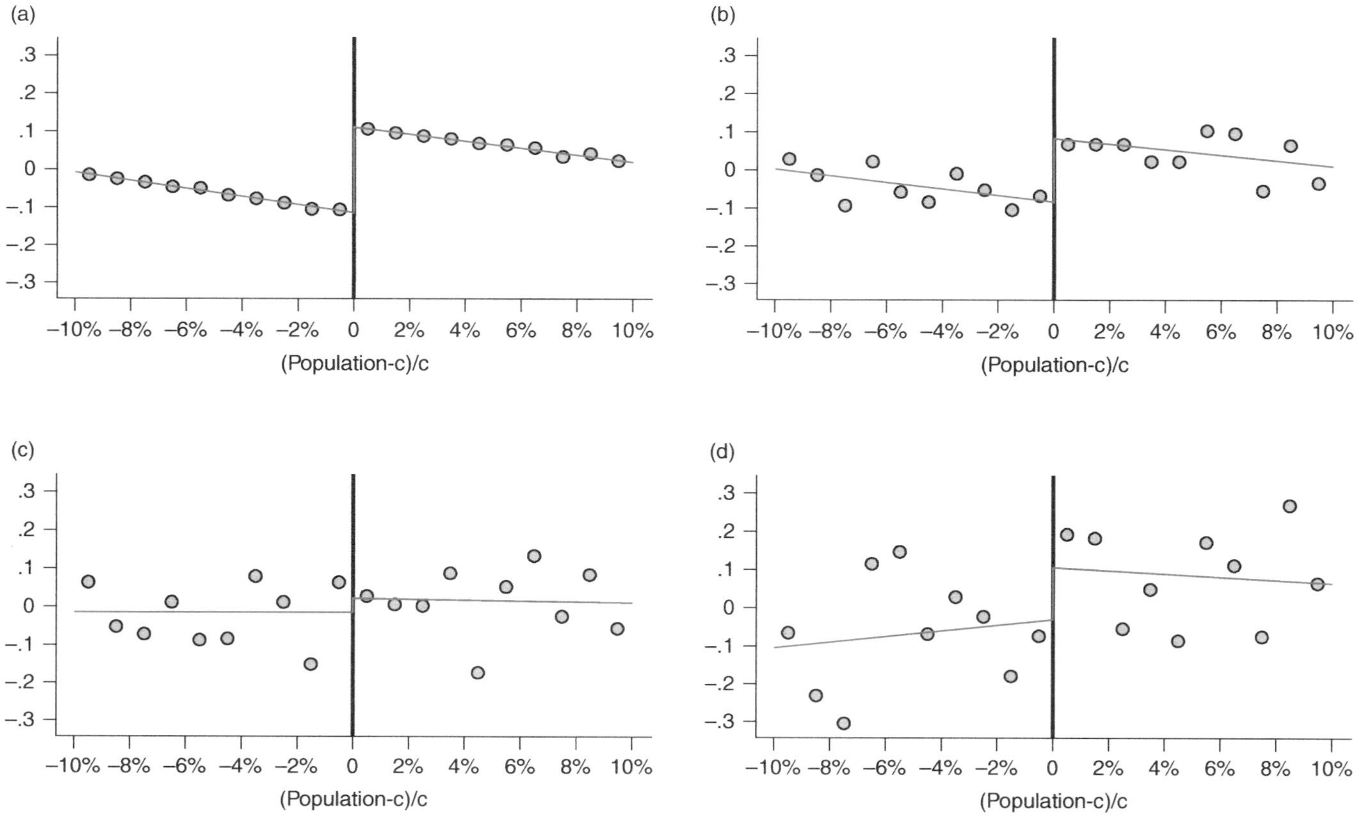

FIGURE 5.4. Discontinuity plots of transfers and their effects on spending and revenue.

Note: All variables are summed over the period 1982–85 and scaled by the 1982 official population. Each dot represents the sample average of the (partialled out) dependent variable in a given bin. The bin width is one percentage point of the respective threshold (10,188; 13,584; and 16,980).

instead of fitting two regression lines through the *ten* dots on either side of the cutoff, this figure were to fit two lines through the first *two* dots on either side of the cutoff, then the result would roughly illustrate the jump estimated in the first column of Table 5.3, the two percent neighborhood without covariates. With this in mind, the figure shows clear evidence of a discontinuity in total spending at the pooled cutoff, and it additionally shows that the discontinuity is visually robust irrespective of the width of the neighborhood examined.

Turning to revenue, Panels C and D of Figure 5.4 graphically represent the results for other revenues (which are composed of other federal and state government transfers) and own revenue, both cumulative over the period 1982–85. They show that there are no significant discontinuities in either.[30] This suggests that the effects on party reelection discussed next can, in this case, be attributed to local spending rather than tax breaks (Litschig and Morrison 2013). This is not particularly surprising, even in the context of the theory in Chapter 3, given the extremely low taxation of municipalities during this time in Brazil (discussed earlier). By the 2000s, taxation made up six percent of municipal revenues, and Brollo et al. (2013) have used our research design to study the relationship between FPM transfers and taxation and spending in that period. They find a negative and significant effect on taxation, as well as a positive and significant effect on spending.

So what effect did that extra spending financed by nontax revenue have? In line with the overall argument in this book, it led to greater rates of reelection in Brazilian municipalities, as Table 5.4 shows. Although some of the estimates focusing on only municipalities close to the thresholds are insignificant, we achieve significance when we include municipalities somewhat farther away (i.e., within 10 and 15 percent), thereby increasing the size of the sample. Importantly, we reach statistical significance not through higher point estimates, but through a monotonic reduction in standard errors: at least a 50 percent reduction compared to the narrowest neighborhoods.[31] Overall, municipalities that received the extra nontax revenue had reelection rates about 10 percentage points higher than those that did not.[32] Figure 5.5 presents graphical evidence of the discontinuity. Note that this figure presents the actual reelection rates, not the residuals after state effects are taken into account, as in Figure 5.4. Even without state effects, this jump is visually robust, irrespective of the width of the neighborhood examined.[33] The jump of about eight

[30] Although the figure suggests a jump up in own revenue associated with the FPM transfer, this is not close to statistically significant.

[31] The same pattern of results arises with the probit estimates, with state-level fixed effects, and with quadratic and cubic polynomial specifications (Litschig and Morrison 2013).

[32] Following Solé-Ollé and Sorribas-Navarro (2008), we checked whether local governments politically aligned with the allocating central government benefited more from the same amount of transfers than other governments. We found no evidence of this.

[33] There is visibly more variance in Figure 5.5 than in Figure 5.4, but this is not surprising given that Figure 5.4 has state effects partialled out.

TABLE 5.4. *The Effect of Extra Transfers on Municipal Party Reelection, 1988*

Specification	Linear	Linear	Linear	Linear	Linear
Neighborhood (percent)	2	2	10	10	15
Pretreatment covariates	No	Yes	No	Yes	Yes
$I[X_{ms}>0]$	0.119	0.186*	0.082	0.103**	0.084**
	(0.112)	(0.107)	(0.051)	(0.048)	(0.042)
Observations	197	197	940	940	1242
R-squared	0.04	0.20	0.02	0.16	0.18

Note: These results are for the pooled sample of the first three population thresholds. The numbers in parentheses are heteroskedasticity-robust standard errors. Neighborhood (percent) is the distance from the respective threshold (in terms of population) from which municipalities were drawn for the sample. $I[X_{ms}>0]$ is the function indicating whether the municipality received the treatment (i.e., extra transfers). Pretreatment covariates (1980 census) include county income per capita, average years of schooling for individuals twenty-five years and older, poverty headcount ratio, illiterate percentage of people older than fifteen years, infant mortality, enrollment of seven- to fourteen-year olds, and percent of population living in urban areas. All specifications allow for differential slopes or curvature by segment and on each side of the cutoff. The asterisks (* and **) denote significance at the 10 percent and 5 percent levels, respectively.

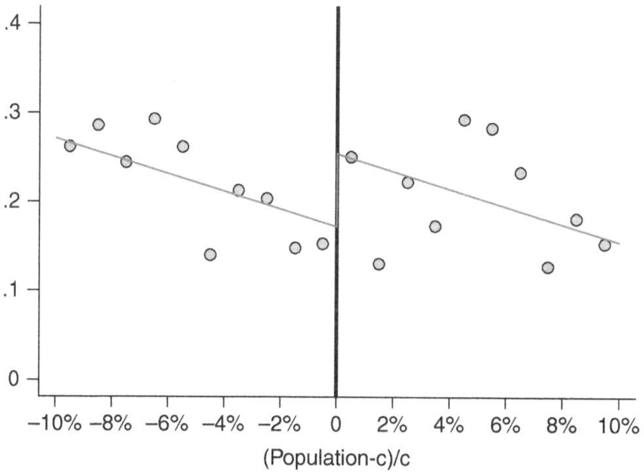

FIGURE 5.5. Discontinuity plot of the effect of extra transfers on reelection.
Note: Party reelection is measured in 1988. Each dot represents the sample average of the dependent variable in a given bin. The bin width is one percentage point of the respective threshold (i.e., 10,188; 13,584; and 16,980).

percentage points at the cutoff corresponds to the coefficient estimate in the third column and first row of Table 5.4.

5.6 Conclusion

This chapter has advanced the argument of this book in three important ways. First, it has demonstrated that the same dynamics demonstrated to hold at the national level in the previous three chapters also hold at the subnational level. Second, it has demonstrated that nontax revenue stabilizes democratic leaders in the same way it does authoritarian leaders (as shown in Chapter 4). And third, it has shown that the results are robust to the use of a design-based research strategy as opposed to a model-based one. We found evidence that a twenty percent increase over a four-year period in the nontax revenue we studied – intergovernmental transfers – increased spending by about the same amount and increased the reelection probability of the incumbent party by about ten percentage points. It had little effect on taxation, but this is not surprising since municipalities taxed so minimally.

As discussed at the beginning of the chapter, one of the concerns with studying one country is how generalizable the lessons are. Indeed, in this case we cannot even say with certainty that our results are valid for all municipalities in Brazil; we only studied municipalities around the first three thresholds, and the effects presented apply only to the municipalities near the relevant cutoffs (as is true in any regression discontinuity analysis).[34] However, these concerns are lessened by the evidence presented in the previous three chapters, showing similar patterns at national levels in other countries. And the reward for focusing only on these small and medium municipalities has been great: a design-based research strategy that supports the theory advanced in this book.

Appendix 5A: The FPM Transfer Allocation

The FPM transfer we study in this chapter is allocated on the basis of population cutoffs. More specifically, based on county population estimates, pop^e, municipalities are assigned a coefficient $k = k(pop^e)$, where $k(\cdot)$ is the step function shown in Table 5.5. For counties with up to 10,188 inhabitants, the coefficient is 0.6; from 10,189 to 13,584 inhabitants, the coefficient is 0.8; and so forth. The coefficient $k(pop^e)$ determines the share of total

[34] However, because our results are qualitatively similar across the first three cutoffs, it seems likely that the effects presented here generalize at least to the subpopulation of municipalities in the approximate population range 8,500–18,700, which represents about 30 percent of Brazilian municipalities during the time period we studied.

TABLE 5.5. *Population Brackets and Coefficients for the FPM*

Population Bracket				Coefficient
up to	10,188			0.6
from	10,189	to	13,584	0.8
from	13,585	to	16,980	1
from	16,981	to	23,772	1.2
from	23,773	to	30,564	1.4
from	30,565	to	37,356	1.6
from	37,357	to	44,148	1.8
from	44,149	to	50,940	2
from	50,941	to	61,128	2.2
from	61,129	to	71,316	2.4
from	71,317	to	81,504	2.6
from	81,505	to	91,692	2.8
from	91,693	to	101,880	3
from	101,881	to	115,464	3.2
from	115,465	to	129,048	3.4
from	129,049	to	142,632	3.6
from	142,633	to	156,216	3.8
above	156,216			4

Source: Decree 1881/81.

FPM resources, rev_t, distributed to municipality m in year t according to the following formula:

$$FPM_{mt} = \frac{k(pop_m^e)}{\sum_m k_m} rev_t.$$

Appendix 5B: Estimating Effects at Individual and Pooled Cutoffs

As discussed in this chapter, we are interested in the effects of additional transfers, and although we are interested in the effects at each of the first three transfers, we are most interested in studying the effects at all three jointly. The specification we use to test the null hypothesis of common effects across the first three thresholds is as follows. Let seg_j denote the four integers (7,500; 11,800; 15,100; and 23,772) that bound and evenly partition the population support into three segments: Y_{ms}, an outcome in municipality m, state s; z_{ms}, a set of pretreatment covariates; a_s, a fixed effect for each state; and u_{ms}, an error term for each municipality. Neither covariates nor state effects are needed for identification. We include them to guard against chance correlations with treatment status and to increase the precision of our estimates. If p denotes the percentage distance from the cutoff that defines the sample (that is, we consider all municipalities within p percent of the cutoff, as illustrated in Figure 5.3), then the testing specification is:

$$\begin{aligned} Y = & [\tau_1 1[pop_{ms} > c_1] + \alpha_{10} pop_{ms} + \alpha_{11}(pop_{ms} - c_1)1[pop_{ms} > c_1]]1_{1p} \\ & + [\tau_2 1[pop_{ms} > c_2] + \alpha_{20} pop_{ms} + \alpha_{21}(pop_{ms} - c_2)1[pop_{ms} > c_2]]1_{2p} \\ & + [\tau_3 1[pop_{ms} > c_3] + \alpha_{30} pop_{ms} + \alpha_{31}(pop_{ms} - c_3)1[pop_{ms} > c_3]]1_{3p} \\ & + \sum_{j=1}^{3} \beta_j 1[seg_{j-1} < pop_{ms} \leq seg_k]1_{jp} + \gamma \mathbf{z}_{ms} + a_s + u_{ms} \end{aligned}$$

$$seg_0 = 7500; \quad seg_1 = 11{,}800; \quad seg_2 = 15{,}100; \quad seg_3 = 23{,}772$$

$$1_{jp} = 1[c_j(1-p) < pop_{cs} < c_j(1+p)], \ j = 1,2,3; p = 2,3,4, \text{ and } 15.$$

We fail to reject the null hypothesis $\tau_1 = \tau_2 = \tau_3$ at conventional levels of significance for all outcomes and in all of our specifications.

For the pooled analysis, we need to make observations comparable in terms of the distance from their respective cutoff. To do this, we rescale population to equal zero at the respective thresholds within each of the first three segments:

$$\begin{aligned} X_{ms} = \; & pop_{ms} - 10188 \text{ if } seg_0 < pop_{ms} \leq seg_1 \\ & pop_{ms} - 13564 \text{ if } seg_1 < pop_{ms} \leq seg_2 \\ & pop_{ms} - 16980 \text{ if } seg_2 < pop_{ms} \leq seg_3. \end{aligned}$$

We then use the scaled variable, X_{ms} (municipality m in state s), for estimation purposes:

$$\begin{aligned} Y_{ms} = \; & \tau 1[X_{ms} > 0]1_p + [\alpha_{10} X_{ms} + \alpha_{11} X_{ms} 1[X_{ms} > 0]]1_{1p}. \\ & + \alpha_{20} X_{ms} + \alpha_{21} X_{ms} 1[X_{ms} > 0]]1_{2p} \\ & + \sum_{j=1}^{3} \beta_j 1[seg_{j-1} < pop_{ms} \leq seg_k]1_{jp} + \gamma \mathbf{z}_{ms} + a_s + u_{ms} \end{aligned}$$

$$1_p = 1_{1p} + 1_{2p} + 1_{3p}.$$

Essentially, this equation allows for six different slopes – one on each side of the three cutoffs (as represented in Figure 5.3), but imposes a common effect τ. Under the continuity assumption discussed in this chapter, the pooled treatment effect is given by $\lim_{\Delta \downarrow 0} E[Y|X = \Delta] - E[Y|X = 0] = \tau$.

As a specification check, we also use a Two-Stage-Least-Squares approach with theoretical FPM transfers per capita (using modal FPM levels from Figure 5.1) as the endogenous variable and the three indicators, $1[pop_{ms} > c_1]$,

$1[pop_{ms} > c_2]$, and $1[pop_{ms} > c_3]$, as multiple instruments. Finally, we use Angrist and Lavy's (1999) instrumental variable approach, putting theoretical FPM transfers per capita as the instrument for actual FPM transfers per capita, controlling for population.[35] The results of these alternative estimation approaches are quantitatively similar to those we get when we divide our reduced-form estimates based on equation (2) by the average jump in FPM per capita funding (R$ 100 per capita across cutoffs c_1, c_2, and c_3 and R$ 110 across c_1 and c_2). These additional results are omitted to save space and are available on request.

[35] For this approach, we impute missing actual FPM amounts with the modal levels shown in Figure 5.1.

6

Conclusions and Implications

The last four chapters have covered a lot of ground, theoretically and empirically. Building on literatures about taxation in Europe, oil in the Middle East, foreign aid in Africa, and intergovernmental transfers in Latin America, among other phenomena and places, I have put forth an argument that I hope provides an overarching theoretical apparatus for understanding the effects of all revenue and spending on political stability. I have also presented a variety of different forms of empirical evidence to support my theory. This chapter reviews the argument and discusses some of its theoretical and policy implications.

6.1 Summary of Argument

In my effort to synthesize existing literature on revenue and political stability, it was first necessary to reinterpret existing conventional wisdom with regard to tax revenue. In Chapter 2, I engaged the literature on taxation and representative government, contending that the well-known hypothesis that "taxation leads to representation" could – and should – be encompassed into a broader theoretical argument that taxation leads to political instability. The manifestation of this theory in authoritarian regimes is that higher levels of taxation lead to representative government; my theory predicted that higher levels of taxation should increase the risk of regime turnover in democracies as well. The flip side of this argument was that government spending should stabilize both authoritarian and democratic regimes. I provided evidence supporting these hypotheses using data on both regime turnover and leadership turnover. Taxation leads to instability and spending leads to stability in all regimes.

This formulation of the relationship between taxation, spending, and stability provided the framework for the analysis of nontax revenue. To begin, in Chapter 3, I built on existing work on government finance to develop a simple model of the effects of an influx of nontax revenue on taxation and spending decisions, assuming that taxation had costs and that spending had benefits for those making the decision (as evidenced in Chapter 2). The resulting prediction was that nontax revenue would reduce taxation and increase spending. Because of the model's flexibility, I was able to argue that the predictions would hold across a wide variety of theories about decision making in both democracies and dictatorships – in other words, the general prediction should be the same in both kinds of regimes. In addition, I argued that the model's predictions should hold in various systems of public finance, and across different kinds of nontax revenue. The conditions that made this possible were that nontax revenue did not change the way a government "weights" the utilities of its citizens, and that the revenue did not come from taxation. Statistical analysis of the effects of nontax revenue on taxation and spending supported these hypotheses: nontax revenue leads governments to reduce taxation and increase spending.

The combined theoretical and empirical results of these chapters led to Chapter 4, in which I argued that nontax revenue should lead to more regime and leadership stability in all regimes. The condition under which this hypothesis held was that tax decreases and spending increases financed by nontax revenue did not have different effects than "normal" tax decreases and spending increases. I reviewed the various theoretical approaches discussed in Chapter 2 and described how nontax revenue would work in each of them. I then also provided a comparative case study of Kenya and Mexico to demonstrate how the dynamics suggested by my theory played out in those different contexts. Finally, I used statistical analysis to examine the effects of nontax revenue on regime stability, as well as the effects of nontax revenue on leadership turnover in authoritarian regimes. The results supported the predictions.

Finally, the quasi-experimental analysis of Brazil in Chapter 5 filled in several gaps in the empirical analysis in preceding chapters. First, it showed that the theory advanced in those chapters not only applied at the national level, but also the subnational level. Second, it showed that the theory applied to democratic leaders, which were not studied in prior chapters because of the nature of the data. And finally, it showed that the theory was robust to analysis with a design-based research strategy.

The result of these chapters is a new account of the effects of revenue on political stability around the world – encompassing various political regimes, levels of government, and sources of revenue – supported by evidence drawn from a variety of different research strategies. In sum, taxation hurts regimes and leaders, spending helps them, and nontax revenue increases political stability by facilitating the lowering of taxes and increasing spending.

I now turn to exploring some of the theoretical and policy implications of this argument.

6.2 Theoretical Implications

This book has clearly taken a different approach to taxation and representative government than the traditional one. I have argued that, as powerful as it has been as a framing device, the hypothesis that taxation leads to representation has led to the mistaken implication that higher levels of taxation will lead a country to have more representative government. This was difficult to reconcile with the existing work on taxation in democracies, showing how difficult taxation can be for democratic regimes and their leaders. Instead, I argued that taxation is simply difficult for all regimes and their leaders.

The suggestion that taxation hurts, and spending helps, both democratic leaders and authoritarian leaders situates this book in a tradition that has emphasized that democracies and dictatorships are often more similar than we might at first expect. Indeed, this has been the overwhelming message of the work in past decades that has informed us about the institutional foundations of authoritarian rule, giving us much insight into how such regimes are based on managing coalitions and key supporters just as democratic regimes are (Geddes 1999; Bueno de Mesquita and others 2003). A particularly relevant early pioneer in this regard was Remmer (1986, 1990, 1991), who challenged the idea that democracies would have a harder time implementing structural adjustment programs in developing countries than authoritarian regimes would. It turned out that raising taxes and cutting spending were hard for all regimes.

In this light, it is interesting to consider whether there still might be important differences that we can discover in the public finance systems of authoritarian and democratic regimes. Even if at the broad level considered in this book taxation and spending in the regimes work similarly, there is still much to be learned about the ways authoritarian and democratic leaders manage the costs and benefits of taxation and spending. Democratic and authoritarian regimes have been compared in broad areas such as their fiscal capacity (Cheibub 1998), size of spending (Boix 2001), and public versus private goods (Bueno de Mesquita et al. 2003), but there is relatively little work systematically comparing the sorts of "micro" decisions they have to make in terms of the sorts of groups to which they respond – in other words, how they balance the costs and benefits discussed in Chapter 2.[1]

Important work in this area has focused on the broad question of whether finance systems tend to be redistributional or contractual – that is, are they characterized by taking from one group and giving to another, or are they characterized by contractual kinds of relationships in which a group is taxed and also receives the bulk of government spending (Timmons 2005, 2010)? Less explored has been the question of whether some countries have one kind

[1] These kinds of decisions formed the foundation of Levi's (1988) seminal argument about the formation of tax systems.

of government system and other countries have the other, and what accounts for these patterns of finance relationships. For example, might authoritarian regimes be characterized by taking from one group and giving to another, whereas democracies are characterized by more contractual relationships? Or vice versa? Understanding these kinds of relationships could add greatly to our understanding of how different kinds of taxation and spending affect stability in different kinds of regimes, and the nature of the threats they elicit or are able to diminish.

Nevertheless, an important result in this book has been that regardless of the details of taxation and spending systems in a country, nontax revenue should be stabilizing, and indeed, the various sources of it are relatively interchangeable. As mentioned in the Introduction, scholars studying nontax revenue have, in general, focused on disaggregated types of it: oil revenues, foreign aid, borrowing, intergovernmental grants, and so forth. In contrast, political scientists studying tax revenue have generally ignored disaggregated types of it – such as taxes on the rich or poor – and focused instead on aggregate tax revenue (although see, for example, Timmons 2005; Scheve and Stasavage 2010; Timmons 2010). This latter approach has also generally been taken with regard to government spending, although an important exception is the study of social spending.

This book offers evidence that leverage may be gained from taking a new approach to nontax revenue, aggregating it to explore its cumulative effect. At the very least, propositions suggesting that certain types of nontax revenue act differently than others need to be defended, not assumed, as do propositions about aggregating tax revenue and spending. I hope that the work in Chapters 3 and 4 will provide some guidance in this regard, in terms of specifying the conditions nontax revenue must have in order to have the effects predicted here. To affect taxation and spending in the way I predict, this revenue must not come from taxation and must not affect the way in which the government "weights" the well-being of its citizens in its decision. And to have the effects I predict in Chapter 4, the tax breaks and spending increases financed by nontax revenue should not act differently than "normal" tax breaks and spending increases.

This theoretical innovation of aggregating nontax revenue has implications for how we understand phenomena in different regions of the world and different levels of government. It helps bridge the important works that have focused on nontax revenues prevalent in particular regions of the world, such as oil in the Middle East and foreign aid in Africa, and demonstrates the similarities in dynamics across regions. Perhaps most strikingly, it suggests that political aspects of the "resource curse" have less to do with natural resources than with revenues, simultaneously broadening the implications of prior research in that area and calling into question the utility of continuing to focus on the resource curse as much as focusing on different revenues. In a similar way, it demonstrates how nontax revenues act the same way at different levels of government in that intergovernmental grants at the subnational level seem to have the same effects as foreign aid at the national level. In addition to bringing many different phenomena under one theoretical umbrella, it gives us more confidence in the external validity of research designs that focus only on one or a few countries.

This focus on revenue has implications for the way we view shifts in different sources of nontax revenue. According to the World Bank (2007), for example, much of the first decade of the 2000s saw a massive decline in net official lending to developing countries. Given the impact of nontax revenue found in this book, one might have anticipated rising instability and conflict in the developing world; however, this book has emphasized the importance of focusing on *all* nontax revenue, and the interchangeability of different sources. The World Bank explained in the same report that the decline in official lending was driven by high oil prices, which allowed major oil-exporting countries (such as Algeria, Nigeria, and Russia) to rapidly repay their debt and alleviated the need for further official borrowing. This broader perspective suggests that nontax revenue did not decline as much as one might have thought.

The recent years of global economic crisis have seen a reversal in this trend in official lending (World Bank 2011), as the World Bank and particularly the International Monetary Fund have attempted to compensate for a massive decline in private capital flows to developing countries. In 2009, debt inflows from official sources to developing countries were larger than those from private creditors for the first time since 2002. Even though this was mainly driven by an increase in multilateral lending, the World Bank (2011) reported something quite notable: "The net inflow of capital from bilateral creditors turned positive for the first time since 2000, in large measure because of increased South-South lending."[2]

This South-South lending (lending from one developing country to another) is indicative of a proliferation of nontax revenue sources around the world, resulting in shifting patterns of international influence and regional stability. In Latin America, the obvious example was Venezuelan President Hugo Chávez, whose influence both within and outside the region revolved around the provision of nontax revenue to other countries. His proposal to form a regional "Bank of the South" (paid for and run by Latin American countries only) – as an alternative to the IMF, the World Bank, and the Inter-American Development Bank – became a reality in September 2009, with an initial $20 billion of capital. In Asia, the desire to maintain exclusive control over large sources of nontax revenue was almost certainly behind the United States' vigorous resistance to the idea of an "Asian Monetary Fund" in the wake of the region's financial crisis in the late 1990s (Lipscy 2003). Although an Asian Monetary Fund remains elusive, in March 2010 the Chiang Mai Initiative

[2] "Bilateral" in this sentence means from one country to another, as opposed to "multilateral," which implies from several countries (through an international institution) to one country.

was launched, forming a currency swap arrangement among thirteen Asian nations with an initial reserves pool of $120 billion that was doubled in 2012 to $240 million.

In Africa as well, where European countries and the United States have long dominated the purse strings, a major new player has entered the nontax revenue game: China.[3] Accurate data on Chinese aid is not available, but the best estimate is probably from Bräutigam (2009), who estimates that China gave approximately $1.4 billion in official development aid to Africa in 2007 (including debt relief). That would have made China the seventh largest bilateral donor to Africa that year. Bräutigam's estimate that Chinese aid would reach $2.5 billion by 2009 would have put China in fourth place that year.[4] Already Western countries are complaining that China's influence will undermine their goals in the region, particularly with regard to democratization (McGreal 2007).

What is likely to be the effect on systemic stability of new and increasing sources of nontax revenue, besides a likely decline in the influence of international financial institutions and the Western donors that have dominated them? This book suggests that these new resources are likely to have a stabilizing effect on the world's regimes, as both democracies and dictatorships access increased nontax revenues. The implication would be a period of less regime transition, reducing a major source of political uncertainty and conflict in the developing world. In contrast, if the global economic downturn present as this book is being finished were to result in a drying up of nontax revenue, the result would presumably be a period of greater political instability.

While so far I have focused on the implications of this book's argument for the study of different revenues, there are similarly important implications for the study of regime stability. One of the central theoretical steps in this book, in Chapter 2, was to reconceptualize the dependent variable of interest in talking about the effects of taxation and spending. Instead of considering the effect of taxation on transitions to democracy, as in the work on taxation and representation, I focused on the effect of taxation on *all* transitions. Doing so led to a very different interpretation of the effect of taxation, moving away from an association between taxation and representative government toward an association between taxation and instability. I showed that this theoretical approach was able to better explain the empirical phenomenon than focusing simply on democratic transitions.

As discussed in this book, existing research regarding different kinds of nontax revenue has generally taken an approach similar to that in work on taxation and representative government. It has tended to assume that certain

[3] Africa is also beginning to receive funds from India and other developing countries (*The Economist* 2011).

[4] These comparisons with other bilateral donors are made using data from the OECD/DAC.

kinds of nontax revenue have what might be called "normative properties." That is, various nontax revenues push countries either toward dictatorship (in the case of oil, for example) or toward democracy (in the case of aid). This book has taken a different approach, arguing that the effects of revenues are similar in dictatorships and democracies: nontax revenues stabilize them, whereas taxation destabilizes them. The results throughout this book, showing that the effects of tax and nontax revenues are respectively similar in dictatorships and democracies, provide support for this latter approach and not the "normative" one.

This approach may have lessons for other work focused on either democratic or authoritarian transitions. For example, many studies of international finance and political regimes have explored whether financial flows are pro- or antidemocratic in general (for example, Rudra 2005). This book indicates the possibility that, at least for flows to governments, this question might be incorrectly formulated. Similar to other nontax revenues, they may simply have stabilizing effects on whatever regime they enter.

Finally, this conception of the dependent variable also has interesting implications for how we conceive of the effects of nontax revenues in democratic regimes. As discussed in Chapter 5, there has been important recent work looking at, for example, the effects of oil revenues on leaders in democratic countries. These papers have tended to cast their findings – that oil and intergovernmental grants lead to less taxation, more spending, and greater margins of victory in democratic elections – in a negative light, arguing that this is evidence of a resource curse in democratic countries. The approach in this book would suggest the need for an alternative interpretation: one less focused on authoritarianism and one more focused on stability.

In particular, the theoretical framework in Chapter 3 suggests that citizens would actually support the decision about government finance observed in these studies: with an influx of nontax revenue, one would want to reduce taxation and increase spending. As a result, when this sort of dynamic is observed in democracies, we should be hesitant to interpret it as some sort of nefarious activity on the part of the government without some other evidence in support of this interpretation. This activity may be perfectly consistent with representative government (Morrison 2007).

More broadly, the association between nontax revenue and greater leadership stability in democratic regimes presents an interesting problem with regard to how to evaluate democracy in these settings. Much debate, for example, has centered on whether or not Venezuela under Chávez was a democracy or a dictatorship. Indeed, the same sorts of questions arise in many settings that are institutionally democratic but have large amounts of nontax revenue, such as diamond-rich Botswana and even earlier periods in Venezuela prior to Chávez's rule. The principal issue, as made clear, for example, by Przeworski and his colleagues (2000), is that contestation is intuitively a central component of democracy (Dahl 1971), and this seems to imply that there should be leadership turnover in democracies. When we see less leadership turnover, we therefore are inclined to believe that there must not be contestation.

We need to think more about this. The theory offered here suggests that even if democratic elections are contested, there may for some reason (such as nontax revenue) be a strong incumbency advantage. This is quite a different phenomenon than a country being authoritarian. The implication is that a country's democracy might have contestation – and representation – but this may not be reflected in turnover.[5] We currently we do not have a good way of conceptualizing democracies in this way, and developing such a method would be a helpful goal of future research.

6.3 Policy Implications

Given the theoretical roots this book has in the *rentier* theories of the resource curse, and the high-profile discussion of the resource curse that has arisen in recent years alongside commodity prices (for example, Friedman 2006; Naím 2009), it seems appropriate to conclude this book with some thoughts about the implications of the argument for policies related to natural resources. In addition to whatever the value the policy suggestions might have, I hope these thoughts will also help to reinforce the differences between the approach of this book and other approaches in the literature.

Much work in the past decade has examined the effects of natural resources and found that a country's existing governing institutions determine those effects (Hodler 2006; Mehlum, Moene, and Torvik 2006; Robinson, Torvik, and Verdier 2006; Boschini, Pettersson, and Roine 2007; Smith 2008; Bhattacharyya and Hodler 2009). The message generally is that natural resources will have negative economic and political effects if a country has poor institutions, and will have no effects or even positive ones if a country has good institutions (Morrison 2013b). This book fits well in that literature; my argument about nontax revenue leading to stabilization can be characterized as saying that these revenues have "good" effects in democracies and "bad" effects in dictatorships. While this literature is important in the sense that it argues that "oil is not a curse" (Jones Luong and Weinthal 2010), it raises a critical question: What is to be done with countries that have bad institutions?

My nontax revenue approach gives me a unique perspective on this issue: it suggests that we might look at experiences with other kinds of nontax revenue to find lessons for natural resources (Morrison 2012). And Chapter 3 suggests an obvious place to start: foreign aid. Indeed, the similarities between foreign

[5] Dahl's (1971: 2) discussion of contestation does not seem to rule out anything regarding democracy as discussed in Chapter 3. Indeed, there are direct parallels, as he says that there is contestation when citizens "have unimpaired opportunities ... 1. To formulate their preferences, 2. To signify their preferences to their fellow citizens and the government by individual and collective action, [and] 3. To have their preferences weighted equally in the conduct of the government."

aid and natural resource rents seem to stretch well beyond the political effects examined in this book. Both natural resources and aid have been linked to an appreciation of the real exchange rate, often referred to as "Dutch Disease" (e.g., Younger 1992; Adam and Bevan 2003; Rajan and Subramanian 2005; van der Ploeg 2011); volatility in revenue (Bulir and Lane 2002; Arellano et al. 2009; Ross 2012); and greater corruption and weaker accountability (Knack 2001; van de Walle 2001; Leite and Weidmann 2002; e.g., Bräutigam and Knack 2004).[6] And just as the resource curse literature has recently argued that institutions can ameliorate all of these problems, the trend in the aid literature is to focus on how domestic institutions condition the effects of aid in developing countries (e.g., Isham, Kaufmann, and Pritchett 1997; Burnside and Dollar 2000; Kosack 2003; Burnside and Dollar 2004; Mosley, Hudson, and Verschoor 2004; Gomanee et al. 2005; Kosack and Tobin 2006; Wright 2008b; Baliamoune-Lutz and Mavrotas 2009).

Despite the apparent similarities between these nontax revenues, however, it turns out that policy makers in the areas of natural resources and foreign aid have recently been taking very different approaches to ensuring that these revenues have good effects. Given that the major problem with natural resources is how governments use the revenue, one of the central thrusts of policy recommendations has been to lessen government control over how these revenues are used. This can be done in one of two ways. The first is to take the resources away from the government or otherwise bypass the government in some way, as suggested by proposals to privatize state-owned oil companies (Weinthal and Luong 2006) or distribute oil wealth directly to citizens (Birdsall and Subramanian 2004). The second way is to keep the resources in the hands of the government but attempt to change the government's actions somehow. Suggestions along these lines have included putting the money in natural resource funds that include some sort of conditions over the way the funds are used and/or overseen (Varangis, Akiyama, and Mitchell 1995).

Having read Chapter 3, the reader may be thinking that these policies seem vaguely familiar. And indeed, as discussed in detail in that chapter, for decades donors tried tactics very similar to those that are now being recommended for natural resources: attempting to change governments' behaviors or bypass them to some degree. Unfortunately, they found them to be largely unsuccessful. Policy conditionality (attempts to change governments' behaviors) and project financing (attempts to bypass the government to some degree) have not attained the results desired by donors.

The lessons learned by donors shed light on the disappointing results – and pessimistic prospects – for the various policy proposals put forward for avoiding the resource curse. For example, consider the proposals to take natural resources out of the hands of the government. Privatization of the resources – one of the ways to do this – has experienced the same type of problems that

[6] See Morrison (2012).

have plagued project-based aid. In the absence of a good institutional environment – such as a developed legal system, a tax administration to collect revenues, and a corporate governance regulatory structure – privatizing the resources has led to a few people getting very rich and countries as a whole seeing little benefit (Stiglitz 2007). Although some may argue that in the longer term the newly rich will begin to demand better institutions, there is no particular historical or theoretical reason to expect this (Hoff and Stiglitz 2005).

Transferring natural resource revenues in lump-sum form to citizens – another way of taking the resources out of the hands of the government – is similarly unlikely to succeed. As Sachs (2007) argues, what poor countries need to develop are infrastructure and primary health and education – services that must be provided by the government. Transferring resources to citizens in the absence of good governance is unlikely to result in any wide-scale development of the country as such development requires a functioning government.

There are also reasons to doubt the ability of these various mechanisms to improve the political situation in a country with natural resources. For example, one might expect that taking money out of the hands of an authoritarian regime – by distributing the money to citizens, for example – would help to destabilize the regime. However, in previous work (Morrison 2007), I have shown that under a broad set of conditions this type of arrangement will not destabilize the dictatorship, even if one assumes that the arrangement works perfectly (e.g., there is no corruption). The reason is that this spending will essentially defuse demands for regime change from lower and middle-income citizens who would benefit under a democracy, as discussed in Chapter 4.

The foreign aid literature also indicates that the other set of policy mechanisms – aiming to change the way governments use natural resource rents – is also unlikely to be successful. The general conclusion has been that in the absence of "ownership" on the part of the government – that is, without the government supporting the policies of its own accord – any policies put in place on the basis of conditionalities are likely to be reversed. Even if one sets up a natural resource fund to finance social spending in a poorly run country, for example, the implication is that eventually this fund will be raided by the government for other purposes (Humphreys and Sandbu 2007). Countries where natural resource funds seem to have worked properly are countries that were already managing their fiscal situation well (Davis and others 2001; Pegg 2006; Independent Evaluation Group 2009).[7]

Perhaps the best example of these problems has been the largest attempt to shield natural resource revenues from bad governance: the Chad-Cameroon pipeline project overseen by the World Bank starting in 2000. Despite the Bank's "unprecedented system of safeguards assuring that the revenues are used to reduce poverty," there were major problems of noncompliance with the Bank's

[7] An example is Chile (Fasano 2000).

various desires (Pegg 2006; Gould and Winters 2011).[8] Chad's President Idriss Déby spent $4.5 million of his country's $25 million "signing bonus" on his military. The IMF (2003) found that the government was not allocating sufficient funds to health, education, and other priority sectors. And the group that monitors Chad's compliance with environmental and social safeguards found that the government was not following the country's stated poverty reduction strategy (International Advisory Group 2004). In 2005, Déby amended his country's revenue law to spend more on the military, in direct violation of Bank conditions. Although the Bank protested initially, it eventually capitulated.[9] In March 2008, Déby used a state of emergency decree to suspend Chad's compliance with the remaining Bank conditions with regard to poverty spending. Finally, in September 2008, the Bank decided to cancel the project.

In other words, the most elaborate measures designed to date to change the way a government uses its natural resources were unsuccessful. An evaluation of the project by the Independent Evaluation Groups of the World Bank and International Finance Corporation concluded that the project's fundamental objective of reducing poverty and improving governance was not achieved. Just as significantly, the review concluded that "no alternative program design or closer supervision would have allowed to achieve [sic] the program's development objectives in the absence of government commitment" (Independent Evaluation Group 2009: viii).[10]

Do these lessons and experiences mean that aid and natural resources can never have beneficial effects? Certainly not, as demonstrated in this book and the literature mentioned in this chapter studying the conditional effects of these revenues in different institutional environments. And largely on account of that research, many donors have begun to change their relationships with recipients in two important ways in order to ensure that aid is more effective.

The first might be seen as a revised attempt to change the institutional environment itself, akin to Chapter 3's discussion of changing the weights of citizens' well-being in governments' decisions. The World Bank and the International

[8] The quotation is from the World Bank's website on the Chad-Cameroon pipeline: http://go.worldbank.org/RQSFYMZPE0 (last accessed October 8, 2008).

[9] The 2005 standoff is particularly indicative of the similarities between this experience and donors' experiences with aid conditionalities. Chad was in the midst of political turmoil and approaching an election. Despite its qualms about Déby, the World Bank and its major shareholders probably preferred him to the alternatives, or to an unstable country (Bank Information Center 2006). The agreement to resume lending to Chad happened just after a U.S. State Department visit to the country, and just before the national elections. In sum, just as with foreign aid, a variety of conflicting interests (principally geostrategic ones) rendered ineffective the attempts to make these resources promote development in a clearly antidevelopment environment.

[10] It is notable that the "Management Response" to the report agreed: "A project of this sort *cannot* succeed without Government commitment and responsibility" (Independent Evaluation Group 2009: xx).

Monetary Fund now require "Poverty Reduction Strategy Papers" – documents outlining the government's poverty reduction policies that are drawn up in consultation with nongovernmental organizations (NGOs), the private sector, and other important actors in society. This venturing into areas of governance has been criticized by some observers (e.g., Srinivasan 2001), who argue that these organizations have no expertise or remit to involve themselves in countries' politics in this way. However, the Bank and Fund hope that this deliberative approach will lead to more sustainable, country-owned policies that donors can support (World Bank 2002: 240). It is unclear whether this will be more successful than previous forms of conditionality. There are some social science theories that indicate building societal consensus may be possible under certain conditions, but these conditions are extremely rigorous, such as complete equality among participants in the deliberation (Morrison and Singer 2007).[11]

The second way that some donors have changed their aid delivery is potentially more important: they are beginning to limit to whom they give it. Following the implications of the research reviewed earlier, some donors have begun to implement a principle of "selectivity," by which they mean that recipient countries should receive more aid if they already have good policies in place. This idea took particular hold of the donor community after work by Burnside and Dollar showed that aid was more effective in certain policy environments (World Bank 1998; Burnside and Dollar 2000). This work has generated a large response, with some scholars confirming their results and others arguing that their results are not robust (a good review is provided by Easterly 2003). However, as one of the critics of their empirical analysis Easterly (2007: 645) writes, "whether the Burnside and Dollar results hold (specifically whether aid has a positive effect on growth when policies/institutions are good) is something of a red herring regarding the issue of selectivity. The idea that aid money directed to governments would be more productive if those governments had pro-development policies and institutions is very intuitive."

Perhaps it is not surprising, then, that evidence indicates that some donors have paid increasing attention to the institutional environment of recipient countries (Dollar and Levin 2006). The World Bank, for example, allocates loans from its International Development Association on the basis of its Country Policy and Institutional Assessment (Morrison 2013a). And the United States now allocates part of its aid through the Millennium Challenge Corporation, which has strict economic and political criteria that must be met before aid is granted to a country (Radelet 2003). The approach has become

[11] And this approach also assumes that the World Bank and IMF will accept whatever policies emerge from the deliberation, an assumption about which many observers are dubious (for example, Dijkstra 2005).

important and influential enough that the Development Assistance Committee of the OECD – the main group of bilateral donors – is concerned that some states will be "left behind" by donors (e.g., OECD/DAC 2002, 2009).[12]

Given this shift among some donors, and if the thrust of this book regarding the similarities between foreign aid and natural resources is correct, the policy community might consider how to formulate a "selectivity" approach to natural resources. After all, the lessons from foreign aid indicate that the disappointing performances of the current policy recommendations with regard to the resource curse are likely to continue. The next section considers what this kind of approach might look like.

6.3.1 A "Selectivity" Approach to Natural Resources (and Nontax Revenue in General)

Implementing a "selectivity" approach to natural resources requires first that a government come up with a list of economic and political characteristics it would like to see in some other country. This is no easy task, perhaps particularly on the economic side, and there is no reason to expect that all countries will have the same criteria. Although at one point there was some agreement regarding the policies necessary for economic development, this consensus began to evaporate in the late 1990s (Stiglitz 1998) and even before the recent global financial crisis, there were reasonable arguments that looking for such a consensus might be misguided (Rodrik 2007).[13] In the foreign aid context, Kanbur, Sandler, and I (1999) have argued that this lack of consensus means that donors should decide for themselves what kind of economic policies and political institutions they want to support. Since donors have different preferences over policies, each of them should support the countries that are closest to its preferences. As mentioned earlier, the United States has done this in the form of its Millennium Challenge Corporation, an agency that doles out part of the U.S. aid budget along criteria meant to reward what the United States considers to be good policy performance (Radelet 2003). Other donors have other instruments and criteria (OECD/DAC 2003).

However, one would hope that in this day and age, "democracy" would be on any country's list of desirable criteria. A lesson to be drawn from the theoretical framework of this book is that one should expect the benefits of any increases in nontax revenue to accrue mainly to the people in a country who receive positive weights in a regime's utility function. Benefiting these people is what keeps a regime – and its leaders – in power. Broadly speaking, this should mean not only that nontax revenues like foreign aid will stabilize dictatorships and democracies, but also that the benefits of these resources will be more widely spread in democracies than dictatorships.

[12] It should be noted that while much academic and policy-oriented work has emphasized the benefits of this approach, many donors continue to deliver aid in more traditional ways.

[13] See Morrison (2011c) for more on this topic.

If democracy were part of a country's list of desirable characteristics in other countries, a selectivity approach would require that foreign aid be directed to such countries and natural resources bought from them. In this light, it is depressing how little democracy seems to matter in rich countries' considerations, if their foreign aid allocations are any indication. Historically, whether or not a country is a democracy seems to have played relatively little role in the allocation of foreign aid (Neumayer 2003). This was perhaps not surprising during the Cold War, but Wright and Winters (2010) and Clist (2011) indicate that things have not improved much since the end of the Cold War. There are some who argue that things are improving (Claessens, Cassimon, and van Campenhout 2009), or that some donors are better than others (Dollar and Levin 2006; Lebovic and Voeten 2009), and one can only hope they are correct. Nevertheless, the majority of all aid around the world goes to countries that are not fully democratic (Morrison 2009). And it seems likely that democratic considerations play even less of a role in countries' decisions about natural resource imports. As an example, in 2012, only four of the top ten sources of oil imports for the United States were democratic.[14]

If one were to care about democracy, how should one approach buying natural resources from a nondemocratic country? The message of this book and the rest of the literature is that we should be quite skeptical that policy instruments can ensure that natural resources have economically and politically positive effects in these countries. The prospects of changing a government's policies are dim, and the ability of projects to spur development without a beneficial policy environment are similarly poor. In other words, it is highly unlikely that – from the donor's perspective – the resources sold by the producer country will have a democratic effect for that country.

In nondemocratic countries, therefore, the best option for natural resources would seem to be "delaying extraction of resources below the ground until the country can reinvest the resources well above the ground" (Stiglitz 2007: 40). Given the political and economic incentives involved in trading natural resources, it is unrealistic to expect rich countries to close their markets to these countries.[15] However, there certainly seems to be no justification in the literature for helping these countries develop their natural resources. In other words, donors might follow a "trade but no aid" strategy, in which they open their markets to natural resources from the producer countries but provide no financial assistance in terms of developing the resource sector. Obviously, if a country's governance improve, so could aid from the donor. And even if the

[14] Although, importantly, the largest source of oil for the United States is the obviously democratic Canada. Based on data from the U.S. Energy Information Administration and 2010 data from *Polity IV*.

[15] An interesting alternative would seem to be a market-driven solution, by which companies offer the equivalent of "fair trade" gasoline to those consumers willing to pay extra for knowing that the gasoline comes from responsible governments. I have, however, seen no discussion of this idea. I am grateful to Macartan Humphries for suggesting this to me.

donor does not provide aid, it might still stay involved with the country in various ways, such as trying to help build capacity in the government where it is possible (OECD/DAC 2009).

Finally, there is a third set of countries. After democracies and "tolerable" dictatorships, these are the countries that export natural resources but which the population in a given importing country views as having truly unacceptable policies. By "unacceptable," I mean that the policies are so undemocratic or inhumane that importing countries may decide against even buying resources from these countries, despite the political and economic incentives pushing otherwise.[16] Given the power of those incentives, this is likely to be an extremely small set of countries. Nevertheless, there are important examples of importing countries pursuing this kind of approach.

Since 1997, for instance, the United States has prohibited U.S. energy companies from trading with the Sudanese government. The Executive Order instituting these sanctions cited Sudan's "support for international terrorism, ongoing efforts to destabilize neighboring governments, and the prevalence of human rights violations, including slavery and the denial of religious freedom."[17] Echoing the focus on revenue highlighted in this book, Secretary of State Madeleine Albright said the sanctions were intended to "deprive the regime in Khartoum of the financial and material benefits of U.S. trade and investment, including investment in Sudan's petroleum sector."[18] It is notable that the United States has continued this policy despite the fact that Sudan is able to sell its oil to other markets. Since 1999, the Sudanese government has received about $500 million a year from petroleum despite the U.S. sanctions, much of it sold to China, which meets about seven percent of its energy needs with Sudanese oil (Baldauf 2007). There is a close parallel here with the issue of selectivity in aid: as mentioned earlier in this Conclusion, Western donors have begun to complain about China's aid policy in Africa because China is giving aid to countries these donors would prefer not receive it (McGreal 2007).

A second important example is the Kimberley Process Certification Scheme (KPCS) instituted by the United Nations to prevent diamond production from fueling rebel groups and human rights abuses in producer countries. The goal of the KPCS is to keep illegitimately produced diamonds out of the international market, an idea that arose out of research indicating that – like other natural resources – producing diamonds in certain environments had terrible consequences for the producer country.[19] As a result of pressure from international NGOs, an agreement was reached between the major diamond trading and

[16] See Wenar (2008) for an interesting treatment of this issue.

[17] See http://www.gpo.gov/fdsys/pkg/CDOC-105hdoc166/html/CDOC-105hdoc166.htm (last accessed June 10, 2014).

[18] See http://1997-2001.state.gov/www/statements/971104.html (last accessed June 10, 2014).

[19] See http://www.globalwitness.org/pages/en/the_kimberley_process.html (last accessed June 10, 2014).

producing countries, the diamond industry, and NGOs to establish a diamond certification scheme. Even though faults in the scheme may remain (NGOs like Global Witness and Amnesty International have argued that improvements are needed), what is important here is the basic principle: an international agreement exists to restrict the buying of an important natural resource for reasons of human welfare.

The Kimberley Process example indicates how NGOs and policy-oriented research helped focus attention on how actions in rich countries encourage the negative effects of diamonds. The selectivity approach indicates that their efforts might be focused more broadly. In fact, the development community is increasingly focusing not just on aid policies, but also on how trade, migration, and other policies affect developing countries. Perhaps the best-known evaluation of these various policies is the Center for Global Development's Commitment to Development Index, which evaluates rich countries in terms of their contribution to development.[20] Importantly, in the Index's evaluation of donors' aid policies, it downgrades countries for giving aid to corrupt and undemocratic regimes, but the analysis of rich countries' finance or trade policies – particularly with regard to natural resources – includes no such devaluation. The approach presented here indicates that these policies may be just as important.

In sum, the lessons in this book argue for taking a "selectivity" approach to interacting with poorly governed countries that have natural resources. Indeed, this would easily apply to all kinds of nontax revenue sources. In well-governed democratic countries, the international community should help in the development of natural resources. Just as with aid, the emphasis here should be on enabling the country to pursue its own agenda. For those countries that do not meet a donor's selectivity criteria for aid, it is unrealistic to expect the donor country to stop buying the resources, but there seems to be no justification (from a democratic governance perspective) for them to finance the country's resource sector. The message from the foreign aid literature is that if one does not like a resource-rich country's agenda, then one should not help that country develop its natural resources rather than trying to condition one's assistance on changing that agenda. Finally, at the worst extreme in terms of governance, there is a serious argument to be made for not purchasing the natural resources – that is, not providing these countries with nontax revenue.

This book suggests that the use of this type of graduated approach should enable the greatest development and governance impact from countries' natural resources. As discussed in the Introduction, this impact is potentially enormous. Natural resources do not have to be a curse – this much has become clear in the literature. If it continues to be one, it will likely be the fault not only of the countries with those resources, but also of the international community.

[20] See http://www.cgdev.org/initiative/commitment-development-index (last accessed June 10, 2014).

6.4 Conclusion

This book started with a series of paradoxes about theories of government revenue, revealing apparent inconsistencies in the effects scholars attribute to various types of revenue. The rest of the book has been devoted to developing a synthetic and systematic analysis of the effects of both types of major government revenue – tax and nontax – on political stability. The resulting argument is fairly simple: taxation hurts regimes and leaders, spending helps them, and nontax revenue increases political stability by facilitating the lowering of taxes and increasing of spending. Yet in its simplicity, it helps to reconcile a wide variety of disparate works focusing on the effects of various sources of government revenue on political stability. And as discussed in this concluding chapter, it also has several important theoretical and policy implications.

As mentioned in Chapter 3, this is no doubt a "lumping" type of argument, attempting to bring a wide variety of empirical phenomena under one theoretical umbrella. It has not only argued that different kinds of tax revenue, government spending, and nontax revenue work similarly, but also that they have similar effects across a wide array of political settings. As such, it suggests a research frontier that, among other questions, examines conditions and revenues for which the argument does not hold. If the baseline of future studies is that under most circumstances, taxation tends to destabilize regimes and their leaders, and nontax revenue tends to stabilize them, then this book will have achieved its goal.

References

Abente, Diego. 1990. "The Political Economy of Tax Reform in Venezuela." *Comparative Politics* 22(2): 199–216.

Acemoglu, Daron, Simon Johnson, and James A. Robinson. 2003. "An African Success Story: Botswana." In D. Rodrik, ed., *In Search of Prosperity: Analytic Narratives on Economic Growth*. Princeton, NJ: Princeton University Press.

Acemoglu, Daron, and James A. Robinson. 2006. *Economic Origins of Dictatorship and Democracy*. New York: Cambridge University Press.

Adam, Christopher S., and David L. Bevan. 2003. *Aid, Public Expenditure, and Dutch Disease, CSAE Working Paper 2003-02*. Oxford: Center for the Study of African Economies.

Afonso, José Roberto R., and Luiz de Mello. 2000. *Brazil: An Evolving Federation, IMF/FAD Seminar on Decentralization*. Washington, DC.

Afrifa, A. A. 1966. *The Ghana Coup*. London: Frank Cass.

Ahmed, Faisal Z. 2012. "The Perils of Unearned Income: Aid, Remittances, and Government Survival." *American Political Science Review* 106(1): 146–65.

Akhmedov, Akhmed, and Ekaterina Zhuravskaya. 2004. "Opportunistic Political Cycles: Test in a Young Democracy Setting." *Quarterly Journal of Economics* 119(4): 1301–38.

Alesina, Alberto, and David R. Dollar. 2000. "Who Gives Foreign Aid to Whom and Why?" *Journal of Economic Growth* 5(March): 33–64.

Alesina, Alberto, and Guido Tabellini. 1990. "A Positive Theory of Fiscal Deficits and Government Debt." *Review of Economic Studies* 57(3): 403–14.

Ames, Barry. 1977. "The Politics of Public Spending in Latin America." *American Journal of Political Science* 21(1): 149–76.

1994. "The Reverse Coattails Effect: Local Party Organization in the 1989 Brazilian Presidential Election." *American Political Science Review* 88(1): 95–111.

2001. *The Deadlock of Democracy in Brazil*. Ann Arbor: University of Michigan Press.

Andersen, Jørgen Juel, and Michael L. Ross. 2014. "The Big Oil Change: A Closer Look at the Haber-Menaldo Analysis." *Comparative Political Studies* 47(7): 993–1021.

Angrist, Joshua D., and Victor Lavy. 1999. "Using Maimonides' Rule to Estimate the Effect of Class Size on Scholastic Achievement." *Quarterly Journal of Economics* 114: 533–75.

Angrist, Joshua D., and Jörn-Steffen Pischke. 2009. *Mostly Harmless Econometrics: An Empiricist's Companion*. Princeton, NJ: Princeton University Press.

Ansell, Ben, and David Samuels. 2010. "Inequality and Democratization: A Contractarian Approach." *Comparative Political Studies* 43(12): 1543–74.

Arellano, Cristina, Aleš Bulíř, Timothy Lane, and Leslie Lipschitz. 2009. "The Dynamic Implications of Foreign Aid and Its Variability." *Journal of Development Economics* 88(1): 87–102.

Bailyn, Bernard, David Brion Davis, David Herbert Donald, John L. Thomas, Robert H. Wiebe, and Gordon S. Wood. 1977. *The Great Republic: A History of the American People*. Boston: Little, Brown.

Baldauf, Scott. 2007. "Hu's Trip to Sudan Tests China-Africa Ties." *The Christian Science Monitor* February 2.

Baliamoune-Lutz, Mina, and George Mavrotas. 2009. "Aid Effectiveness: Looking at the Aid-Social Capital-Growth Nexus." *Review of Development Economics* 13(3): 510–25.

Banani, Amin. 1961. *The Modernization of Iran, 1921–1941*. Stanford, CA: Stanford University Press.

Banco de México. 1973. *La Distribución Del Ingreso En México*. Mexico City: FCE.

Banco Nacional de Desenvolvimento Econômico e Social. 2003. "Carga Tributaria Global Estimativa Para 2002." *Informe-se 54*. Rio de Janeiro: Banco Nacional de Desenvolvimento Econômico e Social.

Bank Information Center. 2006. "World Bank to Resume Lending to Chad after Interim Agreement Reached with Government." Available at: http://www.bicusa.org/en/Article.2750.aspx.

Barkan, Joel D. 1979. "Legislators, Elections, and Political Linkage." In J. D. Barkan and J. J. Okumu, eds., *Politics and Public Policy in Kenya and Tanzania*. New York: Praeger, 64–92.

Barkan, Joel D., and Michael Chege. 1989. "Decentralising the State: District Focus and the Politics of Reallocation in Kenya." *The Journal of Modern African Studies* 27(3): 431–53.

Barr, James, and Otto Davis. 1966. "An Elementary Political and Economic Theory of the Expenditures of Local Governments." *Southern Economic Journal* 33(October): 149–65.

Barro, Robert J. 1979. "On the Determination of Public Debt." *Journal of Political Economy* 87: 940–71.

Bates, Robert H., and Da-Hsiang Donald Lien. 1985. "A Note on Taxation, Development, and Representative Government." *Politics and Society* 14(1): 53–70.

Battaglini, Marco, and Stephen Coate. 2011. "Fiscal Policy and Unemployment." *NBER Working Paper* 17562. Cambridge, MA: National Bureau of Economic Research.

Beblawi, Hazem, and Giacomo Luciani, eds. 1987. *The Rentier State*. London: Croom Helm.

Beck, Nathaniel. 1991. "Comparing Dynamic Specifications: The Case of Presidential Approval." *Political Analysis* 3: 51–87.

2001. "Time-Series – Cross-Section Data: What Have We Learned in the Past Few Years?" *Annual Review of Political Science* 4: 271–93.

Beck, Nathaniel, and Jonathan N. Katz. 1995. "What to Do (and Not to Do) with Time-Series Cross-Section Data." *American Political Science Review* 89(September): 634–47.

2001. "Throwing Out the Baby with the Bath Water: A Comment on Green, Kim, and Yoon." *International Organization* 55(2): 487–95.

Beck, Nathaniel, Jonathan N. Katz, and Richard Tucker. 1998. "Taking Time Seriously: Time-Series-Cross-Section Analysis with a Binary Dependent Variable." *American Journal of Political Science* 42(4): 1260–88.

Becker, Gary S. 1983. "A Theory of Competition among Pressure Groups for Political Influence." *Quarterly Journal of Economics* 98: 371–400.

Benton, Allyson Lucinda. 2012. "Bottom-up Challenges to National Democracy: Mexico's (Legal) Subnational Authoritarian Enclaves." *Comparative Politics* 44(3): 253–71.

Bergstrom, Theodore C., and Robert P. Goodman. 1973. "Private Demand for Public Goods." *American Economic Review* 63(3): 280–96.

Bermeo, Sarah Blodgett. 2013. "Aid Is Not Oil: Donor Preferences, Heterogeneous Aid, and the Aid-Democratization Relationship." Duke University.

Bernstein, Thomas P., and Xiaobo Lü. 2000. "Taxation without Representation: Peasants, the Central and the Local States in Reform China." *The China Quarterly* 163(September): 742–63.

Besley, Timothy, and Anne Case. 1995. "Incumbent Behaviour: Vote-Seeking, Tax-Setting, and Yardstick Competition." *American Economic Review* 85: 25–44.

Besley, Timothy, and Stephen Coate. 1997. "An Economic Model of Representative Democracy." *Quarterly Journal of Economics* 112(1): 85–114.

Bezerra, Marcos Otávio. 1999. *Em Nome Das "Bases," Política, Favor E Dependência Pessoal.* Rio de Janeiro: Relume Dumará.

Bhattacharyya, Sambit, and Roland Hodler. 2009. "Natural Resources, Democracy and Corruption." *European Economic Review* 54: 608–21.

Bienen, Henry. 1974. *Kenya: The Politics of Participation and Control.* Princeton, NJ: Princeton University Press.

Birdsall, Nancy, and Arvind Subramanian. 2004. "Saving Iraq from Its Oil." *Foreign Affairs* 83(4): 77–89.

Birdsall, Nancy, Stijn Claessens, and Ishac Diwan. 2003. "Policy Selectivity Foregone: Debt and Donor Behavior in Africa." *World Bank Economic Review* 17: 409–35.

Black, Duncan. 1948. "On the Rationale of Group Decision Making." *Journal of Political Economy* 56(1): 23–34.

Boix, Carles. 2001. "Democracy, Development, and the Public Sector." *American Journal of Political Science* 45(1): 1–17.

2003. *Democracy and Redistribution.* Cambridge: Cambridge University Press.

Boone, Peter. 1996. "Politics and the Effectiveness of Foreign Aid." *European Economic Review* 40: 289–329.

Borcherding, Thomas E., and Robert T. Deacon. 1972. "The Demand for the Services of Non-Federal Governments." *American Economic Review* 62(December): 891–901.

Bornhorst, Fabian, Sanjeev Gupta, and John Thornton. 2009. "Natural Resource Endowments and the Domestic Revenue Effort." *European Journal of Political Economy* 25(4): 439–46.

Bosch, Núria, and Albert Solé-Ollé. 2007. "Yardstick Competition and the Political Costs of Raising Taxes: An Empirical Analysis of Spanish Municipalities." *International Tax and Public Finance* 14(1): 71–92.

Boschini, Anne D., Jan Pettersson, and Jesper Roine. 2007. "Resource Curse or Not: A Question of Appropriability." *Scandinavian Journal of Economics* 109(3): 593–617.

Bowen, Howard R. 1943. "The Interpretation of Voting in the Allocation of Economic Resources." *Quarterly Journal of Economics* 58(November): 27–48.

Bowler, Shaun, and Todd Donovan. 1995. "Popular Responsiveness to Taxation." *Political Research Quarterly* 48(1): 79–99.

Boyce, James K. 2002. "Aid Conditionality as a Tool for Peacebuilding: Opportunities and Constraints." *Development and Change* 33(5): 1025–48.

Brachet-Márquez, Viviane. 1994. *The Dynamics of Domination: State, Class, and Social Reform in Mexico, 1910–1990*. Pittsburgh, PA: University of Pittsburgh Press.

Brady, Henry E. 2010. "Doing Good and Doing Better: How Far Does the Quantitative Template Get Us?" In H. E. Brady and D. Collier, eds., *Rethinking Social Inquiry: Diverse Tools, Shared Standards (Second Edition)*. Lanham, MD: Rowman & Littlefield, 67–82.

Brand, Laurie A. 1992. "Economic and Political Liberalization in a Rentier Economy: The Case of the Hashemite Kingdom of Jordan." In I. Harik and D. J. Sullivan, eds., *Privatization and Liberalization in the Middle East*. Bloomington: Indiana University Press.

Bratton, Michael, and Nicolas van de Walle. 1997. *Democratic Experiments in Africa: Regime Transitions in Comparative Perspective*. Cambridge: Cambridge University Press.

Bräutigam, Deborah. 2000. *Aid Dependence and Governance*. Stockholm: Almqvist & Wiksell International.

2009. *The Dragon's Gift: The Real Story of China in Africa*. Oxford: Oxford University Press.

Bräutigam, Deborah, Odd-Helge Fjeldstad, and Mick Moore, eds. 2008. *Taxation and State-Building in Developing Countries: Capacity and Consent*. Cambridge: Cambridge University Press.

Bräutigam, Deborah, and Stephen Knack. 2004. "Aid Dependence, Institutions, and Governance in Sub-Saharan Africa." *Economic Development and Cultural Change* 52(2): 255–85.

Brennan, Geoffrey, and James M. Buchanan. 1980. *The Power to Tax: Analytical Foundations of a Fiscal Constitution*. Cambridge: Cambridge University Press.

Broadway, Robin. 2008. "Intergovernmental Redistributive Transfers: Efficiency and Equity." In E. Ahmad and G. Brosio, eds., *Handbook of Fiscal Federalism*. Northampton, MA: Edward Elgar, 355–80.

Brollo, Fernanda, Tommaso Nannicini, Roberto Perotti, and Guido Tabellini. 2013. "The Political Resource Curse." *American Economic Review* 103(5): 1759–96.

Brown, Stephen. 2001. "Authoritarian Leaders and Multiparty Elections in Africa: How Foreign Donors Help to Keep Kenya's Daniel Arap Moi in Power." *Third World Quarterly* 22(5): 725–39.

Bueno de Mesquita, Bruce, and Alastair Smith. 2010. "Leader Survival, Revolutions, and the Nature of Government Finance." *American Journal of Political Science* 54(4): 936–50.

Bueno de Mesquita, Bruce, Alastair Smith, Randolph M. Siverson, and James D. Morrow. 2003. *The Logic of Political Survival*. Cambridge, MA: MIT Press.
Bulir, Ales, and Timothy Lane. 2002. "Aid and Fiscal Management." In S. Gupta, B. Clements, and G. Inchauste, eds., *Helping Countries Develop: The Role of Fiscal Policy*. Washington, DC: International Monetary Fund.
Burnside, Craig, and David R. Dollar. 2000. "Aid, Policies, and Growth." *American Economic Review* 90(4): 847–68.
2004. "Aid, Policies, and Growth: Reply." *American Economic Review* 94(3): 781–85.
Burton, Michael, Richard Gunther, and John Higley. 1992. "Introduction: Elite Transformation and Democratic Regimes." In J. Higley and R. Gunther, eds., *Elites and Democratic Consolidation in Latin America and Southern Europe*. Cambridge: Cambridge University Press, 1–37.
Carothers, Thomas. 2003. "Promoting Democracy and Fighting Terror." *Foreign Affairs* 82(1): 84–97.
Caselli, Francesco, and Guy Michaels. 2013. "Do Oil Windfalls Improve Living Standards? Evidence from Brazil." *American Economic Journal: Applied Economics* 5(1): 208–38.
Cashel-Cordo, Peter, and Stephen G. Craig. 1990. "The Public Sector Impact of International Resource Transfers." *Journal of Development Economics* 32(January): 17–42.
Centeno, Miguel Angel, and Sylvia Maxfield. 1992. "The Marriage of Finance and Order: Changes in the Mexican Political Elite." *Journal of Latin American Studies* 24(1): 57–85.
Chaudhry, Kiren Aziz. 1992. "Economic Liberalization in Oil-Exporting Countries: Iraq and Saudi Arabia." In I. Harik and D. J. Sullivan, eds., *Privatization and Liberalization in the Middle East*. Bloomington: Indiana University Press.
1994. "Economic Liberalization and the Lineages of the Rentier State." *Comparative Politics* 27(1): 1–25.
Cheibub, José Antonio. 1998. "Political Regimes and the Extractive Capacity of Governments: Taxation in Democracies and Dictatorships." *World Politics* 50(3): 349–76.
Cheibub, Jose Antonio, and Adam Przeworski. 1999. "Democracy, Elections, and Accountability for Economic Outcomes." In A. Przeworski, S. C. Stokes, and B. Manin, eds., *Democracy, Accountability, and Representation*. Cambridge: Cambridge University Press.
Chiozza, Giacomo, and Hein E. Goemans. 2004. "International Conflict and the Tenure of Leaders: Is War Still *Ex-Post* Inefficient?" *American Journal of Political Science* 48(3): 604–19.
Claessens, Stijn, Danny Cassimon, and Bjorn van Campenhout. 2009. "Evidence on Changes in Aid Allocation Criteria." *World Bank Economic Review* 23(2): 185–208.
Clist, Paul. 2011. "25 Years of Aid Allocation Practice: Whither Selectivity?" *World Development* 39(10): 1724–34.
Clough, Michael. 1992. *Free at Last? US Policy toward Africa and the End of the Cold War*. New York: Council on Foreign Relations.
Coate, Stephen, and Stephen Morris. 2005. "Policy Conditionality." In J. R. Vreeland and G. Ranis, eds., *Globalization and the Nation State: The Impact of the IMF and World Bank*. London: Routledge.

Cockcroft, James D. 1983. *Mexico: Class Formation, Capital Accumulation, and the State*. New York: Monthly Review Press.

Collier, Paul. 1997. "The Failure of Conditionality." In C. Gwin and J. Nelson, eds., *Perspectives on Aid and Development*. ODC Policy Essay No. 22. Washington, DC: Overseas Development Council.

1999a. "The IMF's Role in Structural Adjustment." *The Economic Journal* 109(November): F634–51.

2006. "Is Aid Oil? An Analysis of Whether Africa Can Absorb More Aid." *World Development* 34(9): 1482–97.

Collier, Ruth Berins. 1999b. *Paths toward Democracy: The Working Class and Elites in Western Europe and South America*. Cambridge: Cambridge University Press.

Córdova, Arnaldo. 1974. *La Política De Masas Del Cardenismo*. Mexico: Ediciones Era, S.A.

Cornelius, Wayne, Ann L. Craig, and Jonathan Fox, eds. 1994. *Transforming State-Society Relations in Mexico: The National Solidarity Strategy*. San Diego: Center for U.S.-Mexican Relations, University of California.

Crawford, Gordon. 2001. *Foreign Aid and Political Reform: A Comparative Analysis of Democracy Assistance and Political Conditionality*. New York: Palgrave Macmillan.

Crespo Cuaresma, Jesus, Harald Oberhofer, and Paul A. Raschky. 2011. "Oil and the Duration of Dictatorships." *Public Choice* 148: 505–30.

Crivelli, Ernesto, and Sanjeev Gupta. 2014. "Resource Blessing, Revenue Curse? Domestic Revenue Effort in Resource-Rich Countries." *IMF Working Paper WP/14/5*. Washington, DC: International Monetary Fund.

Cronin, Stephanie. 1997. *The Army and the Creation of the Pahlavi State in Iran, 1910–1926*. London: I.B. Tauris.

Crystal, Jill. 1990. *Oil and Politics in the Gulf: Rulers and Merchants in Kuwait and Qatar*. Cambridge: Cambridge University Press.

Dahl, Robert A. 1971. *Polyarchy: Participation and Opposition*. New Haven, CT: Yale University Press.

Davis, Jeffrey M., Rolando Ossowski, James Daniel, and Steven Barnett. 2001. "Stabilization and Savings Funds for Nonrenewable Resources." In J. M. Davis, R. Ossowski, and A. Fedelino, eds., *Fiscal Policy Formulation and Implementation in Oil-Producing Countries*. Washington, DC: International Monetary Fund.

Debs, Alexander, and Hein E. Goemans. 2010. "Regime Type, the Fate of Leaders, and War." *American Political Science Review* 104(3): 430–45.

de Navarrete, Ifigenia M. 1967. "Income Distribution in Mexico." In E. Pérez Lopéz, E. Fernández Hurtado, M. R. Beteta, A. Navarrete R., I. M. de Navarrete, and V. L. Urquidi, eds., *Mexico's Recent Economic Growth*. Austin: University of Texas Press, 133–71.

Desai, Raj M., Anders Olofsgård, and Tarik M. Yousef. 2009. "The Logic of Authoritarian Bargains." *Economics & Politics* 21(1): 93–125.

Devarajan, Shanta, David R. Dollar, and Torgny Holmgren, eds. 2001. *Aid and Reform in Africa: Lessons from Ten Case Studies*. Washington, DC: World Bank.

Diamond, Larry, and Juan J. Linz. 1989. "Introduction: Politics, Society, and Democracy in Latin America." In L. Diamond, J. J. Linz, and S. M. Lipset, eds., *Democracy in Developing Countries: Latin America*. Boulder, CO: Lynne Rienner.

Dietrich, Simone. 2013. "Bypass or Engage? Explaining Donor Delivery Tactics in Foreign Aid." *International Studies Quarterly* 57(4): 698–712.

Dijkstra, Geske. 2005. "The PRSP Approach and the Illusion of Improved Aid Effectiveness: Lessons from Bolivia, Honduras, and Nicaragua." *Development Policy Review* 23(4): 443–64.

Dollar, David R., and Victoria Levin. 2006. "The Increasing Selectivity of Foreign Aid, 1984–2003." *World Development* 34(12): 2034–46.

Downs, Anthony. 1957. *An Economic Theory of Democracy*. New York: Harper & Row.

Drake, Paul W. 1996. *Labor Movements and Dictatorships: The Southern Cone in Comparative Perspective*. Baltimore, MD: Johns Hopkins University Press.

Dresser, Denise. 1994. "Bringing the Poor Back In: National Solidarity as a Strategy of Regime Legitimation." In W. Cornelius, A. L. Craig, and J. Fox, eds., *Transforming State-Society Relations in Mexico: The National Solidarity Strategy*. San Diego: Center for U.S.-Mexican Relations, 143–65.

Dunning, Thad. 2004. "Conditioning the Effects of Aid: Cold War Politics, Donor Credibility, and Democracy in Africa." *International Organization* 58(Spring): 409–23.

2008a. *Crude Democracy: Natural Resource Wealth and Political Regimes*. Cambridge: Cambridge University Press.

2008b. "Improving Causal Inference: Strengths and Limitations of Natural Experiments." *Political Research Quarterly* 61(2): 282–93.

2010. "Design-Based Inference: Beyond the Pitfalls of Regression Analysis." In H. E. Brady and D. Collier, eds., *Rethinking Social Inquiry: Diverse Tools, Shared Standards (Second Edition)*. Lanham, MD: Rowman & Littlefield, 273–311.

Easterly, William. 2002a. "The Cartel of Good Intentions: The Problem of Bureaucracy in Foreign Aid." *Journal of Policy Reform* 5(4): 223–50.

2002b. "How Did the Heavily Indebted Poor Countries Become Heavily Indebted? Reviewing Two Decades of Debt Relief." *World Development* 30(10): 1677–96.

2003. "Can Foreign Aid Buy Growth?" *Journal of Economic Perspectives* 17(3): 23–48.

2005. "What Did Structural Adjustment Adjust? The Association of Policies and Growth with Repeated IMF and World Bank Adjustment Loans." *Journal of Development Economics* 76: 1–22.

2007. "Are Aid Agencies Improving?" *Economic Policy* 22(52): 633–78.

Eckstein, Harry. 1975. "Case Study and Theory in Political Science." In H. I. Greenstein and N. W. Polsby, eds., *Handbook of Political Science*. Reading, MA: Addison-Wesley Publishing Company.

Eifert, Benn, Alan Gelb, and Nils Borje Tallroth. 2003. "The Political Economy of Fiscal Policy and Economic Management in Oil-Exporting Countries." In J. Davis, R. Ossowski, and A. Fedelino, eds., *Fiscal Policy Formulation and Implementation in Oil-Producing Countries*. Washington, DC: International Monetary Fund.

Enelow, James M., and Melvin J. Hinich. 1982. "Ideology, Issues, and the Spatial Theory of Elections." *American Political Science Review* 76(3): 493–501.

Entelis, John P. 1976. "Oil Wealth and the Prospects for Democratization in the Arabian Peninsula: The Case of Saudi Arabia." In N. A. Sherbiny and M. A. Tessler, eds., *Arab Oil: Impact on the Arab Countries and Global Implications*. New York: Praeger.

Farag, Marwa, A. K. Nandakumar, Stanley S. Wallack, Gary Gaumer, and Dominic Hodgkin. 2009. "Does Funding from Donors Displace Government Spending for Health in Developing Countries?" *Heath Affairs* 28(4): 1045–55.

Fasano, Ugo. 2000. "Review of the Experience with Oil Stabilization and Savings Funds in Selected Countries." *IMF Working Paper WP/00/112*. Washington, DC: International Monetary Fund.

Fearon, James D., and David D. Laitin. 2003. "Ethnicity, Insurgency, and Civil War." *American Political Science Review* 97(1): 75–90.

Felix, David. 1977. "Income Inequality in Mexico." *Current History* 72(March): 111–14.

Feyzioglu, Tarhan, Vinaya Swaroop, and Min Zhu. 1998. "A Panel Data Analysis of the Fungibility of Foreign Aid." *World Bank Economic Review* 12: 29–58.

Finkel, Steven E., and Edward N. Muller. 1998. "Rational Choice and the Dilemmas of Political Action." *American Political Science Review* 92(1): 37–49.

Finkel, Steven E., Edward N. Muller, and Karl-Dieter Opp. 1989. "Personal Influence, Collective Rationality, and Mass Political Action." *American Political Science Review* 83: 885–903.

Finkel, Steven E., Aníbal Pérez-Liñán, and Mitchell Seligson. 2007. "The Effects of U.S. Foreign Assistance on Democracy Building, 1990–2003." *World Politics* 59(3): 404–38.

Free, Lloyd A., and Hadley Cantril. 1967. *The Political Beliefs of Americans: A Study of Public Opinion*. New York: Simon and Schuster.

Friedman, Edward, and Joseph Wong, eds. 2008. *Political Transitions in Dominant Party Systems*. New York: Routledge.

Friedman, Thomas L. 2006. "The First Law of Petropolitics." *Foreign Policy* May/June: 28–36.

Geddes, Barbara. 1994. *Politician's Dilemma: Building State Capacity in Latin America*. Berkeley: University of California Press.

1999. "What Do We Know About Democratization after Twenty Years?" *Annual Review of Political Science* 2: 115–44.

Gehlbach, Scott. 2008. *Representation through Taxation: Revenue, Politics and Development in Postcommunist States*. Cambridge: Cambridge University Press.

Gerring, John. 2001. *Social Science Methodology: A Criterial Framework*. Cambridge: Cambridge University Press.

Gervasoni, Carlos. 2010. "A Rentier Theory of Subnational Regimes: Fiscal Federalism, Democracy, and Authoritarianism in the Argentine Provinces." *World Politics* 62(2): 302–40.

Gibson, Clark C., and Barak D. Hoffman. 2007. "Can Foreign Aid Help Produce Democracy? A Political Concessions Model of Africa's Transition Period." University of California, San Diego.

Gleditsch, Kristian Skrede, and Michael D. Ward. 2006. "Diffusion and the International Context of Democratization." *International Organization* 60(4): 911–33.

Goemans, Hein E., Kristian Skrede Gleditsch, and Giacomo Chiozza. 2009. "Introducing Archigos: A Dataset of Political Leaders." *Journal of Peace Research* 46(2): 269–83.

Goldberg, Ellis, Erik Wibbels, and Eric Mvukiyehe. 2008. "Lessons from Strange Cases: Democracy, Development, and the Resource Curse in the U.S. States." *Comparative Political Studies* 41(4–5): 477–514.

Gollás, Manuel. 1980. "Orígenes De La Desigualdad En La Distribución Del Ingreso Familiar En México." In N. Lustig, ed., *Panorama Y Perspectivas De La Economía Mexicana*. Mexico City: Colegio de México, 137–54.

Gomanee, Karuna, Oliver Morrissey, Paul Mosley, and Arjan Verschoor. 2005. "Aid, Government Expenditure, and Aggregate Welfare." *World Development* 33(3): 355–70.

Gould, John A., and Matthew S. Winters. 2011. "Betting on Oil: The World Bank's Attempt to Promote Accountability in Chad." *Global Governance* 17: 229–46.

Greene, Kenneth F. 2007. *Why Dominant Parties Lose: Mexico's Democratization in Comparative Perspective*. Cambridge: Cambridge University Press.

Grosh, Barbara, and Stephen Orvis. 1996. "Democracy, Confusion, or Chaos: Political Conditionality in Kenya." *Studies in Comparative International Development* 31(4): 46–65.

Grossman, Gene M., and Elhanan Helpman. 1994. "Protection for Sale." *American Economic Review* 84(4): 833–50.

Guriev, Sergei, Anton Kolotilin, and Konstantin Sonin. 2011. "Determinants of Nationalization in the Oil Sector: A Theory and Evidence from Panel Data." *The Journal of Law, Economics, and Organization* 27(2): 301–23.

Guyer, Jane I. 1992. "Representation without Taxation: An Essay on Democracy in Rural Nigeria, 1952–1990." *African Studies Review* 35(1): 41–79.

Haber, Stephen, and Victor Menaldo. 2011. "Do Natural Resources Fuel Authoritarianism? A Reappraisal of the Resource Curse." *American Political Science Review* 105(1): 1–26.

Haddad, Eduardo A. 1999. *Regional Inequality and Structural Changes: Lessons from the Brazilian Experience*. Aldershot, England: Ashgate.

Haggard, Stephan, and Robert R. Kaufman. 1995. *The Political Economy of Democratic Transitions*. Princeton, NJ: Princeton University Press.

2012. "Inequality and Regime Change: Democratic Transitions and the Stability of Democratic Rule." *American Political Science Review* 106(3): 495–516.

Hagopian, Frances. 1996. *Traditional Politics and Regime Change in Brazil*. Cambridge: Cambridge University Press.

Hahn, Jinyong, Petra Todd, and Wilbert van der Klaauw. 2001. "Identification and Estimation of Treatment Effects with a Regression-Discontinuity Design." *Econometrica* 69: 201–09.

Hamilton, Nora. 1982. *The Limits of State Autonomy: Post-Revolutionary Mexico*. Princeton, NJ: Princeton University Press.

Hansen, John Mark. 1998. "Individuals, Institutions, and Public Preferences over Public Finance." *American Political Science Review* 92(3): 513–31.

Heckelman, Jac C., and Stephen Knack. 2008. "Foreign Aid and Market-Liberalizing Reform." *Economica* 75: 524–48.

Heller, Peter S. 1975. "A Model of Public Fiscal Behavior in Developing Countries: Aid, Investment, and Taxation." *American Economic Review* 65(3): 429–45.

Herb, Michael. 2003. "Taxation and Representation." *Studies in Comparative International Development* 38(3): 3–31.

Herbst, Jeffrey. 2000. *States and Power in Africa: Comparative Lessons in Authority and Control*. Princeton, NJ: Princeton University Press.

Hexter, Jack H. 1979. *On Historians: Reappraisals of Some of the Masters of Modern History*. Cambridge, MA: Harvard University Press.

Hines, James R., Jr., and Richard H. Thaler. 1995. "Anomalies: The Flypaper Effect." *Journal of Economic Perspectives* 9(Fall): 217–26.

Hodler, Roland. 2006. "The Curse of Natural Resources in Fractionalized Countries." *European Economic Review* 50(6): 1367–86.

Hoff, Karla, and Joseph E. Stiglitz. 2005. "The Creation of the Rule of Law and the Legitimacy of Property Rights: The Political and Economic Consequences of a Corrupt Privatization." *NBER Working Paper 11772*. Cambridge, MA: National Bureau of Economic Research.

Hoffman, Philip T. 1994. "Early Modern France, 1450–1700." In P. T. Hoffman and K. Norberg, eds., *Fiscal Crises, Liberty, and Representative Government, 1450–1789*. Stanford, CA: Stanford University Press, 226–52.

Hoffman, Philip T., and Kathryn Norberg. 1994. "Conclusion." In P. T. Hoffman and K. Norberg, eds., *Fiscal Crises, Liberty, and Representative Government, 1450–1789*. Stanford, CA: Stanford University Press, 299–312.

Hornsby, Charles, and David W. Throup. 1992. "Elections and Political Change in Kenya." *Journal of Commonwealth and Comparative Politics* 30(2): 195–6.

Horowitz, Donald. 1985. *Ethnic Groups in Conflict*. Berkeley: University of California Press.

Hsiao, Cheng. 2003. *Analysis of Panel Data*. Second edition. Cambridge: Cambridge University Press.

Humphreys, Macartan, and Martin E. Sandbu. 2007. "The Political Economy of Natural Resource Funds." In M. Humphreys, J. D. Sachs, and J. E. Stiglitz, eds., *Escaping the Resource Curse*. New York: Columbia University Press.

Huntington, Samuel P. 1968. *Political Order in Changing Societies*. New Haven, CT: Yale University Press.

1991. *The Third Wave: Democratization in the Late 20th Century*. Norman: University of Oklahoma Press.

Hyde, Susan D., and Nikolay Marinov. 2012. "Which Elections Can Be Lost?" *Political Analysis* 20(2): 191–210.

Imbens, Guido W., and Thomas Lemieux. 2008. "Regression Discontinuity Designs: A Guide to Practice." *Journal of Econometrics* 142(2): 615–35.

Independent Evaluation Group. 2009. "The World Bank Group Program of Support for the Chad-Cameroon Petroleum Development and Pipeline Construction: Program Performance Assessment Report." Washington, DC: World Bank Group.

INEGI. 1999. *Estadísticas Históricas De México* Mexico City: Instituto Nacional de Estadística Geografia e Informática.

Inman, Robert P. 1978. "Testing Political Economy's 'as If' Proposition: Is the Median Income Voter Really Decisive?" *Public Choice* 33: 45–65.

2008. "The Flypaper Effect." NBER Working Paper 14579. Cambridge, MA: National Bureau of Economic Research.

Instituto Brasileiro de Geografia e Estatistica (IBGE). 2002. "Estimativas Populacionais Do Brasil, Grandes Regioes, Unidades Da Federacao E Municípios." *IBGE background paper*. Rio de Janeiro: Instituto Brasileiro de Geografia e Estatistica.

International Advisory Group. 2004. "Report of Mission 8 to Chad, October 10–26, 2004." Montreal: International Advisory Group.

International Monetary Fund (IMF). 1986. *A Manual on Government Finance Statistics.* Washington, DC: International Monetary Fund.

2001. *Government Finance Statistics Manual 2001*. Washington, DC: International Monetary Fund.

2003. "*Chad: 2003 Article IV Consultation.*" Washington, DC: International Monetary Fund.

2011. *World Economic Outlook*. Washington, DC: World Bank.

Isham, Jonathan, Daniel Kaufmann, and Lant H. Pritchett. 1997. "Civil Liberties, Democracy, and the Performance of Government Projects." *World Bank Economic Review* 11(2): 219–42.

Ivanhoe, L. F. 2000. *World Oil Supply: Production, Reserves, and EOR*. Golden, CO: M. King Hubbert Center for Petroleum Supply Studies, Colorado School of Mines.

Iversen, Torben, and Thomas R. Cusack. 2000. "The Causes of Welfare State Expansion: Deindustrialization or Globalization?" *World Politics* 52(April): 313–49.

Jack, William, and Roger Lagunoff. 2006. "Dynamic Enfranchisement." *Journal of Public Economics* 90: 551–72.

Jones Luong, Pauline, and Erika Weinthal. 2006. "Rethinking the Resource Curse: Ownership Structure, Institutional Capacity, and Domestic Constraints." *Annual Review of Political Science* 9: 241–63.

2010. *Oil Is Not a Curse: Ownership Structure and Institutions in Soviet Successor States*. Cambridge: Cambridge University Press.

Kadera, Kelly M., Mark J. C. Crescenzi, and Megan L. Shannon. 2003. "Democratic Survival, Peace, and War in the International System." *American Journal of Political Science* 47(2): 234–47.

Kanbur, Ravi, Todd Sandler, and Kevin M. Morrison. 1999. *The Future of Development Assistance: Common Pools and International Public Goods*. ODC Policy Essay No. 25. Washington, DC: Overseas Development Council.

Kapur, Devesh, John P. Lewis, and Richard Webb. 1997. "The Bank's Institutional Identity: Governance, Internal Management, External Relations." In D. Kapur, J. P. Lewis, and R. Webb, eds., *The World Bank: Its First Half Century*. Washington, DC: Brookings Institution, 1161–1216.

Karl, Terry Lynn. 1990. "Dilemmas of Democratization in Latin America." *Comparative Politics* 23(1): 1–21.

1997. *The Paradox of Plenty: Oil Booms and Petro-States*. Berkeley: University of California Press.

Kaufman, Robert, and Alex Segura-Ubiergo. 2001. "Globalization, Domestic Politics, and Social Spending in Latin America: A Time-Series Cross-Section Analysis, 1973–1997." *World Politics* 53(4): 553–87.

Kelsall, Tim. 2000. "Governance, Local Politics and Districtization in Tanzania: The 1998 Arumeru Tax Revolt." *African Affairs* 99(397): 533–51.

Khilji, Nasir M., and Ernest M. Zampelli. 1994. "The Fungibility of U.S. Military and Non-Military Assistance and the Impacts of Expenditures of Major Aid Recipients." *Journal of Development Economics* 43(April): 345–62.

King, Gary, Robert O. Keohane, and Sidney Verba. 1994. *Designing Social Inquiry: Scientific Inference in Qualitative Research*. Princeton, NJ: Princeton University Press.

Kinzo, Maria D'Alva G. 1993. "Consolidation of Democracy: Governability and Political Parties in Brazil." In M. D. A. G. Kinzo, ed., *Brazil: The Challenges of the 1990s*. London: British Academic Press, 138–54.

Kitschelt, Herbert. 1992. "Political Regime Change: Structure and Process-Driven Explanations?" *American Political Science Review* 86(4): 1028–34.

Kitschelt, Herbert, and Steven I. Wilkinson. 2007. *Patrons, Clients, and Policies: Patterns of Democratic Accountability and Political Competition*. New York: Cambridge University Press.

Knack, Stephen. 2001. "Aid Dependence and the Quality of Governance." *Southern Economic Journal* 68(2): 310–29.

2004. "Does Foreign Aid Promote Democracy?" *International Studies Quarterly* 48: 251–66.

2009. "Sovereign Rents and Quality of Tax Policy and Administration." *Journal of Comparative Economics* 37(3): 359–71.

Knight, Alan. 1986. *The Mexican Revolution*. Cambridge: Cambridge University Press.

Kosack, Stephen. 2003. "Effective Aid: How Democracy Allows Development Aid to Improve the Quality of Life." *World Development* 31(1): 1–22.

Kosack, Stephen, and Jennifer Tobin. 2006. "Funding Self-Sustaining Development: The Role of Aid, FDI, and Government in Economic Success." *International Organization* 60: 205–43.

Kousser, J. Morgan. 1974. *The Shaping of Southern Politics: Suffrage Restriction and the Establishment of the One-Party South, 1880–1910*. New Haven, CT: Yale University Press.

Lancaster, Carol. 1999. *Aid to Africa: So Much to Do, So Little Done*. Chicago, IL: University of Chicago Press.

2007. *Foreign Aid: Diplomacy, Development, Domestic Politics*. Chicago, IL: University of Chicago Press.

Leal, Victor Nunes. 1977. *Coronelismo: The Municipality and Representative Government in Brazil*. Cambridge: Cambridge University Press.

Lebovic, James H., and Erik Voeten. 2009. "The Cost of Shame: International Organizations and Foreign Aid in the Punishing of Human Rights Violators." *Journal of Peace Research* 46(1): 79–97.

Lee, David S. 2008. "Randomized Experiments from Non-Random Selection in U.S. House Elections." *Journal of Econometrics* 142(2): 675–97.

Lee, David S., and Thomas Lemieux. 2010. "Regression Discontinuity Designs in Economics." *Journal of Economic Literature* 48(June): 281–355.

Leite, Carlos, and Jens Weidmann. 2002. "Does Mother Nature Corrupt? Natural Resources, Corruption, and Economic Growth." In G. T. Abed and S. Gupta, eds., *Governance, Corruption, and Economic Performance*. Washington, DC: International Monetary Fund, 159–96.

Levi, Margaret. 1988. *Of Rule and Revenue*. Berkeley: University of California Press.

Levitt, Stephen D., and James M. Snyder. 1997. "The Impact of Federal Spending on House Election Outcomes." *The Journal of Political Economy* 105(1): 30–53.

Licht, Amanda A. 2010. "Coming into Money: The Impact of Foreign Aid on Leader Survival." *Journal of Conflict Resolution* 54(1): 58–87.

Lindbeck, Assar, and Jörgen W. Weibull. 1987. "Balanced-Budget Redistribution as the Outcome of Political Competitions." *Public Choice* 52(3): 273–97.

Lindert, Peter H. 2004. *Growing Public: Social Spending and Economic Growth since the Eighteenth Century*. Cambridge: Cambridge University Press.

Lipscy, Phillip Y. 2003. "Japan's Asian Monetary Fund Proposal." *Stanford Journal of East Asian Affairs* 3(1): 93–104.

Lipset, Seymour Martin. 1959. "Some Social Requisites of Democracy: Economic Development and Political Legitimacy." *American Political Science Review* 53(1): 69–105.

Litschig, Stephan. 2010. "Financing Development: Quasi-Experimental Evidence from Municipalities in Brazil, 1980–1991." *Working Paper 1143*. Barcelona: Universitat Pompeu Fabra.

2012. "Are Rules-Based Government Programs Shielded from Special-Interest Politics? Evidence from Revenue-Sharing Transfers in Brazil." *Journal of Public Economics* 96: 1047–60.

Litschig, Stephan, and Kevin M. Morrison. 2013. "The Effect of Intergovernmental Grants on Education Outcomes and Poverty Reduction." *American Economic Journal: Applied Economics* 5(4): 206–40.

Lowery, David, and Lee Sigelman. 1981. "Understanding the Tax Revolt: Eight Explanations." *American Political Science Review* 75(4): 963–74.

Lyne, Mona M. 2007. "Rethinking Economics and Institutions: The Voter's Dilemma and Democratic Accountability." In H. Kitschelt and S. I. Wilkinson, eds., *Patrons, Clients, and Policies: Patterns of Democratic Accountability and Political Competition*. New York: Cambridge University Press, 159–81.

Mack Smith, Denis. 1968. *A History of Sicily: Medieval Sicily 800–1713*. London: Chatto & Windus.

Magaloni, Beatriz. 2006. *Voting for Autocracy: Hegemonic Party Survival and Its Demise in Mexico*. Cambridge: Cambridge University Press.

Magaloni, Beatriz, and Ruth Kricheli. 2010. "Political Order and One-Party Rule." *Annual Review of Political Science* 13: 123–43.

Mahdavy, Hussein. 1970. "The Patterns and Problems of Economic Development in Rentier States: The Case of Iran." In M. A. Cook, ed., *Studies in the Economic History of the Middle East: From the Rise of Islam to the Present Day*. London: Oxford University Press.

Mainwaring, Scott. 1991. "Politicians, Parties, and Electoral Systems: Brazil in Comparative Perspective." *Comparative Politics* 24(1): 21–43.

Makoloo, Maurice Odhiambo. 2005. "*Kenya: Minorities, Indigenous Peoples and Ethnic Diversity*." London: Minority Rights Group International.

Mann, Michael. 1980. "State and Society, 1130–1815: An Analysis of English State Finances." In M. Zeitlin, ed., *Political Power and Social Theory*. Greenwich, CT: JAI Press.

Marinov, Nikolay. 2005. "Do Economic Sanctions Destabilize Country Leaders?" *American Journal of Political Science* 49(3): 564–76.

Marshall, Monty G., and Keith Jaggers. 2003. "Polity IV Project: Political Regime Characteristics and Regime Transitions, 1800–2002." Available at: http://www.cidcm.umd.edu/inscr/polity/.

Mas-Colell, Andreu, Michael D. Whinston, and Jerry R. Green. 1995. *Microeconomic Theory*. New York: Oxford University Press.

McCrary, Justin. 2008. "Manipulation of the Running Variable in the Regression Discontinuity Design: A Density Test." *Journal of Econometrics* 142(2): 698–714.

McGreal, Chris. 2007. "Chinese Aid to Africa May Do More Harm than Good, Warns Benn." *The Guardian* February 8.
Mehlum, Halvor, Karl Moene, and Ragnar Torvik. 2006. "Institutions and the Resource Curse." *The Economic Journal* 116(January): 1–20.
Meltzer, Allan, and Scott Richard. 1981. "A Rational Theory of the Size of Government." *Journal of Political Economy* 89(5): 914–27.
Minns, John. 2006. *The Politics of Developmentalism: The Midas States of Mexico, South Korea and Taiwan*. New York: Palgrave Macmillan.
Moisés, José Alvaro. 1993. "Elections, Political Parties and Political Culture in Brazil: Changes and Continuities." *Journal of Latin American Studies* 25(3): 575–611.
Monteiro, Joana, and Claudio Ferraz. 2010. "Does Oil Make Leaders Unaccountable? Evidence from Brazil's Offshore Oil Boom." Pontifícia Universidade Católica do Rio de Janeiro.
Moore, Barrington. 1966. *Social Origins of Dictatorship and Democracy: Lord and Peasant in the Making of the Modern World*. Boston: Beacon.
Moore, Mick. 2001. "Political Underdevelopment: What Causes 'Bad Governance.'" *Public Management Review* 3(3): 385–418.
Morrison, Kevin M. 2007. "Natural Resources, Aid, and Democratization: A Best-Case Scenario." *Public Choice* 131(June): 365–86.
2009. "Oil, Nontax Revenue, and the Redistributional Foundations of Regime Stability." *International Organization* 63(Winter): 107–38.
2011a. "As the World Bank Turns: Determinants of IDA Lending in the Cold War and After." *Business & Politics* 13(2): Article 2.
2011b. "Nontax Revenue, Social Cleavages, and Authoritarian Stability in Mexico and Kenya: 'Internationalization, Institutions, and Political Change' Revisited." *Comparative Political Studies* 44(6): 719–46.
2011c. "When Public Goods Go Bad: The Implications of the End of the Washington Consensus for the Study of Economic Reform." *Comparative Politics* 44(1): 105–22.
2012. "What Can We Learn About the 'Resource Curse' from Foreign Aid?" *World Bank Research Observer* 7(1): 52–73.
2013a. "Membership No Longer Has Its Privileges: The Declining Informal Influence of Board Members on IDA Lending." *Review of International Organizations* 8(2): 291–312.
2013b. "Whither the Resource Curse?" *Perspectives on Politics* 11(4): 1117–25.
Morrison, Kevin M., and Matthew M. Singer. 2007. "Inequality and Deliberative Development: Revisiting Bolivia's Experience with the PRSP." *Development Policy Review* 25(6): 721–40.
Mosley, Paul, Jane Harrigan, and John Toye. 1995. *Aid and Power*. London: Routledge.
Mosley, Paul, John Hudson, and Sara Horrell. 1987. "Aid, the Public Sector and the Market in Less Developed Countries." *The Economic Journal* 97(September): 616–31.
Mosley, Paul, John Hudson, and Arjan Verschoor. 2004. "Aid, Poverty Reduction, and the 'New Conditionality.'" *The Economic Journal* 114(496): 217–43.
Muller, Edward N., Henry A. Dietz, and Steven E. Finkel. 1991. "Discontent and the Expected Utility of Rebellion: The Case of Peru." *American Political Science Review* 85: 1261–82.

Muszynski, Judith, and Antonio Manuel Teixera Mendes. 1990. "Democratização E Opinião Pública No Brasil." In B. Lamounier, ed., *De Geisel a Collor: O Balanáo Da Transição*. São Paulo: Sumaré.

Naím, Moisés. 2009. "The Devil's Excrement." *Foreign Policy* September: 159–60.

Neumayer, Eric. 2003. *The Pattern of Aid Giving*. London: Routledge.

Niemi, Richard G., Harold W. Stanley, and Ronald J. Vogel. 1995. "State Economies and State Taxes: Do Voters Hold Governors Accountable?" *American Journal of Political Science* 39(4): 936–57.

Njeru, James. 2003. "The Impact of Foreign Aid on Public Expenditure: The Case of Kenya." *AERC Research Paper 135*. Nairobi: African Economic Research Consortium.

North, Douglass C., and Barry R. Weingast. 1989. "Constitutions and Commitment: The Evolution of Institutions Governing Public Choice in Seventeenth-Century England." *Journal of Economic History* 49: 803–32.

O'Brien, F. S., and Terry C. I. Ryan. 2001. "Kenya." In S. Devarajan, D. Dollar, and T. Holmgren, eds., *Aid and Reform in Africa: Lessons from Ten Case Studies*. Washington, DC: World Bank.

O'Donnell, Guillermo. 1973. *Modernization and Bureaucratic Authoritarianism*. Berkeley: University of California.

1993. "On the State, Democratization Some Conceptual Problems: A Latin American View with Glances at Some Postcommunist Countries." *World Development* 21(8): 1355–69.

O'Donnell, Guillermo, and Philippe C. Schmitter. 1986. *Transitions from Authoritarian Rule: Tentative Conclusions about Uncertain Democracies*. Baltimore, MD: Johns Hopkins University Press.

O'Donnell, Guillermo, Philippe C. Schmitter, and Lawrence Whitehead, eds. 1986. *Transitions from Authoritarian Rule: Prospects for Democracy*. Baltimore, MD: Johns Hopkins University Press.

OECD. 2008. *Aid Targets Slipping Out of Reach?* Paris: Organization for Economic Cooperation and Development (OECD), Development Cooperation Directorate.

OECD/DAC. 2002. *Development Co-Operation in Difficult Partnerships*. Paris: OECD Development Assistance Committee.

2003. "Aid Effectiveness and Selectivity: Integrating Multiple Objectives into Aid Allocations." *DAC Journal* 4(3): 7–40.

2009. *Ensuring Fragile States Are Not Left Behind*. Paris: OECD Development Assistance Committee.

Olson, Mancur. 1965. *The Logic of Collective Action*. Cambridge, MA: Harvard University Press.

1993. "Dictatorship, Democracy, and Development." *American Political Science Review* 87(3): 567–76.

Omgba, Luc Désiré. 2009. "On the Duration of Political Power in Africa: The Role of Oil Rents." *Comparative Political Studies* 42(3): 416–36.

Osborne, Martin J., and Al Slivinski. 1996. "A Model of Political Competition with Citizen-Candidates." *Quarterly Journal of Economics* 111(1): 65–96.

Ossowski, Rolando, and Alberto Gonzáles. 2012. "Manna from Heaven: The Impact of Nonrenewable Resource Revenues on Other Revenues of Resource Exporters in Latin America and the Caribbean." *IDB Working Paper No. IDB-WP-337*. Washington, DC: Inter-American Development Bank.

Overseas Development Institute. 2006. *Meeting the Challenge of the 'Resource Curse': International Experiences in Managing the Risks and Realising the Opportunities of Non-Renewable Natural Resource Revenues*. London: Overseas Development Institute.

Pack, Howard, and Janet Rothenberg Pack. 1993. "Foreign Aid and the Question of Fungibility." *The Review of Economics and Statistics* 75(2): 258–65.

Paler, Laura. 2013. "Keeping the Public Purse: An Experiment in Windfalls, Taxes, and the Incentives to Restrain Governments." *American Political Science Review* 107(4): 706–25.

Pegg, Scott. 2006. "Can Policy Intervention Beat the Resource Curse? Evidence from the Chad-Cameroon Pipeline Project." *African Affairs* 105(418): 1–25.

Pepinsky, Thomas B. 2008. "Capital Mobility and Coalitional Politics: Authoritarian Regimes and Economic Adjustment in Southeast Asia." *World Politics* 60: 438–74.

Perotti, Roberto. 1996. "Growth, Income Distribution, and Democracy: What the Data Say." *Journal of Economic Growth* 1: 149–88.

Persson, Torsten, and Lars Svensson. 1989. "Why a Stubborn Conservative Would Run a Deficit: Policy with Time-Inconsistent Preferences." *Quarterly Journal of Economics* 104(2): 325–45.

Persson, Torsten, and Guido Tabellini. 2000. *Political Economics: Explaining Economic Policy*. Cambridge, MA: MIT Press.

Philip, George. 1980. "Mexican Oil and Gas: The Politics of a New Resource." *International Affairs* 56(3): 474–83.

Porter, Jack. 2003. "*Estimation in the Regression Discontinuity Model*." Unpublished manuscript. Madison: University of Wisconsin Department of Economics.

Przeworski, Adam. 1991. *Democracy and the Market: Political and Economic Reforms in Eastern Europe and Latin America*. Cambridge: Cambridge University Press.

Przeworski, Adam, Michael Alvarez, José Antonio Cheibub, and Fernando Limongi. 2000. *Democracy and Development: Political Institutions and Well-Being in the World, 1950–1990*. New York: Cambridge University Press.

Purcell, Susan Kaufman, and John F. H. Purcell. 1980. "State and Society in Mexico: Must a Stable Polity Be Institutionalized?" *World Politics* 32(2): 194–227.

Radelet, Steven. 2003. *Challenging Foreign Aid: A Policymaker's Guide to the Millennium Challenge Account*. Washington, DC: Center for Global Development.

2004. "Aid Effectiveness and the Millennium Development Goals." *Center for Global Development Working Paper 39*. Washington, DC: Center for Global Development.

Rajan, Raghuram G., and Arvind Subramanian. 2005. "What Undermines Aid's Impact on Growth?" *IMF Working Paper 05/126*. Washington, DC: International Monetary Fund.

Reiter, Dan. 2001. "Does Peace Nurture Democracy?" *Journal of Politics* 63(3): 935–49.

Remmer, Karen L. 1986. "The Politics of Economic Stabilization: IMF Standby Programs in Latin America, 1954–84." *Comparative Politics* 19(October): 1–24.

1990. "Democracy and Economic Crisis: The Latin American Experience." *World Politics* 42(3): 315–35.

1991. "The Political Impact of Economic Crisis in Latin America in the 1980s." *American Political Science Review* 85(3): 777–800.

2004. "Does Foreign Aid Promote the Expansion of Government?" *American Journal of Political Science* 48(1): 77–92.

Republic of Kenya. 1979. *Statistical Abstract*. Nairobi: Central Bureau of Statistics, Ministry of Economic Planning and Community Affairs.

Reynolds, Clark. 1970. *The Mexican Economy*. New Haven, CT: Yale University Press.

Robinson, James A., Ragner Torvik, and Thierry Verdier. 2006. "Political Foundations of the Resource Curse." *Journal of Development Economics* 79(2): 447–68.

Rodden, Jonathan. 2002. "The Dilemma of Fiscal Federalism: Grants and Fiscal Performance around the World." *American Journal of Political Science* 46(3): 670–87.

2003. "Reviving Leviathan: Fiscal Federalism and the Growth of Government." *International Organization* 57: 695–729.

2004. "Comparative Federalism and Decentralization: On Meaning and Measurement." *Comparative Politics* 36(4): 481–500.

Rodrik, Dani. 1998. "Why Do More Open Economies Have Bigger Governments?" *Journal of Political Economy* 106(October): 997–1032.

2007. *One Economics, Many Recipes: Globalization, Institutions, and Economic Growth*. Princeton, NJ: Princeton University Press.

Roeder, Philip G. 2001. Ethnolinguistic Fractionalization (ELF) Indices, 1961 and 1985. Available at: http://weber.ucsd.edu/~proeder/elf.htm (last accessed March 2, 2005).

Ross, Michael L. 2001. "Does Oil Hinder Democracy?" *World Politics* 53: 325–61.

2004. "Does Taxation Lead to Representation?" *British Journal of Political Science* 34: 229–49.

2008. "Oil, Islam, and Women." *American Political Science Review* 102(1): 107–23.

2012. *The Oil Curse: How Petroleum Wealth Shapes the Development of Nations*. Princeton, NJ: Princeton University Press.

Rousseau, David L., Christopher Gelpi, Dan Reiter, and Paul K. Huth. 1996. "Assessing the Dyadic Nature of the Democratic Peace, 1918–88." *American Political Science Review* 90(3): 512–33.

Rudra, Nita. 2005. "Globalization and the Strengthening of Democracy in the Developing World." *American Journal of Political Science* 49(4): 704–30.

Rueschemeyer, Dietrich, Evelyne Huber Stephens, and John D. Stephens. 1992. *Capitalist Development and Democracy*. Chicago, IL: University of Chicago Press.

Sachs, Jeffrey D. 2005. *The End of Poverty: Economic Possibilities for Our Time*. New York: Penguin Books.

2007. "How to Handle the Macroeconomics of Oil Wealth." In M. Humphreys, J. D. Sachs, and J. E. Stiglitz, eds., *Escaping the Resource Curse*. New York: Columbia University, 173–93.

Sanger, Clyde, and John Nottingham. 1964. "The Kenya General Election of 1963." *The Journal of Modern African Studies* 2(1): 1–40.

Scherlen, Renee G. 1998. "Lessons to Build On: The 1994 Mexican Presidential Election." *Journal of Interamerican Studies and World Affairs* 40(1): 19–38.

Scheve, Kenneth, and David Stasavage. 2010. "The Conscription of Wealth: Mass Warfare and the Demand for Progressive Taxation." *International Organization* 64(Fall): 529–61.

Schumpeter, Joseph A. 1918 (1991). "The Crisis of the Tax State." In R. Swedberg, ed., *The Economics and Sociology of Capitalism*. Princeton, NJ: Princeton University Press, pp. 99–140.

Scott, James C. 1969. "Corruption, Machine Politics, and Political Change." *American Political Science Review* 63(December): 1142–58.

Sears, David, and Jack Citrin. 1985. *Tax Revolt: Something for Nothing in California*. Cambridge, MA: Harvard University Press.

Sekhon, Jasjeet S. 2009. "Opiates for the Matches: Matching Methods for Causal Inference." *Annual Review of Political Science* 12: 487–508.

Shadish, William R., Thomas D. Cook, and Donald T. Campbell. 2002. *Experimental and Quasi-Experimental Designs for Generalized Causal Inference*. Boston: Houghton Mifflin.

Shah, Anwar. 1990. "The New Fiscal Federalism in Brazil." *Working Paper 557*. Washington, DC: World Bank.

Shidlo, Gil. 1998. "Local Urban Elections in Democratic Brazil." In H. A. Dietz and G. Shidlo, eds., *Urban Elections in Democratic Latin America*. Lanham, MD: Rowman & Littlefield, 63–90.

Smith, Alastair. 2008. "The Perils of Unearned Income." *Journal of Politics* 70(3): 1–14.

Smith, Benjamin. 2004. "Oil Wealth and Regime Survival in the Developing World, 1960–1999." *American Journal of Political Science* 48(2): 232–46.

2007. *Hard Times in the Lands of Plenty: Oil Politics in Iran and Indonesia*. Ithaca, NY: Cornell University Press.

Smith, William C. 1986. "The Travail of Brazilian Democracy in the 'New Republic.'" *Journal of Interamerican Studies and World Affairs* 28(4): 39–73.

Sobel, Russell S. 1998. "The Political Costs of Tax Increases and Expenditure Reductions." *Public Choice* 96: 61–80.

Solé-Ollé, Albert, and Pilar Sorribas-Navarro. 2008. "Does Partisan Alignment Affect the Electoral Reward of Intergovernmental Transfers?" *CESifo Working Paper No. 2335*. Munich: CESifo.

Spalding, Rose. 1981. "State Power and Its Limits: Corporatism in Mexico." *Comparative Political Studies* 14(2): 315–50.

Srinivasan, T. N. 2001. "Attacking Poverty: A Lost Opportunity – World Development Report 2000–01." *South Asia Economic Journal* 2(1): 123–8.

Stepan, Alfred. 1985. "State Power and the Strength of Civil Society in the Southern Cone of Latin America." In P. B. Evans, D. Rueschemeyer, and T. Skocpol, eds., *Bringing the State Back In*. New York: Cambridge University Press.

Stiglitz, Joseph E. 1998. "More Instruments and Broader Goals: Moving toward the Post-Washington Consensus." *The 1998 WIDER Annual Lecture*. Helsinki: United Nations University/WIDER.

2007. "What Is the Role of the State?" In M. Humphreys, J. D. Sachs, and J. E. Stiglitz, eds., *Escaping the Resource Curse*. New York: Columbia University Press.

Stokes, Susan C. 2007. "Political Clientelism." In C. Boix and S. C. Stokes, eds., *The Oxford Handbook of Comparative Politics*. New York: Oxford University Press, 604–27.

Stokes, Susan C., Thad Dunning, Marcelo Nazareno, and Valeria Brusco. 2013. *Brokers, Voters, and Clientelism: The Puzzle of Distributive Politics*. Cambridge: Cambridge University Press.

Stroebel, Johannes, and Arthur van Benthem. 2013. "Resource Extraction Contracts under Threat of Expropriation: Theory and Evidence." *The Review of Economics and Statistics* 95(5): 1622–39.

Stubbs, William. 1896. *The Constitutional History of England, Vol. II*. Oxford: Clarendon Press.

Svensson, Jakob. 2000. "Foreign Aid and Rent-Seeking." *Journal of International Economics* 51(2): 437–61.

Svolik, Milan W. 2009. "Power Sharing and Leadership Dynamics in Authoritarian Regimes." *American Journal of Political Science* 53(2): 477–94.

Tabellini, Guido, and Alberto Alesina. 1990. "Voting on the Budget Deficit." *American Economic Review* 80(1): 37–49.

Ter-Minassian, Teresa, ed. 1997. *Fiscal Federalism in Theory and Practice*. Washington, DC: International Monetary Fund.

The Economist. 2011. "Charity Begins Abroad: Big Developing Countries Are Shaking up the World of Aid." Vol. August 13.

Therkildsen, Ole. 2002. "Keeping the State Accountable: Is Aid No Better Than Oil?" *IDS-Bulletin* 33(3): 41–50.

Throup, David W., and Charles Hornsby. 1998. *Multi-Party Politics in Kenya*. Oxford: James Currey.

Tilly, Charles. 1990. *Coercion, Capital, and European States, Ad 990–1990*. Cambridge, MA: Basil Blackwell.

Timmons, Jeffrey F. 2005. "The Fiscal Contract: States, Taxes, and Public Services." *World Politics* 57(July): 530–67.

2010. "Taxation and Representation in Recent History." *Journal of Politics* 72(1): 191–208.

Tordo, Silvana, Brandon S. Tracy, and Noora Arfaa. 2011. "National Oil Companies and Value Creation." *World Bank Working Paper No. 218*. Washington, DC: World Bank.

Treisman, Daniel. 2000. "Decentralization and Inflation: Commitment, Collective Action, or Continuity." *American Political Science Review* 94: 837–58.

Trejo, Guillermo. 2004. "Conflicto Social Y Transición a La Democracia En México." In R. Aguilar, ed., *24 Años De Desarrollo Social En México*. Mexico City: Banamex.

Trejo, Guillermo, and Claudio Jones. 1998. "Political Dilemmas of Welfare Reform: Poverty and Inequality in Mexico." In S. K. Purcell and L. Rubio, eds., *Mexico under Zedillo*. Boulder, CO: Lynne Rienner.

Treviño, Juan, and Alun H. Thomas. 2013. "Resource Dependence and Fiscal Effort in Sub-Saharan Africa." *IMF Working Paper 13/188*. Washington, DC: International Monetary Fund.

van de Walle, Nicolas. 2001. *African Economies and the Politics of Permanent Crisis, 1979–1999*. New York: Cambridge University Press.

van de Walle, Nicolas, and Timothy Johnston. 1996. *Improving Aid to Africa*. Baltimore, MD: Johns Hopkins University Press for the Overseas Development Council.

van der Ploeg, Frederick. 2011. "Natural Resources: Curse or Blessing?" *Journal of Economic Literature* 49(2): 366–420.

Vandewalle, Dirk. 1998. *Libya since Independence: Oil and State-Building*. Ithaca, NY: Cornell University Press.

Varangis, Panayotis, Takamasa Akiyama, and Donald Mitchell. 1995. *Managing Commodity Booms – and Busts*. Washington, DC: World Bank.

Weeks, Jessica L. 2008. "Autocratic Audience Costs: Regime Type and Signaling Resolve." *International Organization* 62(1): 35–64.

Weinthal, Erika, and Pauline Luong. 2006. "Combating the Resource Curse: An Alternative Solution to Managing Mineral Wealth." *Perspectives on Politics* 4(1): 35–53.

Wenar, Leif. 2008. "Property Rights and the Resource Curse." *Philosophy & Public Affairs* 36(1): 2–32.

Wibbels, Erik. 2000. "Federalism and the Politics of Macroeconomic Policy and Performance." *American Journal of Political Science* 44: 687–702.

2006. "Dependency Revisited: International Markets, Business Cycles, and Social Spending in the Developing World." *International Organization* 60(Spring): 433–68.

Widner, Jennifer A. 1992. *The Rise of a Party-State in Kenya: From "Harambee!" to "Nyayo!"*. Berkeley: University of California Press.

Williams, Heather L. 2001. *Social Movements and Economic Transition: Markets and Distributive Conflict in Mexico*. Cambridge: Cambridge University Press.

Winters, Matthew S. 2010. "Choosing to Target: What Types of Countries Get Different Types of World Bank Projects?" *World Politics* 62(3): 422–58.

World Bank. 1985. *Brazil: Finance of Primary Education*. Washington, DC: World Bank.

1992. "World Bank Structural and Sectoral Adjustment Operations: The Second OED Review." *Operations Evaluation Department Report 10870*. Washington, DC: World Bank.

1998. *Assessing Aid: What Works, What Doesn't, and Why*. Washington, DC: World Bank.

2002. *A Sourcebook for Poverty Reduction Strategies*. Washington, DC: World Bank.

2007. *Global Development Finance 2007: The Globalization of Corporate Finance in Developing Countries*. Washington, DC: World Bank.

2011. *Global Development Finance 2011: External Debt of Developing Countries*. Washington, DC: World Bank.

Wright, Joseph. 2008a. "Do Authoritarian Institutions Constrain? How Legislatures Affect Economic Growth and Investment." *American Journal of Political Science* 5(2): 322–43.

2008b. "To Invest or Insure? How Authoritarian Time Horizons Impact Foreign Aid Effectiveness." *Comparative Political Studies* 41(7): 971–1000.

2011. "Curses and Conditionality: Do Oil and Aid Affect Democracy Differently?" Chicago, IL: Presented at the Annual Meetings of the Midwest Political Science Association.

Wright, Joseph, and Matthew Winters. 2010. "The Politics of Effective Foreign Aid." *Annual Review of Political Science* 13: 61–80.

Younger, Stephen D. 1992. "Aid and the Dutch Disease: Macroeconomic Management When Everybody Loves You." *World Development* 20(11): 1587–97.

Index

Bold numbers indicate Figures or Tables. *Italicized* numbers indicate footnotes.

Other Books in the Series *(continued from page iii)*

Carles Boix, *Democracy and Redistribution*
Carles Boix, *Political Parties, Growth, and Equality: Conservative and Social Democratic Economic Strategies in the World Economy*
Catherine Boone, *Merchant Capital and the Roots of State Power in Senegal, 1930–1985*
Catherine Boone, *Political Topographies of the African State: Territorial Authority and Institutional Change*
Catherine Boone, *Property and Political Order in Africa: Land Rights and the Structure of Politics*
Michael Bratton, Robert Mattes, and E. Gyimah-Boadi, *Public Opinion, Democracy, and Market Reform in Africa*
Michael Bratton and Nicolas van de Walle, *Democratic Experiments in Africa: Regime Transitions in Comparative Perspective*
Valerie Bunce, *Leaving Socialism and Leaving the State: The End of Yugoslavia, the Soviet Union, and Czechoslovakia*
Daniele Caramani, *The Nationalization of Politics: The Formation of National Electorates and Party Systems in Europe*
John M. Carey, *Legislative Voting and Accountability*
Kanchan Chandra, *Why Ethnic Parties Succeed: Patronage and Ethnic Headcounts in India*
Eric C. C. Chang, Mark Andreas Kayser, Drew A. Linzer, and Ronald Rogowski, *Electoral Systems and the Balance of Consumer-Producer Power*
José Antonio Cheibub, *Presidentialism, Parliamentarism, and Democracy*
Ruth Berins Collier, *Paths toward Democracy: The Working Class and Elites in Western Europe and South America*
Pepper D. Culpepper, *Quiet Politics and Business Power: Corporate Control in Europe and Japan*
Rafaela M. Dancygier, *Immigration and Conflict in Europe*
Christian Davenport, *State Repression and the Domestic Democratic Peace*
Donatella della Porta, *Social Movements, Political Violence, and the State*
Alberto Diaz-Cayeros, *Federalism, Fiscal Authority, and Centralization in Latin America*
Thad Dunning, *Crude Democracy: Natural Resource Wealth and Political Regimes*
Gerald Easter, *Reconstructing the State: Personal Networks and Elite Identity*
Margarita Estevez-Abe, *Welfare and Capitalism in Postwar Japan: Party, Bureaucracy, and Business*
Henry Farrell, *The Political Economy of Trust: Institutions, Interests, and Inter-Firm Cooperation in Italy and Germany*
Karen E. Ferree, *Framing the Race in South Africa: The Political Origins of Racial Census Elections*
M. Steven Fish, *Democracy Derailed in Russia: The Failure of Open Politics*
Robert F. Franzese, *Macroeconomic Policies of Developed Democracies*

Roberto Franzosi, *The Puzzle of Strikes: Class and State Strategies in Postwar Italy*
Timothy Frye, *Building States and Markets after Communism: The Perils of Polarized Democracy*
Geoffrey Garrett, *Partisan Politics in the Global Economy*
Scott Gehlbach, *Representation through Taxation: Revenue, Politics, and Development in Postcommunist States*
Edward L. Gibson, *Boundary Control: Subnational Authoritarianism in Federal Democracies*
Jane R. Gingrich, *Making Markets in the Welfare State: The Politics of Varying Market Reforms*
Miriam Golden, *Heroic Defeats: The Politics of Job Loss*
Jeff Goodwin, *No Other Way Out: States and Revolutionary Movements*
Merilee Serrill Grindle, *Changing the State*
Anna Grzymala-Busse, *Rebuilding Leviathan: Party Competition and State Exploitation in Post-Communist Democracies*
Anna Grzymala-Busse, *Redeeming the Communist Past: The Regeneration of Communist Parties in East Central Europe*
Frances Hagopian, *Traditional Politics and Regime Change in Brazil*
Henry E. Hale, *The Foundations of Ethnic Politics: Separatism of States and Nations in Eurasia and the World*
Mark Hallerberg, Rolf Ranier Strauch, and Jürgen von Hagen, *Fiscal Governance in Europe*
Stephen E. Hanson, *Post-Imperial Democracies: Ideology and Party Formation in Third Republic France, Weimar Germany, and Post-Soviet Russia*
Silja Häusermann, *The Politics of Welfare State Reform in Continental Europe: Modernization in Hard Times*
Michael Hechter, *Alien Rule*
Gretchen Helmke, *Courts Under Constraints: Judges, Generals, and Presidents in Argentina*
Yoshiko Herrera, *Imagined Economies: The Sources of Russian Regionalism*
J. Rogers Hollingsworth and Robert Boyer, eds., *Contemporary Capitalism: The Embeddedness of Institutions*
John D. Huber and Charles R. Shipan, *Deliberate Discretion? The Institutional Foundations of Bureaucratic Autonomy*
Ellen Immergut, *Health Politics: Interests and Institutions in Western Europe*
Torben Iversen, *Capitalism, Democracy, and Welfare*
Torben Iversen, *Contested Economic Institutions*
Torben Iversen, Jonas Pontusson, and David Soskice, eds., *Unions, Employers, and Central Banks: Macroeconomic Coordination and Institutional Change in Social Market Economies*
Thomas Janoski and Alexander M. Hicks, eds., *The Comparative Political Economy of the Welfare State*

Joseph Jupille, *Procedural Politics: Issues, Influence, and Institutional Choice in the European Union*
Stathis Kalyvas, *The Logic of Violence in Civil War*
David C. Kang, *Crony Capitalism: Corruption and Capitalism in South Korea and the Philippines*
Stephen B. Kaplan, *Globalization and Austerity Politics in Latin America*
Junko Kato, *Regressive Taxation and the Welfare State*
Orit Kedar, *Voting for Policy, Not Parties: How Voters Compensate for Power Sharing*
Robert O. Keohane and Helen B. Milner, eds., *Internationalization and Domestic Politics*
Herbert Kitschelt, *The Transformation of European Social Democracy*
Herbert Kitschelt, Kirk A. Hawkins, Juan Pablo Luna, Guillermo Rosas, and Elizabeth J. Zechmeister, *Latin American Party Systems*
Herbert Kitschelt, Peter Lange, Gary Marks, and John D. Stephens, eds., *Continuity and Change in Contemporary Capitalism*
Herbert Kitschelt, Zdenka Mansfeldova, Radek Markowski, and Gabor Toka, *Post-Communist Party Systems*
David Knoke, Franz Urban Pappi, Jeffrey Broadbent, and Yutaka Tsujinaka, eds., *Comparing Policy Networks*
Allan Kornberg and Harold D. Clarke, *Citizens and Community: Political Support in a Representative Democracy*
Amie Kreppel, *The European Parliament and the Supranational Party System*
David D. Laitin, *Language Repertoires and State Construction in Africa*
Fabrice E. Lehoucq and Ivan Molina, *Stuffing the Ballot Box: Fraud, Electoral Reform, and Democratization in Costa Rica*
Mark Irving Lichbach and Alan S. Zuckerman, eds., *Comparative Politics: Rationality, Culture, and Structure*, 2nd edition
Evan Lieberman, *Race and Regionalism in the Politics of Taxation in Brazil and South Africa*
Richard M. Locke, *Promoting Labor Standards in a Global Economy: The Promise and Limits of Private Power*
Pauline Jones Luong, *Institutional Change and Political Continuity in Post-Soviet Central Asia*
Pauline Jones Luong and Erika Weinthal, *Oil Is Not a Curse: Ownership Structure and Institutions in Soviet Successor States*
Julia Lynch, *Age in the Welfare State: The Origins of Social Spending on Pensioners, Workers, and Children*
Lauren M. MacLean, *Informal Institutions and Citizenship in Rural Africa: Risk and Reciprocity in Ghana and Côte d'Ivoire*
Beatriz Magaloni, *Voting for Autocracy: Hegemonic Party Survival and Its Demise in Mexico*
James Mahoney, *Colonialism and Postcolonial Development: Spanish America in Comparative Perspective*

James Mahoney and Dietrich Rueschemeyer, eds., *Comparative Historical Analysis in the Social Sciences*
Scott Mainwaring and Matthew Soberg Shugart, eds., *Presidentialism and Democracy in Latin America*
Isabela Mares, *The Politics of Social Risk: Business and Welfare State Development*
Isabela Mares, *Taxation, Wage Bargaining, and Unemployment*
Cathie Jo Martin and Duane Swank, *The Political Construction of Business Interests: Coordination, Growth, and Equality*
Anthony W. Marx, *Making Race, Making Nations: A Comparison of South Africa, the United States, and Brazil*
Doug McAdam, John McCarthy, and Mayer Zald, eds., *Comparative Perspectives on Social Movements*
Bonnie M. Meguid, *Party Competition between Unequals: Strategies and Electoral Fortunes in Western Europe*
Joel S. Migdal, *State in Society: Studying How States and Societies Constitute One Another*
Joel S. Migdal, Atul Kohli, and Vivienne Shue, eds., *State Power and Social Forces: Domination and Transformation in the Third World*
Scott Morgenstern and Benito Nacif, eds., *Legislative Politics in Latin America*
Kevin M. Morrison, *Nontaxation and Representation: The Fiscal Foundations of Political Stability*
Layna Mosley, *Global Capital and National Governments*
Layna Mosley, *Labor Rights and Multinational Production*
Wolfgang C. Müller and Kaare Strøm, *Policy, Office, or Votes?*
Maria Victoria Murillo, *Labor Unions, Partisan Coalitions, and Market Reforms in Latin America*
Maria Victoria Murillo, *Political Competition, Partisanship, and Policy Making in Latin American Public Utilities*
Monika Nalepa, *Skeletons in the Closet: Transitional Justice in Post-Communist Europe*
Ton Notermans, *Money, Markets, and the State: Social Democratic Economic Policies since 1918*
Eleonora Pasotti, *Political Branding in Cities: The Decline of Machine Politics in Bogotá, Naples, and Chicago*
Aníbal Pérez-Liñán, *Presidential Impeachment and the New Political Instability in Latin America*
Roger D. Petersen, *Understanding Ethnic Violence: Fear, Hatred, and Resentment in Twentieth-Century Eastern Europe*
Roger D. Petersen, *Western Intervention in the Balkans: The Strategic Use of Emotion in Conflict*
Simona Piattoni, ed., *Clientelism, Interests, and Democratic Representation*
Paul Pierson, *Dismantling the Welfare State? Reagan, Thatcher, and the Politics of Retrenchment*

Marino Regini, *Uncertain Boundaries: The Social and Political Construction of European Economies*
Marc Howard Ross, *Cultural Contestation in Ethnic Conflict*
Ben Ross Schneider, *Hierarchical Capitalism in Latin America: Business, Labor, and the Challenges of Equitable Development*
Lyle Scruggs, *Sustaining Abundance: Environmental Performance in Industrial Democracies*
Jefferey M. Sellers, *Governing from Below: Urban Regions and the Global Economy*
Yossi Shain and Juan Linz, eds., *Interim Governments and Democratic Transitions*
Beverly Silver, *Forces of Labor: Workers' Movements and Globalization since 1870*
Theda Skocpol, *Social Revolutions in the Modern World*
Dan Slater, *Ordering Power: Contentious Politics and Authoritarian Leviathans in Southeast Asia*
Regina Smyth, *Candidate Strategies and Electoral Competition in the Russian Federation: Democracy without Foundation*
Richard Snyder, *Politics after Neoliberalism: Reregulation in Mexico*
David Stark and László Bruszt, *Postsocialist Pathways: Transforming Politics and Property in East Central Europe*
Sven Steinmo, *The Evolution of Modern States: Sweden, Japan, and the United States*
Sven Steinmo, Kathleen Thelen, and Frank Longstreth, eds., *Structuring Politics: Historical Institutionalism in Comparative Analysis*
Susan C. Stokes, *Mandates and Democracy: Neoliberalism by Surprise in Latin America*
Susan C. Stokes, ed., *Public Support for Market Reforms in New Democracies*
Susan C. Stokes, Thad Hall, Marcelo Nazareno, and Valeria Brusco, *Brokers, Voters, and Clientelism: The Puzzle of Distributive Politics*
Duane Swank, *Global Capital, Political Institutions, and Policy Change in Developed Welfare States*
Sidney Tarrow, *Power in Movement: Social Movements and Contentious Politics*, revised and updated 3rd edition
Tariq Thachil, *Social Services as Electoral Strategy in India: Elite Parties, Poor Voters*
Kathleen Thelen, *How Institutions Evolve: The Political Economy of Skills in Germany, Britain, the United States, and Japan*
Kathleen Thelen, *Varieties of Liberalization and the New Politics of Social Solidarity*
Charles Tilly, *Trust and Rule*
Daniel Treisman, *The Architecture of Government: Rethinking Political Decentralization*

Guillermo Trejo, *Popular Movements in Autocracies: Religion, Repression, and Indigenous Collective Action in Mexico*
Lily Lee Tsai, *Accountability without Democracy: How Solidary Groups Provide Public Goods in Rural China*
Joshua Tucker, *Regional Economic Voting: Russia, Poland, Hungary, Slovakia, and the Czech Republic, 1990–1999*
Ashutosh Varshney, *Democracy, Development, and the Countryside*
Jeremy M. Weinstein, *Inside Rebellion: The Politics of Insurgent Violence*
Stephen I. Wilkinson, *Votes and Violence: Electoral Competition and Ethnic Riots in India*
Jason Wittenberg, *Crucibles of Political Loyalty: Church Institutions and Electoral Continuity in Hungary*
Elisabeth J. Wood, *Forging Democracy from Below: Insurgent Transitions in South Africa and El Salvador*
Elisabeth J. Wood, *Insurgent Collective Action and Civil War in El Salvador*